P9-CCC-485

For the Love of Children

SERIES EDITORS
DON S. BROWNING AND IAN S. EVISON

UNIVERSITY LUTHERAN CHURCH
1020 S. Harrison Rd.
East Lansing, Michigan 48823

THE FAMILY, RELIGION, AND CULTURE

For the Love of Children

Genetic Technology and the Future of the Family

TED PETERS

Westminster John Knox Press
Louisville, Kentucky

© 1996 Ted Peters

All rights reserved. No part of this book may be reproduced or transmitted in any form or by any means, electronic or mechanical, including photocopying, recording, or by any information storage or retrieval system, without permission in writing from the publisher. For information, address Westminster John Knox Press, 100 Witherspoon Street, Louisville, Kentucky 40202–1396.

Scripture quotations from the New Revised Standard Version of the Bible are copyright © 1989 by the Division of Christian Education of the National Council of the Churches of Christ in the U.S.A. and are used by permission.

Book and cover design by Jennifer K. Cox

First edition

Published by Westminster John Knox Press
Louisville, Kentucky

This book is printed on acid-free paper that meets the American National Standards Institute Z39.48 standard. ♾

PRINTED IN THE UNITED STATES OF AMERICA

96 97 98 99 00 01 02 03 04 05 — 10 9 8 7 6 5 4 3 2 1

Library of Congress Cataloging-in-Publication Data

Peters, Ted, date.
    For the love of children : genetic technology and the future of the family /
Ted Peters.
        p.   cm. — (The family, religion, and culture)
    Includes bibliographical references and index.
    ISBN 0-664-25468-3 (alk. paper)
    1. Human reproductive technology—Religious aspects—Christianity.
    2. Human reproductive technology—Moral and ethical aspects.
    3. Parenthood—Religious aspects—Christianity.   4. Family—Religious
aspects—Christianity.   5. Children—Religious aspects—Christianity.
    I. Title   II. Series.
    RG133.5.P485   1996
    176—dc20   96-17776

Contents

Series Foreword

There is an important debate going on today over the present health and future well-being of families in American society. Although some people on the political right and left use this debate primarily to further partisan causes, the debate is real, and it is over genuine issues. The debate, however, is not well informed and is riddled with historical, theological, and social-scientific ignorance.

This is not unusual as political debates go. The American family debate, however, is especially uninformed and dogmatic. This is understandable, for all people have experienced a family in some way, feel themselves to be experts, and believe that they are entitled to their strong opinions.

The books in this series, The Family, Religion, and Culture, discuss these issues in ways that will place the American debate about the family on more solid ground. The series is the result of the Religion, Culture, and Family project, which was funded by a generous grant from the Division of Religion and the Lilly Endowment, Inc. and was located at the Institute for Advanced Study in The University of Chicago Divinity School. Part of the project proceeded while Don Browning, the project director, was in residence at the Center of Theological Inquiry at Princeton, New Jersey.

The series advances no single point of view on this debate and gives no one solution. The authors and editors contributing to the volumes represent both genders as well as a variety of religious and ethnic perspectives and denominational backgrounds—liberal and conservative; Protestant, Catholic, and Jewish; evangelical and mainline; and black, white, and Asian. A number of different authors and editors met annually for a seminar and discussed—often with considerable intensity—their outlines, papers, and chapters pertaining to the various books. The careful reader will notice that many of the seminar members did influence one another; but, it is safe to say, each of them in the end took their own counsel and spoke out of their own convictions.

The series is comprehensive, with studies on the family in ancient Israel and early Christianity; on economics and the family, law, feminism, and reproductive technology and the family; the family and American faith traditions; congregations and families; and two summary books—one a handbook; the other, a critical overview of the American family debate.

This book, *For the Love of Children,* addresses one of the most disturbing challenges facing both society and churches—how to deal with the emerging possibilities for the control and management of human reproductive processes that is offered by the scientific advancements of modern biology and medicine. The prospects facing us are truly numbing, not so much because they are immediately and obviously dangerous, but because they are so new, such dramatic departures from the past, and have consequences that are so difficult to assess.

Ted Peters sets out the challenge of these new technologies with great clarity and precision. His review of the literature, the prominent alternative perspectives, and the emerging issues in this vast new field is prodigious. Making positive use of Roman Catholic ethical thought as well as his own Protestant tradition, he courageously and fairly confronts positions that oppose his own, even contending with other authors in the series.

Peters' view of the future is both realistic and hopeful. By applying persistently the measure of what is good for children, he believes that church and society can find their way through the thicket of challenges to more liberating and generous options for individuals or couples facing difficulties with their reproductive goals.

Don S. Browning
Ian S. Evison

Preface

This book is concerned about children, children living, but even more about children yet to be born. Like a cowcatcher on the front of a locomotive, the task in this book is to push aside obstructions in order to roll on track toward a single destination: reproductive decisions that make the love of children primary. The obstructions threatening to derail us include the impulse to try every one of the attractive new reproductive technologies regardless of their moral consequences, an outdated inheritance myth that presumes our genes must be passed on intact to our children, some confusing commitments regarding the relation between sexual pleasure and baby making, and inadequately informed theological spokespersons who unthinkingly take sides in the culture war between the family values and pro-choice armies.

The concept of a *committed, loving relationship* between spouses or lovers, as touted these days by sexual ethicists, is a beautiful ideal. What will need to be lifted up in the near future, however, is the call to a committed and loving relationship between parents and children. My emphasis here will be on commitment as a conscious choice to love a child over a sustained period of time regardless of reciprocal rewards such as the child's ability to return love or the sense of bond gained by passing one's genes on to future generations. My motive here is to protect helpless children who cannot reciprocate and who are dependent on the devotion of their families for their survival and well-being.

Perhaps the most profound quality of the love shared by two lovers is the unconditional accepting or treasuring of the other person as other. When this dimension is doubled by being mutual—that is, when both parties accept and treasure each other unconditionally—the two become enthralled, taken up into a mutual self-giving that seems overwhelming if not mystical in its unitive power. It is a taste of grace.

A graceful mutuality is possible between two mature adults who declare that they love each other and willingly shoulder their respective responsibilities for making a committed relationship work over time. The situation between parents and children is similar but also different. Children come into this world helpless, powerless, and unschooled in the responsibilities of committed and loving relationships. This makes the relationship, at least initially, one-sided. Parents must peremptorily declare their commitment to love and treasure children unconditionally. Regardless of how a child looks, behaves, fails, achieves, suffers, or rejoices, love here takes the form of grace bestowed by the parents on the little ones entrusted to their care. Should children grow up and respond with love toward those who raised them, then this would mark a double grace.

Commitments produce covenants. On May 11, 1996, an exemplary covenant was sealed in the Chapel of the Cross at Pacific Lutheran Theological Seminary, the institution where I teach. It was the wedding of students Philip Holck and Laura Holler. Laura brought into the marriage her five-year-old son Matthew, who that day became Phil's son. After the bride and groom had exchanged their vows, Phil knelt down to face young Matthew and said these words: "I, Philip, take you Matthew to be my son, to join with you, to share my life with you, to play with you, to teach and love you until death parts us." Children need commitments and covenants.

Do I as author have a personal interest in this topic? Yes, indeed. The way my own family has developed over the years has produced a sort of living philosophy for which "for the love of children" is something of a motto. Early in our marriage my wife, Jenny, and I thought consciously that our home should be open to children who need one. Rather than make babies ourselves, we saw our task as making babies feel at home. We had already entered the foreign adoption rigmarole when our son Paul was born. We proceeded with the adoption process and ended up with two precious sisters for Paul, Kathy Kim and Elizabeth. As the years went by, the doors on the Peters's house swung in and out constantly with overnighters and frequently months of residence by other children who found our home a safe and welcoming place. For nearly a five-year-period Martin and Derick, two teenage Zulu boys escaping South African apartheid, joined our family and earned an American college education. They returned home just in time to greet the new South Africa. One family picture reveals that out of seven people four different races are represented. As our children are now making their way through university study and into families of their own, our doors swing less often. Dogs, cats, and rabbits are the remaining life forms. This provides us with time to reflect on these things.

Jenny and I did not visit a genetic counselor or employ reproductive high tech. We experienced the strong desire to serve as responsible parents; but we did not undergo what so many couples have experienced, namely, the frustrating ordeal of infertility combined with the desire to make one's own children. The frustration over infertility is a powerful force deserving of shared understanding.

Infertile couples who strive and struggle to create a growing family are quite likely to become devoted to their children. The fulfillment of a deep need they feel for themselves becomes translated into love of children. Self-fulfillment and healthy parenting are not necessarily competitors; they can be complementary.

Yet at this point in history warning lights should flash and buzzers announce imminent danger. The science of genetics and the technologies of reproduction are leaping forward in so many places at once that few people, if any, completely comprehend what is happening. In fits and starts a glittering array of new opportunities for genetic engineering and baby making will become marketed, and the widespread desire to become parents will bring many new customers to the cash register. Although advertising will cloak the reproductive business in medical language and healthcare symbols to make it more culturally acceptable, the creation of a market and the selling of merchandise will provide the driving force behind a significant transition in our cultural values. Designer children and baby-making businesses belong to our future.

We will experience this as expanded choice. We will find ourselves able to invoke choice in baby-making matters in ways unheard of by our great grandparents. Going well beyond the contraceptive practices begun in the 1960s that virtually permit pregnancy at a chosen time and beyond amniocentesis that now enables us to choose our child's gender, new genetic services will allow us to rid our baby of unwanted genes. New reproductive services will also introduce us to curious combinations of biological and social parents. Choice is the cultural value that supports a free market.

I believe that we have nothing to fear from choice and relatively little to fear from the advance of genetic science or the development of new reproductive technologies. The reason for the warning lights and buzzers is that the commercialization of such marketed services poses a threat to the way we value the children involved. The risk is that children—each of whom is a person in his or her own right—might become "commodified" and "thingified" and passed around like other merchandise. Ends and means may become confused. The high tech means of producing children and of selling reproductive services may become for many ends in themselves. Because the parents-to-be have the money and are ready to pay the bill, the market will appeal to their needs and their desires. These needs will be exploited and desires expanded once reproductive advertising becomes a cultural force. The risk is that we may forget that the child is the end to which technological interventions and commercial transactions are a means of service. In the face of this risk I believe we need to cultivate an ethic "for the love of children." This ethic will take as its fundamental axiom that God loves each of us regardless of our genetic makeup, and we should do likewise.

My own perspective is that of a Christian theologian of the old school who still thinks that systematic theology and ethics belong together. My task in this book will be to examine some of the developments in genetic science and reproductive technology, provide warning about the numerous social issues they are likely to provoke, and then to bring theological resources to bear on developing an appropriate Christian ethic.

There are a number of things this book will not do. It will not provide an encyclopedic inventory of options in reproductive technology. Rather, it will reflect theologically and ethically on a number of issues introduced by the frontier of genetic science and the advances in high-tech baby making.

Neither will this book provide a pocket guide to decision making about family planning. Many other fine works in the field of bioethics would be more helpful in this regard. Rather, my task is foundational or perhaps protoethical. Using the challenge of reproductive technology as a stimulus, I look for an appropriate theological response. What I have discovered is that existing theological resources are not ready-made to help us. The Christian tradition, as insightful as it is in apprehending God's will for the human condition, clouds issues by relying too much on commitments made in a prescientific era in response to stimuli we today have largely forgotten. My task, as I see it, is to filter traditional theological resources for clearer application.

Likewise, this book is not a diatribe against family breakup on behalf of a conservative "family values" program or a liberal "politically correctness." That the family is in major crisis, I fully admit. I also admit that this book will not provide the magic potion that will cure the crisis. In a curious way, however, I will point out that the advance of reproductive options and the willingness of so many couples to take advantage of them represent a cultural affirmation of the family. Even so, elaborating on this is not my task here. Rather, it is to hone in on one thing: keeping the well-being of children central in a situation where it could easily become marginalized.

As a seminary student I read Don Browning's first book, *Atonement and Psychotherapy*. I underlined favorite passages and also encouraged my colleagues to read and discuss this exciting book. Later, when I took up the study of systematic theology at the University of Chicago Divinity School, I took a number of fascinating seminars with Professor Browning on interdisciplinary topics involving theology and psychology. A living example of St. Anselm's "faith seeking understanding," Browning's deep faith exudes as much curiosity as it does passion; this energy propels scholarship with a sense of purpose.

So after the appropriate moments of hesitation and deference, I enthusiastically accepted the invitation to join the ambitious Religion, Culture, and Family research project Don Browning directed from 1990 to 1996. One of the thematic convictions reiterated by Browning that I found instructive and inspiring was this: Intact families are still the best place to raise children! This conviction rings in my ears as I sit down to write this book. In addition to thanking the Lilly Foundation and the University of Chicago for their generous support, I would also like to thank my host institution, Pacific Lutheran Theological Seminary, for refitting my job description and granting sabbatical time so as to make the writing of this book possible. I would also like to thank Lutheran Brotherhood for its seminary sabbatical program, a program that benefits the church through faculty development. Carol Jacobson, my research assistant, has earned my gratitude not only for the quality work she does but also for her constant encouragement. I want to express gratitude to the Hastings Center for hosting me as a guest researcher during the spring of 1994. I also want to acknowledge with appreciation the critical review of my chapter on surrogate motherhood by the seminarians and graduate students who meet Friday afternoons at LaVals Pizzeria for "Tim and Ted's Excellent Theological Adventures." A special note of gratitude I extend to two Massachusetts colleagues, Thomas Shannon and Lisa Sowle Cahill, for giving me conceptual and editorial criticism of the first draft of this manuscript. Other partial and full manuscript readers to whom I owe similar gratitude are Don Browning, M. Christian Green, Julie Bongfeldt, Lisa Dahlen, Grant Miller Francisco, and Susan Ashbourne. For faithfulness in the face of tedium, I say "thanks" to Stan Lanier for the indexes included in this book. Finally, I would like to acknowledge my colleagues with whom I work at the Center for Theology and the Natural Sciences at the Graduate Theological Union who readily and steadily offered constructive criticism of my work: Bob Russell, Carl York, and Mark Richardson.

I dedicate this book to Paul William, Kathleen Kim, Elizabeth Anne, Martin, Derick, Helen, Matthew, Stephen, Pam and Joey, Kevin, Erika, and to all other children by destiny and by choice.

Ted Peters

1

Choosing for Children in an Era of Disintegrating Families

*We recommend a limited definition of the primary task
of families: raising children.*
—Don Browning and Carol Browning[1]

Susan Smith had an estranged husband and a wealthy boyfriend. She feared that her two children, three-year-old Michael and fourteen-month-old Alex, stood in the way of her boyfriend's making a long-term commitment to her. In 1994 she strapped them into their child safety seats in her Mazda. Then she sent the car rolling down the embankment into John D. Long Lake near Union, South Carolina. The two boys drowned. The nation was shocked and horrified: If helpless children cannot trust—of all people—their own mother, then is there any hope at all? In his sensitive analysis based on an interview with Susan Smith's pastor, Ron Rosenbaum describes her action as a "terrible choice . . . according to her own handwritten confession—the choice she's facing the electric chair for." The depth of evil here seems so ominous, perhaps even satanic, reflects Rosenbaum. Yet "she had a choice between good and evil. She had a choice and knew what she was doing when she made it."[2]

Much could be said by way of interpreting this shocking event. But I would like to limit my observations here to two: First, choice can override biologically based loyalties and, second, life for children can be dangerous even when the biological connection to a parent is intact. No doubt Susan Smith cared for her children, as her sense of grief and guilt testifies. Yet neither the sense of loyalty to these children who carried her DNA nor the duties of motherhood dictated by her biological connection to her children could stand up to her choice to pursue a relationship with the man she desired. The safety and security of her children could not be guaranteed by the fact that they were in the care of their birth mother.

The world is becoming a much more dangerous place for children. The cover of the July 1995 issue of *Life* magazine shows the face of a tender and innocent young girl. "How Can We Keep Our Children

Safe?" reads the challenging headline. Bordering the girl's face are the words: sexual abuse, abduction, television, accidents, neglect, violence, drugs, vulgarity, and alienation.

The central evidence of this growing danger is the deterioration of the physical and emotional well-being of children, argue Don Browning and Ian Evison. Today's children are worse off than children of their parent's generation. Between 1960 and 1988, we saw standardized test scores fall significantly. Twenty percent of children ages 3 to 17 now have a developmental, learning, or behavioral disorder. Obesity is up 50 percent. In 1970, 15 percent of children lived in poverty; now more than 20 percent do. Teenage suicide and homicide rates have more than doubled.[3]

Neglect is the primary cause. Ours is becoming a culture of neglect. Oh yes, the overt values favor children.[4] On the banks of John D. Long Lake, memorial crosses and comforting signs and makeshift altars stood for months after the drowning, marking the shared remorse of many people for whom the lives of children are very precious. Yet at another competing level, the previously forecasted shift in our culture toward sensate and individualist values has taken place. These values emphasize self-expression, personal fulfillment, and the pursuit of happiness for the individual. What has become marginalized and subordinated is loyalty to the family bond—that is, a loss of parental fidelity to children who are dependent on adults to support and guide their lives.

As partial evidence for the shift we note the increase of people *disagreeing* with the following statement: "When there are children in the family, parents should stay together even if they don't get along." In 1962, 51 percent disagreed. This figure had jumped to 82 percent by 1985.[5] Such data lead most social interpreters to attribute the massive disintegration of North American families to the unbridled pursuit of individual self-fulfillment on the part of grown-ups. This explanation may turn out to be somewhat oversimplified; it is, however, currently the dominant interpretation, and I believe there is sufficient truth to it to be worth working with.

Essential to this understanding of family breakup and a growing systemic neglect of children is the element of choice. Choice—along with its sister values such as freedom, autonomy, individuality, responsibility, self-actualization—is a symbol of the triumph of the liberal ideals that guide our Enlightenment society. We think of ourselves as experiencing liberation when we experience the advent of choice in areas of life previously bound to cultural or biological determinants. In the modern world we have been liberated from the now out-of-date custom of arranged marriages; we may now choose our own partners. As the revolution in genetics and reproductive technology advances, we will experience increased choice in domains we previously thought were biologically determined. Previous biological constraints will soon seem just as out-of-date as the shunned cultural practices of our great grandparents.

As a liberal society striving for and celebrating our ever-increased liberty, we can easily fall into the trap of thinking that increased choice is an end in itself, that more choice is itself an ethical achievement. But the achievement of choice is only a condition for ethical deliberation, only a prerequisite for moral decision making. Susan Smith had a choice. Each day she had the opportunity to choose whether or not to continue serving her children as their faithful mother. One day in 1994, she decided to do differently. She chose to murder her children. Ethically speaking, this was not the right choice to make. Rather than choosing for the well-being of her children, she chose against it.

The fact of choice needs to be supplemented by the criteria of choice. The discipline of ethics helps us distinguish better choices from worse choices. Ethics presupposes choice, as well as the values or other factors that distinguish better decisions from worse decisions. The point of this book is that if concerned Christians are to meet the moral challenges posed by the advance of reproductive technology, we will have to acknowledge and accept increased choice and construct our ethics on a culture of choice. One corollary is this: Any attempt to bypass choice and construct our ethics on a foundation of now-outdated cultural or biological constraints is bound to fail us. A second corollary is that the concept of covenant—the concept of a freely entered into promise to remain faithful—could and should be applied to the relationship parents enter into with their children. Whether or not the promise to love "till death us do part" has shown itself effective in holding marriages together, a covenantal promise of this sort is desperately needed in our era of the growing marginalization of children.

A third corollary, the one that will occupy most of our attention in this volume, is that a covenant to love children means that we will treat children as ends and not merely as a means to fulfill someone else's desires. This is important because as high-tech genetics and reproductive services enter the medical marketplace, there is some risk that children may be treated as merchandise to be bought and used and eventually disposed of. There is some risk that children may become "commodified." To help avoid this, we need to cultivate ethical deliberation as a cultural exercise that declares children as persons, objects of love, and worthy of covenantal commitment.

The guiding principle for an ethics that acknowledges choice is this indicative observation and prescriptive admonition: God loves each of us regardless of our genetic makeup, and we should do likewise. When children become produced with designer genes, our love for the designed child should trump the desires of the designers. The love of children should serve as the primary guide for the choices we make.

Perhaps this seems obvious. Yet two significant social trends threaten to obscure it. The first is the difficult-to-understand shift in the structure of family life—that is, the widespread disintegration of the family unit we have known since the advent of the industrial era. The nuclear family is breaking down everywhere primarily because of divorce but also because of the following: nonmarital motherhood, single-family households, growing poverty, and child neglect and abuse. In this situation children are increasingly seen as impediments to parental happiness, as psychological drains and economic liabilities that prevent individual men and women from achieving self-fulfillment.

The second trend is the explosive advance of science and technology that will soon be translated into marketable services for designer baby making. The advance of reproductive technology will yield more and more choice for persons about to become parents. Technical reproductive services will begin to make procreation look more and more like business deals and consumer purchasing, and if children come to be seen as the merchandised product, they will be evaluated according to standards of quality control. Customer satisfaction may supersede the intrinsic good of the child. The increase in reproductive choice within the cultural context of family breakdown could be a deadly combination for children of the future.

In what follows we will look briefly at the analysis of family disintegration proffered by two sociologists, David Popenoe at Rutgers University and Robert Bellah at the University of California at Berkeley, along with two recent studies—*Families in Focus* by the Population Council and *Marriage in America* by the Institute for American Values. What all these hold in common is the observation that family breakup is caused by a certain set of cultural values, specifically our Enlightenment values of individual choice and the pursuit of self-fulfillment. Because these are individualist values and because families constitute communities, the apparent conclusion is that these values are undermining family fidelity and stability with the result being that children are neglected.

For the most part I accept the logic of these analyses. However, as we proceed toward constructive ethics, I will register my reluctance to seek a solution that bypasses these individualist values. So long as we live in a liberal society, no ethic that ignores or disregards choice and self-fulfillment can be expected to have persuasive force. What we want from an ethical vision in our time is a powerful lure that will draw people to make choices on behalf of the well-being of children.

Is the Family Disintegrating?

Is the family really on the decline? David Popenoe, at least, would say yes. By this he means that "the institution of the family is growing weaker; it is losing social power and social functions, losing influence over behavior and opinion; and generally becoming less important in life."[6] With the decline of the family comes a decline in the quality of life for children.

Popenoe has studied a number of advanced modernized societies, with a focus on Sweden but also including the United States. His key observation is that the "traditional" family of the industrial era—characterized by a lifelong sexually exclusive marriage between one man and one woman with children, where the man is the primary provider and the ultimate authority—is being rapidly replaced by some form of postnuclear family system, or nonsystem. The difference between decline and disappearance is enormous, and Popenoe wants to say that the decline of the traditional nuclear family in no way indicates that it will disappear completely. Rather, he believes that its influence is waning while modern societies engage in the ongoing process of restructuring themselves.

Some, especially the religious right, have decried family decline as "the equivalent of moral decay" that is "seriously weakening the very fiber of the nation." However, "some left-wing groups, especially radical feminist groups, who regarded family decline as a positive human achievement because it meant the decline of patriarchal tyranny and the continued liberation of the individual" have not felt that the decline of the traditional family is deleterious.[7] Popenoe's own position is that the family is in decline, to be sure, and that this is liberating news for those pursuing individualist values and self-fulfillment. It is bad news, however, for children. The postnuclear trend is an adult-oriented trend that is void of a vision of responsibility toward children.

The rise and fall of the nuclear family is a long-term trend spanning the history of the Industrial Revolution. On the eve of the Industrial Revolution, multiple generation kinship systems gave way to the conjugal or nuclear household with one mother and one father plus children. As the nuclear family form adapted to the modern industrial way of life, the man took a job outside the home while the wife remained at home. Now referred to as the "traditional" family, this form of the marital union tends to be sexually exclusive and lifelong. Divorce is uncommon. The family strives to achieve and maintain an intimate and protective environment that focuses on the nurture and care of the children.

Key to understanding the industrial family is the rise of the two spheres, home and work. The preindustrial family functioned as the primary economic unit, whether a sedentary farm family at home or an immigrant family running a restaurant in a foreign city. The family was the principal unit of production as well as consumption. In the modern nuclear family, however, work and home have become separated. The married woman is given the task of creating what Popenoe calls the domestic "nest" from which she can look after the welfare of her husband and children. The married man, in sharp contrast, devotes his professional time outside the home earning a living for the family.[8] Gender roles become more specifically distinguished and defined.

Industrialization and this bourgeois family form seem to come together, but Popenoe reminds us that "one should be careful not to conclude that industrialization is the cause of family change."[9] Economics is not the sole factor determining such social change. Cultural forces need to be independently assessed for their influence, and it just may be that the rise of the traditional family was a partial cause of the Industrial Revolution. Regardless of which is the cause and which is the effect, the traditional family and modernity have come together.

The period known as the 1950s, which actually began in the post–World War II 1940s and extended through the first half of the 1960s, marked a brief interlude in the otherwise giant trend toward family breakup. The real stake in the family revival of the 1950s was held by the rising lower middle class experiencing rapid economic advance in the postwar reconstruction years. For one generation the man could earn a living wage and support an unemployed wife and children in a single-family home that was being purchased.

The major flaw in the nuclear family, from the modern point of view, is that the situation for women has fallen short of full gender equality. Certainly women gained status as they took responsibility for the household, but they lost considerable control over their working conditions. The shift to the nuclear family system on the eve of modernity had marked a relative release of the power of patriarchy and a step toward the liberation of women—a small step, not a giant step. Previously, virtually all extended family kinship systems had been patriarchal in their authority structure. With the rise of the nuclear family the kinship structure was weakened, and this in turn weakened the patriarchal authority structure. The division of labor within the modern family momentarily led to relatively greater equality and authority for women. However, in the twentieth century with the husband as the principal breadwinner, the woman as head of the household found herself located in suburbia and somewhat isolated from much outside social contact. With the privatization of family life, especially in the suburbs of the 1950s, women who were not involved in volunteer work in churches or charities became socially isolated. Many women of the 1950s and early 1960s felt the malaise reported by Betty Friedan in *The Feminine Mystique.* The next step toward full equality of women would require employment outside the home, the professionalization of women, and a postnuclear family.

Although the intact nuclear family remains the ideal in the minds of most people in the industrialized West, especially in America, family breakup is rapidly becoming the norm. Statistically speaking, one in two marriages in the United States will end in divorce. More than one-fourth of all households are now headed by a single parent. The percentage of single-parent households in the United States doubled during the fifteen-year period of 1970 to 1985, where it now rests at 26.3 percent. The highest rates of family instability can be found in the underemployed underclass in large urban areas where inner-city families are marginalized from the mainstream. Here 60 percent of babies are born out of wedlock. But high divorce rates and single parenting occurs among the country's wealthiest classes as well. As the material standard of living improves, so does the overall divorce rate. This leads Popenoe to conclude that divorce is caused not only by poverty but also by affluence.[10] It appears that divorce is committed to be with us, for richer or poorer, even in the middle class.

What might follow the nuclear stage? Communal living? Not likely. "There is virtually no evidence that communal living will become an important alternative to the nuclear family, at least not in America."[11]

The clearly identifiable trend is toward increased individualism and the pursuit of self-fulfillment, and this trend leads to the dissolution of the traditional family without necessarily replacing it with a more durable social institution. The dissolution of nuclear families leads to single-parent households. It also leads to stepfamilies or blended families, but these dissolve into divorce at a rate even higher than the original marriages.

Children indisputably are the victims of divorce. Longitudinal studies have shown that after divorce two-thirds of the children show symptoms of stress, and one-half would say, in effect, that their life had been destroyed. Five years after the divorce, a third of the children are still seriously disturbed and another third are having psychological difficulties. "Marital disruption is associated with psychological problems in children that may persist for many years."[12]

The constant in both the nuclear and postnuclear stages will be pair-bonding between two adults. Marriage among Americans is at a high rate, and most western adults engage in pair-bonding one or more times in their lives. During the nuclear family period, sexual intercourse was restricted to the marital pair-bond. Even though some sexual activity took place outside the marital bond, there was less premarital and extramarital sexual intercourse than in the emerging postnuclear era. In the nuclear family, sex and procreation were closely identified. Today's advances in contraception among other factors permit a greater severing of the connection between sex and procreation in the postnuclear age. "Sexual activity today starts earlier in life, takes place with a larger number of sex partners, and seldom has procreation as the goal."[13]

Yet what is important to note here is that the desires for pair-bonding among adults show no signs of diminishing. "Adults still desire a relatively permanent relationship with one other person, usually one of the opposite sex; indeed, pair-bonding (but not marrying) now takes place at an increasingly younger age than before. But most adults now pair-bond with more than one other adult during their lifetimes."[14] Although most women are likely to have one child or more during their lifetime, pair-bonds are not set up with parenting as the primary purpose. Rather, what is paramount is satisfying the need for intimate relationship. "Indeed, it is the strong desire for meaningful relationships that has led, as much as anything else, to the high rate of marital breakup. People's expectations of what a marital relationship can and should be have escalated. They are no longer willing to tolerate a relationship that is unfulfilling; and there is always a chance that they can find a better one."[15] On a large scale this marks a cultural "shift from child-centeredness to adult-centeredness. . . . Parents seldom break up a relationship to benefit the children; it is to benefit themselves; that is, typically their needs for intimacy are not being met. If children had a say in such matters, the rate of family dissolution most assuredly would drop."[16]

The split between the ideal and the actual is significant for Popenoe. At the level of the ideal, the single lifelong marriage has not lost its currency.

> Probably the vast majority of people, regardless of political persuasion, agree on the family ideal of a lasting, heterosexual pairbond, based on affection and companionship, which provides devoted and continuing love and support to children of the union. Even if their actual behavior would suggest otherwise, people's espousal of that ideal in advanced societies is remarkably persistent. In this sense, at least, the great majority of people agree on the ideal of a strong family.[17]

Despite the ideal of a strong family, in actual practice dissolving a marriage to pursue a higher level of personal happiness is the accepted norm. With this normative practice, children suffer. "It has become clear that adults no longer need children in their lives, at least not in economic terms. The problem is that children, as much as they ever did, still need adults."[18]

What does Popenoe recommend? At first, he recommends a change in values. "Some shift in values is required, namely, a partial retreat from the predominance of self-fulfillment."[19] But then, as if giving in to the self-fulfillment juggernaut, he tries to redefine fulfillment so as to include the responsibility for raising children.

> Lasting personal fulfillment is better achieved as a by-product of the pursuit of extraindividual goals, which reflect high ideals and whose pursuit involves action in concert with others. Perhaps the most meaningful experience of life is the feeling of oneness with others in the pursuit of some common purpose of great intrinsic worth. On a large scale this may consist of significant humanitarian ventures; on a small scale it can involve the raising of children.[20]

Children, it would seem, have gotten caught in the middle of the battle between individual and extraindividual values. For another report from the battlefront we turn to the work of Robert Bellah.

The Not-so-good Society
for Children

Robert Bellah and his colleagues involved in "The Good Society" project say that we no longer understand the institutional logic of family life. This is due in large part to the cultural shift away from family identity to individual identity, to emphasis on the primacy of personal satisfaction or fulfillment.

The pursuit of the individual self in an increasingly fragmented society, where all institutions are losing their moral moorings, has a major consequence; namely, no one is left to care fully for the children. No matter how frail or faltering, families remain the primary theater in which children can realize their full capacities. The relationships between husbands and wives, and between parents and children, liberate the growing self for expression and provide a safe and affectionate context for each child to explore the range of experiences from joy to suffering, frustration to discipline, and dependence to independence. Even if our era watches as the nuclear family goes by the board, the institution of the family in some form is absolutely necessary if our society is to show love to its children.

Can we blame the women's movement for this? No, not exactly. Although it is factually wrong and morally insensitive to blame feminism for the dissolution of family life, Bellah is willing to acknowledge that the movement toward increased rights for women is driven by this larger cultural shift toward individual autonomy and self-fulfillment. Divorce and the abandonment of children is the result. Yet the fact remains that men, even more than women, shirk their family responsibilities to pursue self-fulfillment. Hence, there is no warrant for returning to a time when women had fewer rights on the pretense of saving the family.

> Returning women to a situation where they lack legal rights, cannot own property if they are married, and have no higher education so as to "save the family" would be not only repugnant to women but wholly incompatible with our current understanding of the dignity befitting any human being. Yet there is a small grain of truth in relating "women's liberation" to the decline of the nuclear family, and it has to do with the fact that in recent decades individual fulfillment has ranked ever higher as a central cultural value.[21]

During the late 1960s and early 1970s sexual liberation was a component of women's liberation. "Women enjoy sex too" was the slogan. This combined with the "choice" position on abortion led to a sharp

separation between sexual pleasure and baby making. Sexual fulfillment could now be spoken of as a value in its own right apart from its
role in marriage and family life. Bellah and his colleagues today are willing to separate the sexual from the procreative; however, they are
unwilling to give up on families entirely: "We do not argue that the
modern nuclear family, which combines the emotional intimacy and
sexuality of the parents with the nurture of children, is the only possible or morally respectable form of the family; but because of its importance in bringing children into the world and raising them, it has a kind
of centrality and value that we cannot afford to ignore."[22]

If we acknowledge the breakdown of a sense of the common good
for the whole of society and a corresponding loss of identity determined
by family life, where does this leave us? It leaves us squarely in the domain of individual choice. Whether we like it or not, the end of the road
for a disintegrating liberal society is individual choice. There is no escape. There will be no road back to a robust family life that does not begin with individual choice. This leads Bellah and company to press for
a new kind of teaching, a teaching that lifts the ideal of self-fulfillment
found in mutuality, love, and commitment.

As Bellah points out, "When marriage is a choice rather than a necessity, a choice between two people with a good deal of autonomy and
independence, it is still a choice we want to make, an obligation we
want to assume, a commitment we want to keep, because loyalty is a
virtue essential to our sense of a genuine self."[23] The trick will be to
show how commitment to family life and the loving of children is an
expression of, rather than an alternative to, choosing the path of self-
fulfillment.

With regard to family form, there is no getting around one fact: Two
parents in a mutually supporting relationship provide children with the
best opportunity for healthy growth. It is true that many children who
are raised in single-parent households become strong, self-reliant, and
loving adults; so single-parent families deserve social support, not criticism. In addition, childless heterosexual couples or even homosexual
couples can enjoy a rich family life and should not be seen as a threat
to the so-called normal family. Nevertheless, the two parents committed to a long-term responsible relationship deserve special attention
when the question of children is raised.

> The two-parent family with children has special significance be-
> cause it is the family form that has carried primary responsibility
> for raising children and because it has become harder and harder

to sustain. But recognizing the symbolic as well as practical centrality of this family form in no way means a derogation of other family forms. . . . What is important is the quality of family life, not the diversity of its forms.[24]

I would simply agree with Bellah's concept of the good society on this point, namely, that the form of the family is less important than the quality of family life. And the quality of family life I'm most concerned with here has to do with the well-being of children. I would like to add that the door we must pass through to lead to the well-being of children in our era is the door of choice. Even if Bellah's description of the current cultural situation is accurate, we ought not fool ourselves into thinking that a simple return to the nuclear two-parent family form will have the moral muscle to meet the current challenge. This description of two-parent family success does not lead automatically to a prescription regarding family form. The inescapability of increased choice in people's lives must be met with an ethic based on choice, an ethic in which parents—regardless of the number or gender of the parents—choose to make a covenant that they will love their children to such an extent that the well-being of the children is regarded as equal to, if not given priority over, their own striving for self-fulfillment.

If the analyses of Bellah and Popenoe are reasonably accurate, the temptation on the part of those wishing to think in terms of Christian ethics might be to disavow personal self-fulfillment and give priority to some premodern or modern family form. Because the concept of self-sacrifice is so highly valued in the Christian tradition, the temptation is to identify self-fulfillment with selfishness and then repudiate both of them. The temptation is to repudiate individualism and endorse some form of communitarian ethic that dissolves personal striving into family striving. By blunting personal striving, we might naively assume that we have struck a blow for family stability and, thereby, for the well-being of children.

Both Bellah and Popenoe themselves flirt with this temptation, but they also recognize that the drive for individual self-fulfillment will not easily be blunted; nor is it necessary to do so. The trick they both ponder pulling off is to somehow paint responsibility toward others—in this case responsibility toward children—into the self-fulfillment picture. To pull off this trick, I believe, we would need to frame the picture with choice. People will be responsible only if they choose to be responsible. The task of ethics is to hold up the vision of the child's well-being and encourage individuals to choose to commit themselves to this vision for the lifetime of the child.

Children as a Sign of Hope

Duke ethicist Stanley Hauerwas embraces such a vision. Hauerwas would agree with Popenoe, and he would advise even more strongly that the marital bond seek a higher purpose than mere self-fulfillment through intimacy. That higher purpose is the raising of children.

Hauerwas notes that the crisis of the family in our society does not indicate the absence of a moral ethos for the family. Rather, Hauerwas says the crisis reflects exactly how the family is in fact formed by the deepest moral convictions we have about ourselves.[25] In our liberal society those convictions can be identified as individualism, autonomy, and self-fulfillment. We pursue marital relationships out of an ethic of self-fulfillment, and then destiny plays a trick on us; namely, we repeatedly discover that we have married the wrong person. Hauerwas tries to point out that our moral task ought not to be to choose the right person. Rather, our moral task should be to learn how to love and care for this stranger to whom we find ourselves married. The ethic of self-fulfillment in a marital relationship leads to divorce unless complemented with another higher-minded ethical task. "For marriage to be sustained today," says Hauerwas, "we need a sense of contributing to a people through having children."[26]

Children and hope belong together, says Hauerwas. This leads him to place a high value on bringing children into the world.

> Christians do not place their hope in their children, but rather their children are a sign of their hope, in spite of the considerable evidence to the contrary, that God has not abandoned this world. Because we have confidence in God, we find the confidence in ourselves to bring new life into this world, even though we cannot be assured that our children will share our mission. For they, too, must be converted if they are to be followers of the way.[27]

Hope is not what children experience, however, if they feel unwanted. The actual problem that North American society and other societies around the world face is having too many children in the unwanted or at least uncared for category.[28] By recommending that Christians have more babies, Hauerwas seems to be recommending that we put out a grass fire by spraying charcoal lighter on it. Would it not be more consistent with Christian principles to go outside the established community and bring in existing children from the highways and byways to be cared for? To the issue of unwanted children we now turn, noting as we do that this subject inevitably begins with a concern for marriage and marriage breakup.

Unwed Homes,
Unwanted Children

Two studies published in 1995—one a U.N. global study by the Population Council and the other a U.S. domestic study by the Council on Families in America—both conclude that the institution of marriage is suffering badly and that children are suffering because of it. "The parent-child relationship is the fundamental building block of human society," writes Judith Bruce and her colleagues at The Population Council; but this building block is cracked and disintegrating and no longer able to support a healthy and viable society virtually anywhere in the world.[29]

Although families are as adaptable as they are diverse in form, they are changing faster today than ever before. Based on data gathered during the United Nation's International Year of the Family in 1994, their *Families in Focus* report identifies five global trends in family formation, structure, and function: (1) rising age at which women first marry and first give birth, delaying the formation of new families; (2) decreasing size of households; (3) increasing financial burden on working-age parents for supporting children, as well as older dependents, in their household; (4) increasing percentage of female-headed households; and (5) shifting the balance of financial responsibilities for family support onto the shoulders of women as their share of the labor market increases and the share of men decreases. The combined impact of these trends at work, with only modest differences in different cultures and classes, is a disproportionate loading of financial and other burdens onto the mother's shoulders, a weight too heavy for one parent alone to bear.

The difficulties for women around the world are poignant, showing that in many societies choice may be more of a goal sought than a power possessed. Due to cultural traditions and stereotyped sex roles that support the subordination of women to the men in their lives, their increased family responsibilities do not translate into liberation. For example, husbands and wives often think differently about the need for protection against sexually transmitted diseases or about the number of children the family should bring into the world. Citing fear of disapproval or even of abuse from their husbands, women frequently succumb to pleas to abandon contraceptives. "Women's lack of control over their own sexuality and fertility remains one of the most threatening aspects of their lives." In a subsection titled, "Marriage and Motherhood as Free Choices," the Population Council report says,

By all indications women want and need satisfying sexual relationships. Most women probably also want to have a close partnership with a man and want to have children (whether because of innate desire or socialization). The issue for most women is not the value of these experiences, but rather the conditions under which they experience them. Women's weak bargaining power in the areas of sexual relationships, childbearing, and childrearing is the difficulty.[30]

The contrast with men is striking. While women's lives are characterized primarily by motherhood, men's lives are characterized largely without reference to fatherhood. The biological connection through supplying half a child's genes amounts to the sum total of the definition of fatherhood in many cases. An ethnographic look at 186 different societies reveals that in only 2 percent of societies do fathers have "regular close relationships" with their babies, and in only 5 percent of societies do they have such close relationships with their toddlers during early childhood. When we add to this relative lack of involvement the worldwide rise in cases of divorce or family abandonment where the father is geographically estranged, children in large numbers are deserted to a destiny of living with an overburdened mother, inadequate financial support, and lack of parental attention.

The definition of *father* offered by the Population Council is relevant to our study here. Defined narrowly, a *father* is the man who provides half of a child's genetic material. Indeed, many men throughout history have restricted their fathering to this reproductive contribution. But the Population Council wishes to broaden the concept of fatherhood to embrace what it dubs as "functions," such as feeding, cleaning, playing, holding, showing affection, teaching, socializing, disciplining, and modeling appropriate behavior. It also wishes to include indirect activities that benefit children such as providing economic resources, shelter, protection, and emotional support to the mother.

> In sorting out the fathers' roles, the focus should be on the functional impact of fathers in children's lives. An abusive or economically noncontributing father is not likely to be an asset to a child, while a caring and contributing father is—regardless of whether or not the father and child live together or are biologically related. . . . Engaged fathering increases children's emotional and social wellbeing.[31]

Significant here is that the social value of the father takes clear precedence over the biological.

This is the Population Council's fatherhood ideal. However, overall

global trends toward nonmarital childbearing and marital breakup give
the lie to our traditional image of ideal father and mother making a safe
and secure home for children. Unwantedness is spreading. The percentage of nonmarital births has jumped over the last two decades in
the United States from 5.4 percent to 28 percent and in Northern Eu-
rope from 8.8 percent to 33.3 percent, while remaining quite low in
Japan. Although many sub-Saharan African societies have low premarital birthrates, a quarter of births in some countries such as Kenya and
Liberia are nonmarital. The figure jumps to 77 percent, however, in
Botswana. The percentage of marriages ending in divorce or other forms
of separation for women under age 50 in England and Wales is 41.7
percent; Canada, 38.3 percent; Sweden, 44.1 percent; Kenya, 24.2 percent; Sri Lanka, 25.6 percent; Indonesia, 37.3 percent; and Peru, 26.1
percent. These figures lead us to generalize that a quarter or more of
marriages the world over will dissolve during the childrearing years.
Single-parent households with dependent children now account for
14.9 percent of the total in Australia, 17 percent in Sweden, and 23.9
percent in the United States. To these statistics the Population Council
adds the category of "unwanted" children, those who are born after a
family has already reached its desired limit. By this definition, 32 percent of all children born in Colombia are unwanted, 44 percent in Peru,
and 26 percent in Sri Lanka. Whether due to nonmarital birth, divorce,
or born too late to be wanted, the unwanted children of the world are
more likely to be poor in economic resources and also in health.

Signs of unwantedness are appearing everywhere. "More recent evidence of abandoned baby girls in orphanages in China, and the growing numbers of street children in many large cities in less-developed
countries, further illustrate the most extreme consequence of unwantedness: severe neglect and abandonment of children."[32] The Population
Council registers its worry. "Our analysis reveals that the present and
future wellbeing of significant numbers of the world's children is in
jeopardy because of adverse family circumstances beyond their control,
including their parents' sexual and marital choices."[33]

Broken Homes,
Broken Children

The second study, *Marriage in America*, published by The Council on
Families in America and co-chaired by Jean Bethke Elshtain and David
Popenoe, offers a forceful argument for garnering cultural support for

marriage as the only way to improve the lot of children in our society. What they call the "divorce revolution"—that is, "the steady displacement of a marriage culture by a culture of divorce and unwed parenthood—has created terrible hardships for children. It has generated poverty within families. It has burdened us with unsupportable social costs. It has failed to deliver on its promise of greater adult happiness and better relationships between men and women . . . . It is time to rebuild a family culture based on enduring marital relationships."[34]

The well-being of children in America is deteriorating, according to all relevant indicators: rates of juvenile delinquency and crime, drug and alcohol abuse, suicide, depression, and the growing number of children living in poverty. Since 1960, juvenile violent crime has increased sixfold, from 16,000 arrests in 1960 to 96,000 in 1992, a period when the total number of juveniles had remained relatively stable. Reports of child neglect and abuse have been multiplied by a factor of five since 1976. Teen suicide has nearly tripled. Poverty has shifted from the elderly to the young, so that today 38 percent of the nation's poor are children.

No doubt many factors have contributed to the deteriorating circumstances in which children today find themselves. Yet Elshtain and Popenoe rank as the most fundamental factor of all *the weakening of marriage as an institution.* Unless we reverse the decline of marriage, they argue, no other achievements—no tax cut, no government program, no new idea—will be powerful enough to stop the decline in the well-being of children. So the goal they have set is to increase the proportion of children who grow up with their two married parents and decrease the proportion of children who do not.

Every child needs and deserves the love and provision of two parents, a mother and a father. The loving two-parent family is the best environment for children to gain identity, discipline, and the moral education essential for their full individual development. Surveys show that as children from broken homes become teenagers, they have two or three times as many behavioral and psychological problems as those children from intact homes. The evidence is mounting that the weakening of marriage is having devastating consequences on the well-being of children.

Why is marriage weakening? Elshtain joins in the Popenoe analysis we reviewed earlier, locating the cause not in economics but in culture. The root cause is in the values that we as a society hold. We no longer value marriage with sufficiently high regard. Rather, we place our primary values on choice and happiness for the individual. Individual choice in the pursuit of individual happiness has become the de facto summum bonum. "In our view, marriage has declined primarily because we no longer value the institution as highly as we once did. . . . We now put a much higher value on individualism, choice, and unrestricted personal liberty. . . . 'Till death us do part' has been replaced by 'as long as I am happy.'"[35] The emphasis on individualism and choice has wrought a shift in cultural support away from marriage toward divorce. Once we were a nation in which marriage and family values were inherent to the American dream. Now we have become a nation in which divorce is commonly seen as the path to personal liberation. Recognizing that in individual cases, of course, divorce is sometimes the best solution for a highly troubled marriage, Elshtain and Popenoe are registering their concern that our culture has accepted divorce as a normative experience for millions. Rather than accept this as the norm, they want to sound the alarm. Rather than resignation, passivity, and excuse making, they want to call us to arms.

To contribute to the well-being of children, marriages need to be permanent and loving. This is why phrases such as "till death us do part" appear so frequently in wedding ceremonies. Maintaining a permanent covenant between a woman and a man is no easy task; so religious and other cultural supports need to be invoked. Elshtain and Popenoe recognize that affective ties between men and women, "no matter how biologically based they may be, are notoriously fragile and breakable."[36] This is why weddings, in both their legal and religious contexts, include vows of fidelity and permanence. In large measure, of course, these vows are directed toward the man; they are "designed to bind males to long-term commitment in order to foster the social institution of fatherhood." In saying this, they recognize that we human beings may not be suited perfectly to monogamous relationships. Our biological dispositions are not enough to guarantee successful homemaking. This is why we need the full weight of culture in the form of pro-marriage values to help create an atmosphere within which children can enter the world and enjoy trustworthy love and nourishment.

Toward the end of influencing cultural values and public policy, Elshtain and Popenoe offer numerous constructive proposals. Relevant here are their four broad goals. First, we should reclaim the ideal image of the permanent marriage and affirm that such a marriage provides the best environment in which to raise children. Second, we should assert unequivocally that out-of-wedlock childbearing is wrong, that we should reduce our divorce rate, and that every child deserves to have a father. Third, we should resolve to increase the proportion of children who grow up with two married parents and decrease the proportion who do not. Fourth, we should resolve that parents increase the amount of time they spend with their children. This means that no one should engage in paid employment for more than sixty hours per week if it takes him or her out of the home.

To the religious community they say specifically that we need to restate theologically that marriage is sacramental and covenantal and that these religious dimensions have implications for the natural, economic, social, and legal components of marriage. They also recommend that we not equate marriage with "committed relationships," in general, but rather support marriage as a legal and binding institution.

If the threat to the well-being of children is the disease, then in my judgment these prescriptions will not provide a cure. They are unfortunately only a cure for ailing marriages. To simply garner religious validation for permanent, legal, two-parent households will provide too little therapy for the disease. This would be like putting a Band-Aid over a three-inch gash. More is needed to sew up the wound. Intact families may be in the broad sense necessary for the love of children, but in themselves they are not sufficient. Even if we are able to establish a persuasive ethic that draws people to this family form, we still require commitment to children. Commitment to children can no longer be taken for granted. If we can do it for marriage, then up-front, public, legal, articulated promises to love and care for children for life should be the minimum starting point.

Now let me be clear on one point. I am not devaluing the passion by which the *Marriage in America* report calls for a renewed commitment to marriage as a means to getting at commitment to children. I am not seeking a child-oriented ethic that completely bypasses a sexual ethic or marriage ethic. My point is that the commitment to love children calls for more than what we normally associate with committed relationships between consenting adults or lifelong marriages. Scientific advances in the technology of baby making have shocked our consciousness, so we need to consider other factors beyond merely what makes for a rich sexual relationship or a faithful marital bond.

The Male Problematic
and the Inheritance Myth

In addition to focusing on rising divorce rates, another way to view the disintegration of families is to look at the *male problematic*. The male problematic, as Don Browning identifies it, is the widespread tendency for men to father children and then fail to shoulder sufficient responsibility to support them. The *male problematic* is defined as biological procreation without social responsibility.

When we think of nonmarital births, for example, we immediately think of single mothers supporting their children alone. We should be reminded, however, that for these women to become mothers, at some point a man had to make a contribution. As we have seen, nearly a third of children being born in the United States now enter the world out of wedlock. Such nonmarital birthing is growing around the world. In Barbados only 22 percent of fathers live with their children, and in Chile 42 percent do not support their children. In both countries these neglected children are more poorly nourished and perform more poorly in school than children from intact two-parent families. Browning trumpets, "Men are procreating around the world, contributing to the population explosion, but doing less and less to support their children. Population explosion and deepening poverty due to lack of family formation are going hand in hand around the world."[37]

We know these men in North America as "deadbeat dads." Governmental pressures are increasing to use newly developed DNA testing to establish paternity and then to make those deadbeat dads pay. In California a man who fathers a child outside of marriage is liable to the same financial responsibility as one who does so within marriage. On the surface, this may sound like the government is striking a blow for family values. This is but a thin charade, however. The sole motive for law enforcement is to reduce the government's commitment to support impoverished single-parent families by imposing court-ordered financial payments by absentee fathers. The assumption our society makes here is significant: If DNA testing can prove biological paternity, then the deadbeat dad must pay. The biological connection defines fatherhood, so it is assumed.

This biological definition of fatherhood lies at the root of the male problematic. To get at a deeper understanding of the male problematic, Browning appeals to sociobiology and to theology. The sociobiologists—now operating under other assumed names such as *human evolutionary ecology* or *evolutionary psychology*—have a materialist explanation for the social attachment of biological fathers to their children.[38] The explanation can be found in the twin concepts of *kin altruism* and *paternal certainty*. The concept of kin altruism, reminiscent of the selfish-gene theory of the 1970s, holds that we have a natural inclination to prefer genetic kin over outsiders or strangers. When we sense that our children or other relatives are biological copies of ourselves—even if only partial copies—we dedicate our lives and pledge our fortunes to defend their welfare. *Kin altruism* is "the tendency to care and even sacrifice for those who carry one's genes."[39] Here is a prayer that I've long thought expresses well the theology of kin altruism.

> God bless me and my wife.
> My son John and his wife.
> Us four.
> No more.

Now, according to Browning, to release the energies of male paternal investment (MPI), the father needs to have certainty that the child in question is his. Mothers can easily be certain that a child is theirs; men at best can have only degrees of certainty. For paternal investment in their children to be unleashed, men have to have a high degree of certainty that the infants are in fact theirs. Kin altruism depends on paternal certainty.[40]

Browning feels that these concepts borrowed from sociobiology illuminate the contemporary male problematic. In part, I too find them illuminating. However, what we have here is certainly insufficient for ethical construction. It is insufficient for a couple reasons. The irresponsibility of biological fathers seems to run rampant regardless of paternal certainty. Even when fathers are confident that the children they have fathered are genetically theirs, they may still abandon them. DNA testing, which confirms paternity usually beyond doubt, does not automatically persuade a deadbeat dad to stand up cheerfully and say, "OK, now I'll gladly pay."

In addition, it is theologically problematic. Even if kin altruism had the power to motivate fathers to engage in self-sacrificial love for their children (and to be good husbands as well), it would be only a partial ethical victory. Certainly kin love is better than neglect. Yet it falls far short of the Christian vision regarding how human beings should relate to one another. Jesus stressed beyond-kin altruism. When he enjoined us to love our neighbor, he frequently illustrated the teaching with stories of foreigners such as the Good Samaritan. He told us to love our enemies. He gave no priority to one's biological kin, family, tribe, or nation. Applied internally to families, this translates into love of social kin even when they are not biological kin. Sociobiology may be illuminating but, in my judgment, it certainly is insufficient for such an ethical foundation a Christian could embrace.[41] One might counter, of course, that our concern here is much more modest: supporting love within the family, not exhorting us to neighbor love or enemy love.

Focusing on the family, Don Browning works diligently to develop a two-step ethic. The first is a premoral step, sociobiology. The second step is a theological and ethical one. Biology is premoral but morally relevant, argues Browning, and the fields of ethics and theology should draw on biology through the lens of sociobiological theory. In preparation for taking the theological step, Browning finds Thomas Aquinas offering an astute diagnosis of the male problematic and Martin Luther offering a healing prescription. Aquinas observed what sociobiologists observe, namely, that men "indulge at will in the pleasure of copulation, even as in the pleasure of eating."[42] This medieval scholastic also noted that parents care for their children for the simple reason that their offspring bear their biological makeup. He further noted that fathers need reasonable assurance that their children belong biologically to them. "Man naturally desires to be assured of his offspring; and this assurance would be altogether nullified in the case of promiscuous copulation."[43] Then Aquinas appeals to Eph. 5:25 to argue that, just as Christ is steadfast and does not forsake the church, so fathers should steadfastly serve their wives and children.

Luther picks up where Aquinas leaves off to tell us *how* fathers should love their children. With considerable drama and eloquence Luther admonishes men to pray to God that they may be made worthy to embrace the divinely appointed tasks of caring for children. Men should rock the baby, make the bed, wash the diapers, smell the stench, stay up nights, comfort its cries, heal its rashes and sores, and show care to both child and mother. Although these appear to be "insignificant, distasteful, and despised duties," Luther says men should pray to God; "I am serving thy creature and thy most precious will."[44] Browning believes both Aquinas and Luther "saw Christianity as overcoming, or at least stabilizing, their respective versions of the male problematic."[45] Browning is right on this point, in my judgment.

The larger conceptual framework within which Browning places this prescription for healing the male problematic is the two-step ethic based on natural reason and divine revelation. Sociobiology provides the equivalent of natural reason. Whereas Aristotle's biology provided the light of natural reason for Aquinas, sociobiology could do the same for today's theologians.

The sociobiological lens views civil responsibility as an expanded form of kin altruism. Communal love grows out of early parent-child investments and attachments. Parents love their children. Parental love is the model for all human love. This parental love is actually a form of self-love because it is based on the underlying biological demand of our DNA to replicate itself through human reproduction. Thus, sociobiology gives genetic reasons for the special love relationship between parents and children. What the theologian needs to do, argues Browning, is acknowledge this and proceed to cultivate a broader social dimension of love that capitalizes on family love and expands it to include nonkin. Family affections should be elaborated and expanded to nonfamilial circles. Rather than self-sacrificial *agape* love, Browning supports *caritas* as the desired form of Christian love because it builds on enlightened self-regard. To love our enemies, as Jesus commands, would then be an expansion of loving our friends, which in turn is an expansion of loving our children.

Browning distinguishes *altruism,* defined as behavior that appears at first to sacrifice one's immediate reproductive advantage but in the long run contributes to one's reproductive advantage, from *Christian love;* but he sees them as connected rather than disjointed. If the concept of Christian love means *agape* in the sense of true self-sacrifice, then of course no connection can be made with biological altruism. But a more "mellow" form of Christian love, *caritas,* which includes self-love and self-regard at the core, could be conjoined in a fruitful and productive way. The self-love of a parent toward his or her biological children could be connected with genuine care for others in society. Browning wants to harness the power of admittedly selfish familial forces for wider social good; therefore, the distinctively Protestant—distinctively Lutheran—understanding of *agape* must be rejected as inadequate.

> Extreme self-sacrificial formulations of the Christian concept of love may themselves unwittingly work against the spread of our kin and reciprocal altruism to the wider community. Formulations of Christian love that exclude all self-regarding motives . . . may fail to harness the natural forces fueling kin, reciprocal, and group altruism and therefore fail to extend them to wider circles.[46]

If I could rewrite the kin altruism prayer in light of Browning's sociobiological-theological ethic, it might go like this:

> God bless me and my wife.
> My son John and his wife.
> Us four.
> And more.

The more Roman Catholic notion of love as *caritas*—in Browning's view *caritas* is an extension of healthy eros—works better when drawing out the power of kin love for wider communal love. Granting that we need to make a jump from loving one's own to loving the other, from loving family to loving those outside the family, Browning invokes God's grace to make the jump. We must build on, not repress, natural kin affections.

> Christians will insist, however, that the grace of God must transform and extend our affections, reason, and culture for the other reaches of self-sacrificial love to be achieved. In the end we must conclude that sociobiological altruism and Christian love are distinguishable, but that sociobiology can help clarify the natural foundations of love that the grace of God, along with reason and culture, extends.[47]

This construction of a Christian love ethic on a sociobiological foundation points Browning toward the invaluable role that family life plays in society, namely, the family mediates love to the body politic.

I can agree to a modest extent with Browning. Setting aside for now the mellowing of *agape* love to make an easier fit with sociobiology, Browning is simply right in noting that we first learn love from our parents, and if this love is healthy, we are enabled to extend that love to others we know and to the human race at large. It could be a good idea to start with a very small circle and then, like ripples from a stone thrown into a still pond, expand. So long as what we have going on within families is love, then we have a resource that can be cultivated and expanded so that others benefit. But, I ask, what if we find that within families love is missing? What if Browning's starting point—intrafamilial eros or *caritas*—is just what is missing?

The problem with using sociobiological theory here is that its explanations are only partial. The concept of kin altruism can explain why one family or tribe or race will rally to fight against an enemy family, tribe, or race, but it fails to explain internal violence in families. The first violence mentioned in the Bible is the murder of Abel by Cain, his own brother.[48] What has prompted the whole discussion here is the present lack of kin altruism; it is the list of problems internal to kinship relations: marital breakdown, unwed mothers, absentee fathers, child abandonment, and child abuse. Sociobiology attempts to explain why fathers care for their children, not why they run away.[49] The very problem that exercises Browning—the male problematic—cannot be solved by calling us back to the genes; because the genetic bond has shown itself too weak to inspire parental commitment to children. Rather, we need to press forward to an ethic that will accept as the current given that people have choice. We should avoid trying to circumvent choice by ethical appeal to an at best weak biological determinism.

With or without sociobiology, any Browning proposal to strengthen the family is likely to employ culture rather than genetic engineering; it is likely to press religion into the service of culture for the purpose of getting deadbeat dads to become responsible. One of the most visible Christian programs aimed at combating the male problematic today is "Promise Keepers." Founded by former University of Colorado head football coach Bill McCarney, this program draws men together in large groups for rallies that inspire them to honor Christ; pursue relationships with other men; practice sexual purity; and, of course, build strong marriages and families. The thirteen events of 1995 drew about 700,000 men. The method here is to use the Christian faith as a cultural weapon—not a genetic weapon—in the war against the male problematic.

Is this good enough? One of the reasons that Don Browning finds distinctively Christian arrows in his quiver insufficient and that he wants to add sociobiology to his arsenal is this: He believes that appeal to the apparent science behind sociobiology has apologetic value. Assuming that the non-Christian public is more likely to accept the logic of sociobiology, he feels he can effectively proffer his arguments regarding family responsibility without appealing to the authority of the Christian tradition. The task goes beyond strengthening only Christian families; public policy per se needs to support responsible fatherhood. Despite my doubts regarding the value of sociobiology for this enterprise, I recognize with Browning that Christian reflection on this issue needs to offer something of value to society as a whole and not merely to the Christian community.

Another conceptual point where I must part company with Browning's reliance on sociobiology is that it inadvertently supports the inheritance myth. It seeks human definition in the past—that is, it seeks ethical grounding in our biological inheritance—rather than in the eschatological future that God has promised. Who we are is now in process, a process that looks forward to God's new creation and not backward to our own procreation. Liberated at least in part from our origins, faith in the God of the future is faith in a better reality than the one we have inherited, and this includes our biological inheritance. But more about this theological perspective later. For the moment, I simply wish to reformulate the theme of this work to apply to the male problematic: Fathers should love children regardless of genetic continuity or discontinuity. This theme is not a description of what fathers are in fact doing; rather, it is blatantly an ethical exhortation telling fathers what they ought to do. And, if they don't, they should not be dealt any DNA trump cards in order to win back the children they have abandoned.

High-profile court cases have brought tears to America's eyes when adoptive families have been broken apart by the inheritance myth, injustices that sociobiology could only endorse. In the cases of Baby Richard in Illinois and Baby Jessica in Michigan, biological fathers were awarded custody after challenging the rights of their adoptive families.[50] Bucking the trend, a 1995 Florida Supreme Court decision granted three-year-old Baby Emily's adoptive parents, Stephen and Angel Welsh, the right to keep their child. Emily's biological father, Gary Bjorkland, had abandoned the child after breaking off his relationship with the biological mother. The unmarried man who failed to provide emotional support to the woman he impregnated and the child he fathered lost his right to challenge Emily's adoption. In saying this, the Florida Supreme Court had to override the inheritance myth.

Overcoming the Inheritance Myth

What is the inheritance myth? It is the misleading assumption that the biological connection between parents and children is definitive of their relationship. Because biological connection, especially biological paternity, played so big a role in ancient agrarian cultures including those described in the Bible, it is the default position taken by most cultures including our modern culture.

The energy emitted by the inheritance myth is the cultural force driving the current accelerated progress in reproductive technology. Although nearly invisible on the surface, an underlying psychocultural desire to pass on one's genes through biological procreation is a primary—if not the primary—motive for baby making, not only in individual families but in the wider medical marketplace. Why? Could we be thinking preconsciously that biological continuity between parent and child constitute some sort of ballast to steady us in the rough seas of family breakdown? Will genetic identity help us to weather the storm of divorce? One analyst, Michelle Stanworth, argues that the accelerating rates of divorce and remarriage with children growing up in stepfamilies lead us to look for nonsocial ties that will bind individual parents to individual children. Suspicious that the search for biological continuity will only exacerbate rather than solve the problem, Stanworth observes that "the importance of blood ties is further underscored by scientific theories—from the very dubious accounts of intelligence as a largely genetic characteristic, to the equally contentious claims of biologically based prenatal bonding—that make it their business to explain human qualities and relationships of biological inheritance."[51] In other words, the advance of genetic science that seems to explain more and more of human health and behavior in terms of genes makes us think—wrongly think—that biological inheritance is more and more important. This in turn fuels the flames of reproductive passion.

Yet an ironic reversal appears just here. The very technologies that enable some infertile couples to conceive and bring a child into the world also undercut the notion of genetic continuity. Artificial insemination by donor, surrogate motherhood, and similar techniques (which we will discuss at length in subsequent chapters) actually separate biological parenthood from social parenthood. "The same technologies that enable some infertile people to become genetic parents also place the whole notion of genetic parenthood in jeopardy," comments Stanworth, "thus, reproductive technologies carry the threat (or the promise) of delegitimating genetic parenthood, and even of fracturing common sense understanding of what 'the biological' is."[52]

In light of this we need to ask: What is our theological stake in the inheritance myth? My answer: none. Despite its long and venerable tradition, and despite its apparent rootedness deep within the human and cultural psyche, a theology based on the revelation of God's will in Jesus Christ looks at the human condition without giving moral priority to our inherited biology. Jesus' low regard for what today we might call the priority of DNA inheritance or kin altruism is as uncanny as it is dramatic. When a messenger came to tell Jesus that his family was outside waiting for an opportunity to talk to him, Jesus grasped the occasion to make the point that our true family is God's family. "Who is my mother, and who are my brothers?" he asked. After pointing to his disciples he went on, "Whoever does the will of my Father in heaven is my brother and sister and mother" (Matt. 12:46–50). Is this a positive view of family? Yes, of course. Jesus takes our positive experience of intrafamilial love and then expands it beyond genetic kin limits. Membership in the divine family supersedes limited human kinship.

Jesus' appeal to the heavenly Father is relevant here. This is the divine Father who adopted Israel. In contrast to the mythical self-understanding of so many ancient cultures that saw their respective races of people as descendants from the gods spoken of in the myths, Israel is not the child of God in the same way. There is no fertility imagery here, where the sky impregnates the land and procreates a people. Israel is not the firstborn of a marriage between heaven and earth. Israel is created, not procreated.

If not by celestial-terrestrial procreation, then how does God become Israel's Father? By choice. By adoption. By covenant. Israel is God's chosen people. They are a special nation by divine choice. God chooses to be bound to this nation through the making and fulfilling of promises. God makes a commitment, an everlasting covenant. It is to the God of the covenant that Jesus addresses the Lord's Prayer, "Our Father, who art in heaven." When asking us to share this prayer, Jesus asks us to accept our adoption into God's kingdom. Once we find our identity with God the adopting Father and our new brother, Jesus Christ, we are no longer subject to the boundaries of kin altruism. Nor, to return to the subject of deadbeat dads, can paternal certainty be decisive in determining our moral responsibilities.

Although we are here applying the teachings of Jesus to specific questions of family relations, the biblical teachings are framed more generally to deal with insiders and outsiders and with the nature of godly loving. John Calvin, exegeting the message of Jesus' parable of the Good Samaritan, says that "the term neighbor includes even the most remote person." Therefore, "we are not expected to limit the precept of love to those in close relationships." Calvin does observe that the more closely people are bound together "by the ties of kinship, of acquaintanceship, or of neighborhood, the more responsibilities for one another they share." This does not offend God, he conjectures, for divine Providence, as it were, leads us to it. Then Calvin adds: "But I say: we ought to embrace the whole human race without exception in a single feeling of love; here there is no distinction between barbarian and Greek, worthy and unworthy, friend and enemy, since all should be contemplated in God, not in themselves."[53] I enlist Calvin here not for the grand purpose of developing a global ethic; rather, I wish simply to show that love for someone who is other lies deep within the Christian understanding of the godly life.[54] This is important because the advance of genetic science and reproductive technology will increase the number of children within families who are biologically other—that is, children who are genetically other from their parents.

Beyond the extended family metaphor that moves us from biological families into love for the larger family of God, Christian anthropology has still more to say: Our identity is determined less by where we have come from and more by where we are going. That the genes we have inherited biologically from our parents have a significant influence on our identity is a fact that would be foolhardy to deny. But the promise of God's still outstanding future that includes our transformation is the decisive influence on our identity. Death is not the end. Following the Easter Jesus, resurrection awaits us in the future and retroactively influences our identity today. For a person of Christian faith to ask, "Who am I?" is to ask for an answer that transcends this life to include new life. The past underdetermines the future; the genes underdetermine the person. Who we are is determined less by our biological genesis and more by our spiritual epigenesis, less by our creation and more by our re-creation.

These anthropological and eschatological commitments in themselves do not constitute a family ethic. Yet they are definitely relevant when seeking theological resources to bring to bear on the current family crisis. The temptation in a moment of crisis is to fall back on unquestioned assumptions, and the inheritance myth just may be one of these unquestioned assumptions.

By severing the priority given to the tie between genetics and fatherhood here, I do not suppose that I am solving the male problematic. And, most assuredly, I am not trying to excuse deadbeat dads from their family responsibilities. Nor do I have a magic potion that will cure the epidemic of broken homes and unwanted children. My contribution is a modest one; namely, if we could shed the inheritance myth, we will gain a number of advantages. First, we would avoid the temptation to define fatherhood in strictly biological terms. The biological view provides only a minimalist definition that perpetuates the male problematic rather than give us a handle on an ethics of fatherhood. Second, we would avoid the tempting but misleading shortcut into an ethical way of thinking that pretends we have not achieved the level of freedom and choice that we have. Finally, we would avoid the temptation to ground our ethic in an understanding of biology that is rapidly becoming out-of-date because of the advances in science and technology.

Any attempt by Christian theologians to think ethically about the future of the family must take into account the rapid impact the new reproductive technologies will have on increasing the degree of choice people will have in baby making. More and more the responsibility will fall on the shoulders of the social family who plans for the child's future, not the biological sources of the child's DNA. Any definition of fatherhood we wish to promulgate should derive from our vision of the future well-being of children, and this will include among other things a lifelong commitment—a covenant freely entered into.

No Choice but Choice

What we need to conclude from the above is this: Choice is invading the family. Like a walled city, the family citadel is being penetrated by the forces of choice. Once thought to be an inviolate private dominion made up of involuntary subjects under parental or sometimes even patriarchal rule, the family domain is being overrun by the armies of advancing technology and ever new applications of individual human autonomy.

Modern liberal society appears to be energized by the unquenchable thirst for freedom, the demand for more choice. Relationships become social contracts, voluntarily chosen connections established by autonomous individuals. In this context the traditional nuclear family appears like a bulwark of anachronism. It is largely involuntary. Oh yes, husband and wife choose to marry one another. Beyond this, however, the children simply arrive and, because of no choice of their own, find themselves subject to parental dominion. Relatives and family trees are inherited. No one chooses his or her own genes nor the genes that they share with the rest of the family around them. Up until now, that is.

The juggernaut of Enlightenment individualism rolls on relentlessly, crushing every vestige of immutable communal ties and family bonds. In addition to the decision to get married, staying married has become de facto a choice. Most of the cultural and social supports for intact marriages have fallen away, so that we expect half of all weddings to be followed by a divorce. "Till death us do part" is no longer the default position. Covenant keeping becomes a series of repeat decisions to keep one's promise.

With the advance of birth control technology in the 1960s, the decision to have or not to have a baby became much more a matter of choice than it had been previously. With the legalization of abortion on demand by the U.S. Supreme Court in 1973, "choice" has become the watchword.

The first day cover of a U.S. stamp dedicated to family planning issued March 18, 1972, included a portrait of Margaret Sanger with the words, "No woman can call herself free . . . until she can choose whether or not to be a mother." This was the U.S. Postal Service's response to the women's liberation movement of the late 1960s that came on the eve of *Roe v. Wade,* a landmark case in which abortion on demand was legalized, in 1973. In a 1968 Gallup poll, only 15 percent of those polled favored abortion choice. This figure had climbed to 64 percent by 1972 and even included an affirmation of 54 percent of Roman Catholics. Regardless of one's ethical stance on abortion, history has borne us across the Rubicon into the land of choice.

It does not help in the present moment to blame the women's movement for family breakup. To try to do so would constitute scapegoating. The women's movement has added one more voice to the chorus intoning the Enlightenment values leading us to sing freedom songs and to march toward greater autonomy and self-fulfillment. To think that feminists sing solo in the cultural concert is to fail to hear the music at all. In addition, feminist thinkers and advocates raise some of the strongest voices on behalf of the well-being of children, and I rely heavily on feminist insights here in this book.

Feminism, understood as support for the full dignity and equality of women in home and society, is generating caring concern for the dignity and equality of others. It is but a short step to include children in this concern. One of my colleagues in the Religion, Culture and Family Project, Mary Stewart Van Leeuwen, formulates the agenda this way: "How can we put children first without putting women last and putting men on the sidelines?"[55]

Neither does it help to whimper about individual choice and decry the pursuit of self-fulfillment. These are simply the cultural givens of our epoch. They describe the situation within which we must live and work and raise our children. Attempts to formulate an ethic of the family that bypasses choice or self-fulfillment will fall on the rocks of self-contradiction when we ask: Just what are the rearing and educational goals of the modern intact family? When we put together economic, psychological, and educational goals, what every family wants is for their children to grow up to be independent—that is, grow up with the ability to make individual life choices—and achieve self-fulfillment.

Therefore, I for one would not like to see ethicists appeal to any premodern formalism based on divine dicta or traditional authority or natural law that would try to make an end run around choice and surreptitiously undercut the achievements of the women's movement. Rather, we need to press on, to walk through the door of choice and present a vision of what ought to be chosen. What ought to be chosen, I believe, is the love of children.

A Covenant with Children

Choosing for children might take the form of a covenant. Ordinarily we associate our culture of individualism and choice with contracts, not covenants. We freely enter into contracts and stipulate the rules to which we will abide. When abiding by the contract rules no longer seems mutually beneficial, we try to break the contract.

The concept of covenant is more profound. Like a contract, we enter into a covenant by choice. Yet the rules by which we agree to live come from beyond; they transcend our own benefit. They come from God. Devotion to children is a divinely ordained vocation. Parents are called by God to be ministers to children. They can choose to answer or ignore this call. This puts an element of adoption into every adult's relationship to a child, even if the child carries the adult's genes. This is due to the choice element: The decision to adopt or not to adopt a life-long commitment to love a child for better or worse, for richer or poorer, until death us do part.

2

Multiple Choice
in Baby Making

Christian faith affirms covenant relationship to be
the basis of all human integrity.
—Christopher Morse[1]

Like the Mississippi River after the spring snow melt, the family land-
scape is being flooded with new technologies, which affect the decision as to whether or not to have children. The explosion of progress
in reproductive technologies is creating choice in a dimension of life we
previously consigned to destiny, namely, procreating children. Fertile
women can terminate a pregnancy by using the following alternatives:
Norplant, RU-486, or an abortion. Infertile couples can still make babies with the help of artificial insemination (AI), in vitro fertilization
(IVF), donor semen or eggs, frozen embryos, and surrogates. Soon we
will be able to exact quality control regarding the health and perhaps
the genetic makeup of future children with the aid of genetic screening
and engineering, nuclear transplantation, egg fusion, cloning, selective
abortion, and in utero fetal surgery. A woman can even become a
mother at age 62, and if experiments in ectogenesis and interspecies
gestation prove successful, a woman will be able to become a mother
without becoming pregnant herself.

Technology and choice quickly translate into markets. The already
nascent reproductive industry is likely to expand as new technologies
open up more possibilities for terminating pregnancies, baby making,
and baby selecting. Infertility clinics will soon expand the range of services they offer. This expansion of services may increase the clientele to
include fertile couples and perhaps even individuals who are willing to
pay for designer babies.

Under market conditions will babies become commodities? Perhaps
yes. But the commodification of children will not be due to the fact that
money is exchanged for reproductive services. Rather, it will be due to
quality control. What is at stake is the value children will have for us when
they are the result of engineering or selection in order to manufacture a

superior product. Of course parents want their children to enjoy good health. But choice at the level of reproductive technology means selecting the healthy baby and discarding the unhealthy one. Of course parents may yearn for a child with certain genetic traits or talents or abilities. But choice at the level of genetic testing for acceptable embryos or engineering for superior genetic configurations may lead to the *perfect child syndrome,* wherein the neighborhood children conceived by sexual intercourse may be led to feel inferior. Or worse, something might go wrong—technology is seldom perfect—and something less than the perfect child will be produced causing the parents to deprive the child of unconditional affection. Quality control is the commodification factor.

The possibility of treating children as commodities raises the specter that human dignity will be threatened. So, based on observations of how Jesus behaved with poor and diseased outcasts, and also on the theology of the incarnation wherein God loves the imperfect world enough to become a part of it, I submit the following as a fundamental principle: God loves each of us regardless of our genetic makeup, and we should do likewise.

Even those less interested than I am in basing an ethic on Jesus might hold some reverence for the Enlightenment commitment to human dignity, to Immanuel Kant's dictum that we treat each person as an end and not merely as a means. My central concern here is that children— perfect or imperfect, by choice or by destiny—receive unconditional love from their parents and equal opportunities in society. I cede a certain presumptive primacy not to the parents but to the babies being made by reproductive technology, so that they are treated as ends in themselves and not merely as means for attaining some other social or parental values. I want an ethic that successfully places the love of children first and foremost and that orients all secondary concerns for parental fulfillment and technological means toward this end.

In the meantime, the array of new ways to make babies created by advances in reproductive technology need to be briefly inventoried. That will be our initial task here. What will become immediately obvious is that the array of new possibilities for baby making give rise to an equal array of ethical puzzles. Our additional task will be to identify some of these ethical puzzles and, in a later chapter, to analyze in greater depth one of them, namely, surrogate motherhood. Still in this chapter we will identify two competing ethical sensibilities in North American culture, the libertarian and egalitarian views. We will proceed to examine the work of University of Texas law professor John A. Robertson, a representative voice for the libertarian view, and ethicist Lisa Sowle Cahill, along with Pope John Paul II, who are representatives of a more egalitarian view. We will then finish with a brief exposition of the concept of love found in the work of theologian Vladimir Solovyev, applying it to sexual union and to love for children. In this context I will conclude that, as long as ethical discussion focuses solely on freedom of choice in using reproductive technology—that is, focuses solely on the achievement of choice rather than the criteria for choosing what is good or right—commodification will be virtually inevitable. It will be difficult to find an entrée wherein we can encourage unconditional love for the children.

How Many Ways Can We Make Babies?

Sexual Intercourse

In the traditional manner, sexual coitus results in the insemination of the woman's egg. The fertilized egg or conceptus then drops from the fallopian tube into the womb and remains there throughout the gestation period and, after nine months or so, a new baby glimpses the light of day. This is the way it has been done since the dawn of the human race, and we can predict that sexual intercourse will still be responsible for quite a few of our world's children for the foreseeable future. Even if sex is pursued strictly for pleasure and results in an unplanned pregnancy, the child may still be "wanted" and still be given the love and nurture leading to human well-being. Children from unplanned pregnancies do not constitute a loss of freedom; rather that freedom can be expressed through the willingness or lack of willingness on the part of the parents to be ethically responsible in childrearing.

But if a man and woman are intent on procreating, sex does not always achieve this end. One or both may be infertile, making the couple infertile. Confronting infertility can be a devastating experience for couples who desire children. More than mere frustration of the desire to procreate may be at stake, especially if one or both interpret infertility to be a sign of their inadequacy. Infertility can arouse feelings of guilt, lowered self-esteem, depression, and even conflict between the partners that in extreme cases leads to divorce.

Here it is important to distinguish what can be medicalized and what should not be medicalized. We can rightly think of the physiological dimensions of infertility as a matter for medical analysis and treatment.

But the stigma is not medical; it is social. The stigma—real or imagined—against persons who cannot, or by choice do not, have children of their own ought not be considered a medical problem. Neither should the accompanying psychological distress that the internalization of this stigma causes. Stigma and low self-esteem are moral and spiritual problems and should be addressed as such. To treat infertility as strictly a medical problem would inadvertently mask these other important dimensions of stigma.[2]

Be that as it may, the medicalized dimension of infertility has provided the occasion for the constant cooking up of new reproductive recipes and the cafeteria of options in baby making. To these options we now turn.

Artificial Insemination
and In vitro Fertilization

Of the assisted reproductive technologies, AI is the most widely used, leading in the United States to nearly 30,000 births with donor sperm—that is, artificial insemination with donor sperm (AID)—and 35,000 with the husband's own sperm (AIH). A simple syringe procedure at the clinic is all that is required to place the sperm and egg into proximity so that fertilization can occur. During intrauterine insemination (IUI) a concentration of five million sperm, sometimes washed to remove some of the seminal plasma and increase sperm motility, are placed within the uterus using a thin plastic tube that is passed through the cervix. This procedure is usually painless and takes only a few minutes. The success rate ranges from 40 percent to 70 percent, even though numerous inseminations may be required to initiate pregnancy.

A more complicated variant is IVF. As a laboratory technology, IVF consists of placing the egg and the sperm together in a petri dish, stimulating fertilization, and then implanting the fertilized egg into the woman's womb. The semen may come from the woman's own husband or from another donor, known or anonymous. Fertilization consists of the penetration of a single egg by a single sperm, and this creates the new and unique genome of the pre-embryo. In the petri dish, the initial single cell begins to divide. Standard IVF procedure is to wait 48 to 72 hours and then transfer the now six or eight cell pre-embryo directly into the gestational woman's uterus. A variant procedure is zygote intrafallopian transfer (ZIFT) which is performed earlier: The one-cell zygote is transferred directly into the fallopian tube via laparoscopy. The developing zygote becomes a blastocyst. Whether standard IVF or ZIFT procedures are used, at six to nine days, the blastocyst implants itself with a placenta in the uterine wall, marking the beginning of pregnancy. A variant procedure is gamete intrafallopian transfer (GIFT) in which a sperm and egg mixture is introduced into the fallopian tubes where fertilization then occurs.

Those considering IVF should know in advance that the success rate is not high. Only one out of ten such implanted embryos come to term. Even with multiple simultaneous implants, the take-home baby rate is only 20 percent at best. At this writing the average cost of a test-tube baby, using the above methods, is between $67,000 and $114,000.[3]

A spinoff of IVF is cryopreservation. Because semen can be frozen and stored for several years, fertilization can still occur when the sperm donor is no longer living. We can have birth beyond death. This may lead some families to make long-range plans by depositing semen or embryos in a cryopreservation bank for future use, guarding against loss of progeny because of the father's early death. Ova banks may someday serve a similar purpose for women. Here we get procreation without sex. The usual motive for IVF is not the avoidance of sexual pleasure, of course; rather it is to help couples who want children but, for one reason or another, confront the challenges of infertility.

Another future possibility may be that of a genetic mother having a child even if she herself had been aborted in the womb. Such an uncanny event is possible because the ovaries in an unborn female fetus are well developed; so a well-timed abortion could provide usable ovaries. Fetal tissue obtained from abortions is already often used for research and therapeutic purposes. One could easily imagine a fertility clinic taking aborted fetal ovaries and making them available for IVF. The result would be a child whose genetic mother had never lived. Successful experiments have already been performed on mice but, at this writing, none yet on humans. The specter of legions of test-tube babies whose biological mothers had never been born has caused an outrage in England, however. Even Parliament found itself debating the issue. The Human Fertilization and Embryology Authority (HFEA) has ruled that ova from aborted female fetuses may be used for research only but not to service infertility.[4]

Occasionally moral issues are raised regarding AID. First, for those traditions opposed to masturbation, this procedure is problematic since masturbation is the technique that is used to obtain semen. Sometimes the semen donor will find pornographic literature in the clinic, which is used as an aid in the masturbation process. Second, some fear that the use of sperm from a man other than the mother's husband constitutes adultery. This fear is usually dismissed as a nonissue when adultery is defined in terms of sexual intimacy. No sexual intimacy is involved in AID. Third, the anonymity of AID leads to the statistically low, yet possible, event that two AID children with the same biological father will grow up, meet one another, fall in love, marry, and not know that they are brother and sister. David Feldman gives voice to these worries from a Jewish point of view.

> Adultery is a conscious violation of the marriage vow by illicit intimacy, none of which takes place in this clinical procedure; hence, no adultery or illegitimacy can be associated with artificial insemination by donor. Nonetheless, it does sever the human, family bond, and—more serious from the standpoint of practical consequences—it does conceal paternity. When the children grow they may unwittingly marry their siblings, meaning that unknown paternity has led to the grave sin of incest.[5]

We will see as we proceed that AIH finds few detractors; AID, however, finds more.

Renting a Womb:
Surrogate Motherhood

The option of renting a womb makes it possible for the legal mother of a child to miss pregnancy altogether. Here the fertilized ovum is transferred from the womb of one woman to another—now called the *surrogate mother*—for the period of gestation. With surrogacy we enter the field of collaborative reproduction: reproduction involving donated sperm, egg, or embryo, or involving surrogacy, or any combination of these. In collaborative reproduction the reproductive parents can be distinguished from the social parents who, as a family, will rear the resulting children.

There are different types of womb renting, all of which separate gestational parenting from either genetic parenting or family parenting or both. *Traditional surrogacy* or *genetic-gestational surrogacy* consists of the direct artificial insemination of the ovum produced by the surrogate mother. The sperm comes from the intended father. Here the surrogate mother has a genetic connection with the child she carries, even though at birth the baby is turned over to the contracting family. Genetic-gestational surrogacy is usually chosen by families in which the mother for one reason or another cannot produce ova or is unable to give birth.

Another type is *IVF-gestational surrogacy,* in which the surrogate has no genetic connection to the child she carries. In this case the intended mother may be able to produce ova, but because she has no uterus, or for some similar reason, she cannot complete a natural pregnancy. Here the father's sperm and the egg harvested from the mother undergo fertilization in a petri dish, and then the conceptus is placed in the host womb for gestation. Many variants become immediately possible. One could place donor sperm or even a donor egg, or both, into the petri dish. In the most complex case, a child could end up with two fathers and three mothers: one father for the sperm and a different father in the social family; one mother for the egg, a second for gestation, and a third in the resulting social family.

The technology of freezing embryos increases convenience. One of the major difficulties with egg donation or IVF-gestational surrogacy is matching the ovulation cycles of the two women. The implantation must take place at the proper time in the cycle. When the embryo is frozen, however, it can be simply unfrozen and transferred when the surrogate mother is ready.

Why might a woman offer her body for surrogacy? Out of benevolence or love of children, perhaps. More specifically, some surrogates feel pleased, as organ donors frequently do, that they can offer the "gift of life" to an infertile couple. Some women confess that through surrogacy they are working out residual feelings of guilt left over from a previous pregnancy that ended in abortion or adoption. Other women may become surrogates for monetary reasons. The surrogate mothers quite clearly state their plans to purchase a new car, make a down payment on a house, or finance an education. At this writing, the lump sum fee surrogates typically receive is in the range of $10,000, with an additional $15,000 going to the brokering lawyer, making the womb rental cost about $25,000 plus medical expenses to the rearing family.

Who is the real mother? The egg donor? The surrogate? The woman who plans and pays for the whole thing? What about attachment to the baby? If a woman carries the child for nine months, does she experience such bonding as to make it impossible to surrender the infant to its legal parents? In some cases, evidently not. Frequently an affectionate rapport develops between surrogate and parents; so that on delivery day the surrogate can say, "Goodbye. It's yours. Good luck." In other cases, the surrogate has developed such a bond that she goes to court or even kidnaps the child to maintain that bond. We will look at this nest of issues later, because it is here that the ethical puzzles take shape.

External Gestation

Although clearly not yet a normal reproductive technology, we can envision an artificial womb or incubator-type container that would host the fetus throughout the gestation period. This procedure would be called *ectogenesis* because the child's genesis would take place outside the mother's womb. Perhaps more realistically, we can envision placing a human embryo into the womb of another species of animal, say a cow, and take advantage of that animal's natural birthing processes.

Cloning

Nuclear transplantation, otherwise known as cloning, consists of removing a fertilized ovum or zygote from the woman's oviduct and placing it in a petri dish. Its nucleus is then removed and replaced with a somatic cell nucleus—that is, a complete cell nucleus from some other part of the body. In principle the somatic cell could be taken from anywhere on the body because each nucleus contains the full complement of forty-six chromosomes. A skin cell is already differentiated, however, so that the genes to produce skin tissue are turned on and the genes to produce a brain are turned off. The genes in each cell similarly are turned on for some functions and off for others. The ideal cloning nucleus is one that is as yet undifferentiated—functionally undifferentiated cells appear only within the first eight divisions of the zygote—so to date the success of cloning has been very limited. Nevertheless, nuclear transplantation followed by transfer back to a host womb might some day produce a fully cloned child. Cloning would constitute nonsexual or asexual genesis because it does not rely on the nucleus of either germ cell. No conception takes place; cloning is a monogenetic process. Here we can have birth without conception. Bioethicist Joseph Fletcher refers to this as technological or artificial virgin birth.[6]

The Children of Martha and Phil

One of the salient characteristics of the new situation being created by options in baby making is the increase in choice, the increased sense that people can take control of their destiny. The advances in repro-

ductive technology provide a sense of empowerment in the face of a biological destiny that in previous generations was a brute given. Science
is providing hope. Yet with increased choice comes increased responsibility for new and delicate ethical concerns. I have found the experience
of my friends, Martha Maier and Phil Isensee, to be paradigmatic for
many of the issues that will concern us in this book. Their story will be
instructive; so I tell it here.

"I was shooting blanks," Phil told me, meaning that the active half of
his sperm seemed to be unable to penetrate and fertilize his wife's ovum.
He had had a vasectomy reversal in order to ready the family for bringing children into the world, but it wasn't working. After a year of unsuccessful attempts with sperm concentration, AIH, and other measures
to assist impregnation, Phil was judged to be infertile. It was the mid-
1980s and the Midwest clinic helping the couple suggested alternative
birth technologies.

Martha reports experiencing some confusion and even anger when
realizing that she and her husband would not become parents through
sexual intercourse. "I'd always wanted to have children," she says, "so
the infertility news came as a serious disappointment." It was comparatively less disappointing to Phil, noting that he had undergone vasectomy before marrying Martha and had not been planning on becoming
a father. Yet he and Martha are a very close couple, so he shared her initial grief and sought with enthusiasm to jump the hurdles necessary to
create a family.

Martha and Phil moved to Berkeley, California, where Martha en-
rolled in seminary and became my student. Now on the west coast they
began to pursue adoption and to attend meetings held by Resolve, a national organization offering referral, education, and support services for
people dealing with infertility.[7] Discussions at Resolve regarding ethical issues surrounding adoption, especially private adoption, began to
stir up doubts. Private adoption requires searching for a pregnant
woman who might consider giving up her baby and then convincing
her that these are the people she should place the child with. "Is this
right" quizzed Phil, "to be in a position where you want a mother to give
up a child?" Typically the adopting parents provide the birth mother
with financial support for four to seven months, paying medical expenses, and such. "Am I buying a baby?" Phil asked himself. Martha and
Phil are highly reflective people and investigated the ethical ramifica-
tions of what they were doing while they were doing it. The adoption
process as they understood it left them feeling uneasy.

Compared to adoption, AID seemed to this conscientious couple to have no greater ethical risk. The East Bay Fertility Clinic in Berkeley provided the reproductive services that led ultimately to the birth of two children by artificial insemination. The sperm donors for both Emily and Jeffrey are anonymous. I asked Phil if he had any feelings of jealousy regarding the presence of another man's sperm in his wife's body. "For me it was no big deal," he said, "for in my mind I'd already separated sexual intercourse from procreation back when I got my vasectomy. I look on the donated sperm as a gift, a gift that made my family possible."

Martha told me that at first she thought nearly daily about the connection between her egg and the sperm of a strange man, wondering whether or not this might have a dramatic impact down the road. Now, with two youngsters romping around the home, she says she almost never thinks about it any more. Attending to the needs of growing children is totally occupying. She agrees with Phil: The donated sperm is a "gift."

The two of them went together for the insemination appointment. "Everything was ready," Phil reported and, without pausing, went on to say, "I held her hand and then they inseminated her."

This matter-of-fact remark deeply impressed me. "Why did you hold her hand?" I asked.

"Because we needed to show it was the two of us doing this together," he said. The technology could be impersonal, he went on to explain; but these children are "the product of our relationship" regardless of the means of fertilization.

While a seminary student in Berkeley, Martha read widely in feminist literature, being influenced in particular by the relational epistemology and ethics of Carol Gilligan.[8] I asked whether the coldness or impersonalness of the reproductive technology was disruptive to the relational dimension of her life. "No," quite to the contrary. She stressed that she and Phil had employed the technology as a means whereby the existing marital relationship could be enhanced by incorporating a relationship to children.

So far, so good; but the story gets considerably more complicated. Emily, the firstborn, is a healthy happy child, who could be the apple of any parent's eye. Jeffrey, equally loved and treasured by his parents, is finding life somewhat more difficult to negotiate. He has a genetic disorder known as Williams syndrome.

Affecting perhaps one in twenty thousand newborns, Williams syndrome is a genetic defect due to a missing piece of chromosome 7, which stimulates the production of protein elastin that gives strength and elasticity to vessel walls. This disorder is the result of a spontaneous mutation. Symptoms typically include congenital heart defects, slow physical development, mild mental retardation (IQ around 70), growth deficiency, propensity for high blood pressure, and loose joints. It is difficult for three-year-old Jeffrey to run straight down the hall without falling to one side or the other. Because knowledge of Williams syndrome is relatively new—only identified in 1961—not enough is known to predict life span. Some persons who have Williams syndrome, however, are currently in their sixties. Very few persons with this syndrome, it is assumed, will ever develop to the point where they can live and support themselves independently. Jeffrey is likely to be dependent on his parents for support for his entire life. Now, we might ask, who will live longer?

A century or two ago a child born with Williams syndrome, then unidentified as such, might have simply appeared as the weakling in the family. Many such children might not have survived beyond the postnatal period, and those who did certainly would not outlive their parents. They probably did not live long enough to procreate and pass the mutated chromosome 7 on to another generation. But with the aid of recent advances in medical technology, Jeffrey may outlive the parents whom he depends on for support. Who will care for Jeffrey in his old age? What if Jeffrey as a young man decides to procreate? What if he passes his defective chromosome 7 on to another generation? He would have a 50–50 chance of doing so. Who will care for the two generations of dependents?

I probed Phil to see if he might be holding a grudge against the man who donated the sperm. "No," he said. He could not resent the donor. Because Williams syndrome results from a spontaneous mutation, it is not necessarily the case that the donor actually passed the defective DNA on to Jeffrey. Nevertheless, the geneticist reported the problem to the clinic, asking that the donor be told what had happened in the event that this news might influence the donor's decisions to donate in the future.

When Martha was pregnant with Jeffrey, she underwent prenatal genetic testing. The test showed no known genetic defects in the fetus. At that time no test for Williams syndrome existed, so prenatal knowledge of this disease was impossible. I asked the couple a speculative question, "If you had known at the time of genetic testing that

Jeffrey would be born with Williams syndrome, would you have seriously considered an abortion?"

This was a disturbing question, and Martha could say that it was disturbing. "Maybe," she conceded, "but I'm really glad that I did not have to face that decision at that time. Now that we have Jeffrey and love him, I could not conceive of not having him in our family. If I could decide now what to do back then, I would not have an abortion."

"Did you make the right decision to pursue your family through reproductive technology?" I asked as a global question. Martha answered affirmatively and confidently. Phil too was affirmative. Then he added a piece of philosophical wisdom he had gained from theologian Joseph Sittler that he thought applied to their situation: "Make a decision and then offer up a prayer."

Libertarian Choice
versus Egalitarian Values

The reproductive adventure of this family is packed with ethical issues that we plan to unpack as we proceed. For the moment, however, we want to focus on choice. Advancing technology opened up new possibilities for Martha and Phil to create a family. Had they decided not to avail themselves of AID, this would have been a choice to frustrate a strong desire and commitment. Fully cognizant of what they were getting into, they decided to follow through with AID and accept the puzzling risks by committing themselves unconditionally to loving the children that would come into their family. Whether sitting still or taking action, they had choice. This situation leads John A. Robertson to exclaim:

> Like Caesar crossing the Rubicon, there is no turning back from the technical control that we now have over human reproduction. The decision to have or not have children is, at some important level, no longer a matter of God or nature, but has been made subject to human will and technical expertise. It is now a matter of choice whether persons reproduce now or later, whether they overcome infertility, whether their children have certain genetic characteristics, or whether they use their reproductive capacity to produce tissue for transplant or embryos and fetuses for research.[9]

Thrilled with the opportunities provided by technological advance, Robertson exhibits a touch of hubris in taking what used to be "a matter of God or nature" and subjecting it to "human will and technical expertise." Robertson's colossal mistake is to ignore the fact that technology in the modern world has a life and a power of its own, so it is unlikely that we humans will subject it completely to "human will." Nevertheless, he is right when he says that the flooding of new reproductive technology inundates us with choice. We are becoming overwhelmed with choice. We have no choice but to swim in a sea of choice.

The American ethical psyche is schizoid. Like two house cats who sometimes hiss competitively and other times nap together in a single ball of fur, Americans operate out of two ethical visions—the libertarian and the egalitarian—that sometimes compete and other times complement one another. On the one hand, American culture is deeply committed to the libertarian vision that maximizes individual liberty. This view assumes that each of us is born free and that the ethical or political task is to prevent criminals or government from eclipsing this freedom. Despite the fact that these values derive from the liberal vision of the eighteenth-century Enlightenment, many today call this the conservative position. In complementary contrast, the egalitarian vision assumes that regardless of how we are born we are imprisoned by cultural prejudices or economic forces or political structures. The ethical and political task of government, then, is to liberate, to set us free. Legislation and law enforcement in behalf of equal opportunity or equal access to resources is the primary method for the egalitarians. Also deriving from the Enlightenment vision of a better world, today we dub this the liberal position. Here we will look briefly at the libertarian perspective taken by John A. Robertson and then turn to a representative of the egalitarian view, Lisa Sowle Cahill.

Procreative Liberty:
The Libertarian View

Robertson, mentioned above, belongs squarely in the libertarian camp. He advocates a comprehensive philosophy he calls *procreative liberty*. At its most general level, procreative liberty refers to the freedom either to have children or to avoid having them. Even though the freedom to choose whether or not to have a child is most frequently exercised by couples, Robertson is well aware that he is cultivating a rights-based political philosophy rooted in modern individualism. It follows that procreative liberty belongs not just to traditional married couples but also to gay and lesbian couples or even individuals.

Yet this is not unbridled individualism, but rather presumptive individualism. To take a strong stand in favor of procreative freedom does not mean that procreative choice should always triumph. There may be occasions in which community interest in protecting persons from harm overrides a couple's choice. Such choice is not absolute. Robertson emphasizes that procreative liberty should always be presumed; so that those who would limit it are burdened with the task of showing overriding concerns that the exercise of this choice would do harm to someone else.

We must recognize the anxiety rising in our culture over the prospects of noncoital baby making. Some people are worried that noncoital reproduction will undermine the deep cultural need for having a clear social framework that defines the boundaries of families, sexuality, and procreation. The worry is that "the technical ability to disaggregate and recombine genetic, gestational, and rearing connections and to control the genes of offspring may thus undermine essential protections for offspring, couples, family, and society."[10]

Ambient anxiety is insufficient warrant for restricting or discouraging its use, however. So, when this anxiety gives rise to criticisms of the new reproductive technologies, the criticisms need to be fairly evaluated. Robertson is aware that criticisms arising from this anxiety take on a moral tone, frequently buttressed by one or another specific religious or deontological ethic. Robertson is unsympathetic to religious ethics or deontology, however, feeling they have no place in making public policy for a pluralist society. So his criterion for limiting presumptive procreative liberty is quite clear: demonstrable harm to others. "These criticisms seldom meet the high standard necessary to limit procreative choice . . . without a clear showing of substantial harm to the tangible interests to others, speculation or mere moral objections alone should not override the moral right of infertile couples to use those techniques to form families. Given the primacy of procreative liberty, the use of these techniques should be accorded the same high protection granted to coital reproduction."[11]

What about the risk of commodification? He notes that the Human Genome Project—a worldwide research project to sequence human DNA and locate all the genes—will increase the capacity to screen out what some might consider undesirable traits "by identifying new genes for carrier and prenatal testing, including, potentially, genes for alcoholism, homosexuality, and depression."[12] We already test fetuses in utero for such things as cystic fibrosis or Down's syndrome and screen out the unhealthy ones by aborting those with defective genes. This method is also used to discriminate between genders, usually resulting in the aborting of female fetuses. In the future, through selective abortion or the more sophisticated selection of embryos in vitro, couples will be able to engage in quality control by screening out potential children with undesirable genes. Past experience teaches clearly that "most affected fetuses will be discarded based on a judgment of fitness, worth, or parental convenience."[13] Because abortion is currently the simplest method of selection, these developments will make all pregnancies "tentative" until prenatal testing certifies that the fetus is acceptable.

The question of commodification arises at this point. Parental choice may mean that criteria such as fitness, worth, and convenience will determine which, if any, children will see the light of day. "The danger is that selection methods will commodify children in a way ultimately harmful to their welfare. Carried to an extreme, parents will discard less than 'perfect' children and engineer embryos and fetuses for enhanced qualities. A worst-case scenario envisages repressive political regimes using these techniques to create a government-controlled Brave New World of genetically engineered social classes."[14]

Yet after alerting us to the dangers of commodification, Robertson returns to his defense of individual liberty: "The perceived dangers of 'quality control' appear to be insufficient to remove these choices from the discretion of persons planning to reproduce."[15] Unless we can establish on a case-by-case basis that harm will be done to someone other than the planning parents, then the presumptive right to procreative choice requires social and legal protection. It is Robertson's view that no religious ideals or cultural norms regarding family life are sufficient to justify restricting procreative liberty.

This doctrine of procreative liberty also seeks to protect the right to refuse to use the new technologies. Public action to prevent the birth of genetically handicapped offspring by mandatory means—a potential public threat as the current debate over community rating of healthcare insurance reveals—is not justified. Families should be permitted to have children through sexual intercourse, relying on the luck of the genetic draw, and still retain their rightful place in the communal healthcare system. The result will be some couples employing the new reproductive technologies to the maximum, with others continuing to accept the roll of the procreative dice.

The Relational Challenge to
Individual Choice: The Egalitarian View

Robertson represents the libertarian side of the current values debate. On the egalitarian side we find the nuanced position of Lisa Sowle

Cahill. As a feminist and a Roman Catholic ethicist at Boston College in Massachusetts, Cahill challenges the ideology of choice because it isolates the individual from society. Reproductive libertarianism leaves decisions about whether and how to combine intentional meanings with biological ones strictly to individuals and protects them with policies of informed consent. Such libertarianism also tends to be governed by the scientific model of rationality. Here the justifiability of actions and policies is strictly pragmatic, measured only by their efficiency in gaining ends autonomously chosen.

Autonomy is the unquestioned modern value espoused by the ideology of reproductive choice. This relativizes, if not marginalizes, concomitant values having to do with kinship, community, and the public good. In cases such as third-party gamete donation, wherein the child born has no genetic tie to its family parents, choice advocates can only render moral judgments based on potential harm to the child or to the marriage. Cahill, in contrast, registers concern for the intrinsic value of the embodied nature of the parent-child relationship, an issue that should concern the donor as well as the child's family. A family ethic based on biological kinship cannot be replaced by an ethic based solely on choice.[16] With the concept of embodiment Cahill, like Don Browning, seeks to retrieve an essential role for biology in constructing a family ethic.

When choice becomes more fundamental than the moral criteria by which better and worse choices should be measured, a value vacuum is created into which existing cultural power interests easily flow. Into this vacuum Cahill foresees the rush of bourgeois patriarchy and unscrupulous marketeers who will capitalize on the deep desire many have to procreate their own child. The ideology of choice pervading our culture opens the economy to the free market; the free market owes allegiance solely to the paying customer, and not to any larger vision of the common good.

Cahill charges that practices such as donor insemination, IVF with donor gametes, and surrogate motherhood depend on questionable assumptions: (1) that choice is a universal and nearly absolute value; (2) that individuals alone have the right to choose whether and how to recognize other moral values, such as the value of a biological relation to one's child; (3) that trading with a donor who may be uninterested in a social relation to a child to which he or she is a co-parent is legitimized solely by its instrumental value; and (4) that a biological asymmetry of the family parents' relation to the child will normally make no difference in family ecology. "The end result socially and morally," she fears, "is a dearth of resistance to patriarchal socializations of embodiment, including men's need for guarantees of biological paternity; women's social and self-definition through motherhood; the sale of gametes, embryos, and, in surrogacy, children; as well as the services of economically disadvantaged women."[17]

What is needed to redress this situation? Cahill recommends a reevaluation of intersubjectivity and biology as together normative for sex, marriage, parenthood and family, a reevaluation in which biology has a subordinate but important and protected meaning in these social relations. The challenge she sees is one of reinstating the connection between the unitive and procreative dimensions of sexuality, to affirm embodiment of sexuality through the bodies of mother and father as well as children, and to make this affirmation in the context of gender equality.

Cahill is both an egalitarian and a feminist. Her egalitarianism comes to expression in her emphasis on the inescapably social and political nature of the family as an institution, and also in her retrieval of the classic Roman Catholic commitment to an ethics rooted in a concept of the common good. Her feminism comes to expression as an advocate for gender equality. However, her feminism is in for rough sailing when it sets a course against maximizing free choice. Relevant here is the debate between pro-choice and pro-life advocates in the abortion controversy, a topic we will take up briefly here and more extensively in a later chapter.

Pro-Choice versus Essentialism

The libertarian element in procreative choice poses a significant challenge to feminist thinking. On the one hand, those within the feminist movement who advocate pro-choice will likely see Robertson's notion of procreative liberty as an extension of the same rights it advocated just before and after the *Roe v. Wade* Supreme Court decision, which permitted abortion on request. New reproductive technologies provide women (with or without spouse) with an increased range of options from which to choose. On the other hand, feminists who operate with a more essentialist vision—a vision of some essential quality unique to women or unique to a woman's biological relationship to her child—will find the choice ideology unacceptable. There are many pro-life feminists in this camp, and they argue that the relational bond between mother and child taps into an ontological quality rooted in the human reality that cannot be surrendered through choice.[18]

Some pro-choice feminists may be tempted to employ an essentialist argument against the likes of Robertson. But if they do they will have to deal with an inconsistency: Advocating freedom to choose to abort is inconsistent with the claim that the mother-fetus bond is more fundamental than choice. The Robertson argument is finally an extended form of the pro-choice position that "assures women a large measure of control over their reproductive lives."[19]

What we need to recognize here is that the advance in reproductive technology is carrying us into complexities unanticipated by *Roe v. Wade* in 1973. The key to the legalization of abortion on request was the identification of the fetus with the mother's body during the first trimester, thereby ceding to the mother the right to do with her body what she wills. The court consciously denied the fetus protection under the Fourteenth Amendment. Such legal logic depends entirely on the premise that the child-to-be is part of the mother's body. But what about phases in embryo development outside the mother's body? What about cases where the genetic bond between mother and child is broken?

Take the case of IVF for example. Here fertilization and the creation of a genetically unique individual takes place in a petri dish, perhaps miles away from the mother-to-be. Normally, many eggs are fertilized at once. In some cases, genetic selection takes place right in the petri dish, choosing those with desirable traits and discarding the others. At some point in the future, actual engineering of genetic inheritance will take place at this point. Then, after quality control has been exacted, the desired pre-embryos will be transferred to the woman's uterus, or in some cases the fallopian tube. By law, it then becomes part of the mother's body. But what about prior to implantation? What is the legal or moral status of the preimplanted embryo?

To complicate matters, a family planning to bring a new baby into the world may use donor semen, donor eggs, or cryopreservation. They may also employ a surrogate mother to bring the baby to term. Choice after choice after choice is being made here even apart from the mere choice to abort or not to abort a fetus in utero. We find ourselves in a new situation.

What is the ethical status of the pre-embryo whose genes are subject to parental choices and the clinic's technological capabilities? The Vatican's Congregation for the Doctrine of the Faith in its *Instruction on Respect for Human Life in Its Origin and on the Dignity of Procreation: Replies to Certain Questions of the Day*—also known as *Donum Vitae* (the gift of life)—offers an answer: The human being must be respected—as a person—from the very first instance of his or her existence as a fertilized egg. In *Evangelium Vitae*, Pope John Paul II enlists genetic science to support the position that from the time the ovum is fertilized a new life is begun, a "new human being."[20] This implies a number of things such as the right to life over against the mother's right to an abortion, and, as in the case of IVF, extracoital baby making is judged to be contrary to the moral law. In addition to the dignity of the child at the embryo stage, the Vatican seeks to protect the integrity of marriage. The Vatican's ideal child is one produced by a sexual union of two married parents. Marriage and sexual union within marriage belong to the essence of human nature, and the connection between genes, gestation, and family life should not be broken. Like the essentialist feminists, the Vatican appeals to a depth dimension in human ontology that goes deeper than choice and that would justify restricting procreative liberty.

As I introduce these problems, I along with Cahill and the Vatican do not presume that individual freedom of choice must be the bottom line in every ethical deliberation. However, given where we are in the history of culture, I am not inclined to follow Cahill or the Vatican in restricting choice based on appeal to an essentialist ontology or to increasingly outmoded assumptions about the necessary ties between sex, baby making, and family life. I am single-mindedly interested in one thing: the love of children, children who are already here, and children yet to be born. This view derives from a theological truth and an ethical response: God loves us unconditionally and we should similarly love one another (see 1 John 4:11). Robertson makes no room for such religious ideals or deontological mandates, but I do. Cahill and the Vatican are concerned about upholding an exalted theology of marriage. This theology may be laudable, to be sure, but my focus is different: My priority is the well-being of children regardless of the contribution or noncontribution of the marital sex act or the mother-fetus bond.

In itself, taking advantage of new reproductive technologies will neither enhance nor diminish a parent's motive for bringing a new child into the world. Even so, Robertson makes room for optimism on this score. When it comes to genetically enhancing a child's IQ or physical strength or whatever, he comments: "Enhancement could be seen as an act of love and concern, rather than a narcissistic effort to make the child a product or commodity."[21] Or, when advocating the use of donors and surrogates, he says: "Rather than undermine family, these practices present new variations of family and community that could help fill the void left by flux in the shape of the American family."[22] I like such optimism.

Nevertheless, we need to remind ourselves of just where the ethical burden for loving children and avoiding their commodification lies; namely, in the commitment by the parents and by the community to treat each child as an end and not merely a means—that is, a commitment to love each child by seeking his or her life fulfillment regardless of the child's genetic makeup or form of procreative origin. No ethical shortcuts that appeal to traditional family values or some alleged intrinsic value to sexual mating will allow us to escape the challenge posed by new reproductive options: We must choose whether or not to commit ourselves to loving the babies we make. This choice was laid on our ancestors when coital reproduction was their only option, and it remains our choice today as well. The glitter and glitz of the new reproductive technologies may dazzle us with options, but the sparkle should not blind us to the need children have to know they are wanted, loved, and will be cared for.

Dignity Conferred
and Dignity Claimed

For the purposes of the argument in this book, I am putting the concepts of love and dignity together. As already mentioned, my fundamental ethical axiom is this: God loves each of us regardless of our genetic makeup, and we should do likewise. This is my proposed application of 1 John 4:11: "Beloved, since God loved us so much, we also ought to love one another." Among the ways God has manifested divine love toward us is through the ministry of the incarnate Son that took him to the most humble persons in first-century Israel: the beggars, the lepers, those crippled or blind from birth, and to social outcasts such as adulterers or traitorous tax collectors. In addition, Jesus spoke over the stern objections of his disciples when he uttered the words, "Let the little children come to me, and do not stop them; for it is to such as these that the kingdom of heaven belongs" (Matt. 19:14).

Among its many benefits, love creates dignity in the humble. We feel valuable and have self-worth when we are the object of someone's love. Once we feel this sense of worth imputed to us by the one who loves us, we may then begin to own it. We may begin to claim self-worth. Worth is first imputed, then it is claimed.

It is often assumed that human dignity is innate, that it is inborn.

Legally this makes sense, because such a dignity doctrine permits us in court to defend the rights of every individual regardless of how humble he or she might be. But phenomenologically, this view is mistaken. Dignity—at least the sense of dignity understood as self-worth—is not simply inborn. Rather, it is the fruit of a relationship, an ongoing loving relationship. A newborn, welcomed into the world by a mother and father who provide attention and affection, develops a self-consciousness that incorporates this attention and affection as evidence of self-worth. As consciousness becomes constituted, this sense of worth can be claimed for oneself, and individual dignity develops.

Dignity has a proleptic as well as a relational structure—that is, it is fundamentally future oriented. The conferring of dignity on someone who does not yet in fact experience or claim it is a gesture of hope, an act that anticipates what we hope will be a future actuality. The final dignity, from the point of view of the Christian faith, is eschatological; it accompanies our fulfillment of the image of God. Rather than something with which we are born that may or may not become socially manifest, dignity is the future end product of God's saving activity that we anticipate socially when we confer dignity on those who do not yet claim it. The ethics of God's kingdom in our time and in our place consists of conferring dignity and inviting persons to claim dignity as a prolepsis of its future fulfillment.

How does dignity function ethically? By *dignity* here I mean the Enlightenment notion that a human person should be treated as an end and not merely as a means to some further end. There is nothing in this world we may value more highly than the existence and welfare of a human person. Phenomenologically, however, as we look around us we see dignity denied in almost every quarter. Clan rivalry in Africa is producing genocide, and several hundred thousand people are brutally murdered. Repressive political regimes with their death squad terror prevent the exercise of basic rights in Latin America. Reports of the staggering amount of child abuse in North America indicate that the most helpless among us are not receiving even basic care and loving attention. Whether or not dignity is inborn, the fact is that millions of persons the world over are not being treated as ends in themselves. Actualized dignity is relational, and destructive relations make dignity into an unrealized ideal rather than an authentic human experience. The biblical mandate to love one another means, among other things, the imputing of dignity to all persons in such a way that they may rise up and claim self-worth for themselves and share in the benefits of living together on this planet.

The task of this book is to alert us to what challenges to human dignity might be coming in the near future as the science of genetics and the technology of reproduction continue to shape our life choices. The focus here is on the babies we make, on the children coming into our world who will need to be loved for themselves if they are to grow up claiming self-worth and realizing their full potential as creatures of God. One significant threat is that children will become "commodified" because of the commodification of so many things surrounding the making of children. As the industry of reproductive technology expands in the free market, are we likely to treat the products—the babies being born—like other products we purchase; namely, as commodities that we choose by taste, and then consume if they please us? Or, will we be able to differentiate between products and persons, consuming the former and loving the latter?[23]

Dignity for Persons or Dignity for Sex?

Perhaps it is a curiosity, but at this point in history it is the Vatican that champions the cause of human dignity for the world. I suggest that it is a curiosity because we normally identify the Enlightenment as the torchbearer for dignity, noting that Enlightenment humanism precipitated a vigorous conservative reaction by the Roman Catholic Church during the late nineteenth and early twentieth centuries. But now the baton has been passed, and it is the church who sees itself struggling to keep the dignity lamp lit as the fierce winds of impersonal technology and postmodernist relativism threaten to blow it out.

Perhaps at this point I should make clear where I stand regarding the forceful positions taken recently by the Vatican. In *Donum Vitae,* the Vatican's Congregation for the Doctrine of the Faith appeals to dignity as its fundamental anthropological principle.[24] Our dignity is established because we are persons who are "endowed with a spiritual soul and with moral responsibility, and who are called to beatific communion with God." Dignity elicits an ethic of "respect, defense, and promotion" of human being. On this basis, argues *Donum Vitae,* each person has a "primary and fundamental right" to life.

The distinctively theological foundation for positing human dignity by the Vatican is creationism. This term, *creationism,* ought not be confused here with the fundamentalist Protestant school arguing for a six-day creation in opposition to standard theories of evolution; but rather, in the context of *Donum Vitae,* it is the doctrine that God creates *de nihilo* a fresh soul for each human person at conception.[25] The document is clear: The "spiritual soul" of each person is "immediately created" by God.[26] Human life is sacred because from the beginning—that is, from conception—it involves the creative action of God and remains forever in special relation to God. God is Lord from beginning to end, even to the end that never ends. It follows that no one can claim the right to destroy what God has created for eternity.

It follows further from this creationist version of human dignity that science and technology must be oriented toward serving human dignity. Science and technology are valuable resources, to be sure. When it comes to values, however, they are silent. In themselves they cannot show us the meaning of existence or call us to moral responsibility. "Thus science and technology require for their own intrinsic meaning, an unconditional respect for the fundamental criteria of the moral law; that is to say, they must be at the service of the human person, of his inalienable rights and his true and integral good according to the design and will of God."[27] Such an assertion is more than a mere philosophical observation. Revealing the foreboding anxiety that must have led to the writing of this document, its authors announce that "science without conscience" will only lead to our ruin. The task of the church, then, becomes one of providing science with a conscience.

From the Vatican's point of view, not only do persons have dignity, so also do certain acts—in this instance the act of sexual intercourse. The event in which God intervenes in human affairs to deposit a soul in the fertilized zygote imputes dignity not only to the zygote but also to the act of sexual intercourse that brought sperm and ovum into proximity. This is the assumption that comes to the fore when *Donum Vitae* prohibits the most innocent of the possible reproductive techniques, homologous techniques such as AIH or embryo transfer (ET). During an ET procedure, the egg that was fertilized in vitro is transferred to the mother. "A homologous IVF and ET procedure that is free of any compromise with the abortive practice of destroying embryos and with masturbation, remains a technique which is morally illicit because it deprives human procreation of the dignity which is proper and connatural to it."[28] Because the conjugal sex act retains its own independent dignity, it takes on moral valence going two directions. In one direction, if a married couple engages in sexual intercourse then they must avoid contraception and embrace openness to forces that transcend them, forces that determine if they will procreate a child. In the other direction, a married couple ought not to pursue bringing a child into their family by any means other than sexual intercourse. Sexual intercourse is the only way. A closer look at this argument, I think, will reveal some slippage in logic: The dignity that should accrue to a human person suddenly applies not to a person but to an act, namely, the sex act.

Returning to the dignity of the child conceived, the Vatican combines the forces of grace and exhortation in support of the love of children. "Although the manner in which human conception is achieved with IVF and ET cannot be approved, every child which comes into the world must in any case be accepted as a living gift of the divine Goodness and must be brought up with love."[29] Although I am grateful to the Vatican for including this final exhortation to love children regardless of their procreative origin, I believe the unquestioned connection between the sex act and the making of a baby needs to be questioned. With the advent of improved birth control methods in the 1960s, and presently the exploding frontier of advancing reproductive technologies, increased choice means increased separation between sex and baby making. That the quality of sexual love enjoyed by two parents might indirectly affect the atmosphere of love in a child's household is a connection that will perdure, to be sure. But we must wake up to the fact that the connection between a specific sex act and the bringing of a child into the world is becoming less and less necessary. So to make an ethical argument that borrows moral capital from the rich idea of human dignity, and try to make it pay duty on the moral purchase of the sex act, is a form of ethical embezzlement.

It seems to me that if we press the notion of human dignity as an ethical principle to help us forage through the jungle of reproductive technology, and if we acknowledge that the connection between sexual intercourse and baby making is losing some of its sense of necessity, then we will have to find another basis for establishing the value of sexual bonding. Sexual intercourse is not justifiable solely on the grounds that it makes babies; it must have some other more independent value. Perhaps this other value is intuitively obvious; but those of us afflicted with ethical minds find we must try to spell out what is obvious, noting that we then discover that it may not have been so obvious after all. The obvious value of sex is that it is fun. But many things are fun, and fun all by itself is insufficient to justify such a complicated phenomenon as a sexual relationship. Love is involved too, and love elicits the interest of theologians.

Theologically, the Vatican does not have a patent on ethically justifying the value of sexual relationship. The turn-of-the-century Russian

Orthodox theologian Vladimir Solovyev offers an alternative. He emphasizes that human loving has the capacity to lift the self up and go beyond itself. Love, especially sexual love, has the power to overcome egoism and self-centeredness. "Love is of importance," he writes, "not only as one of our feelings, but as the transfer of all our interest in life from ourselves to another, as the shifting of the very center of our personal life. This is characteristic of every kind of love, but *par excellence* of sex-love; it is distinguished from other kinds of love by greater intensity, by a more engrossing character, and by the possibility of more complete all-around reciprocity."[30]

What is the relationship between "sexual love" and the begetting of children? Because sexual love has a beauty and value in and of itself, the making of babies—as important as it is—is by no means entailed in the love relationship of a man and a woman. "The coincidence of a strong passion of love with the successful begetting of children is merely fortuitous," says Solovyev, "and even so is sufficiently rare; historical and everyday experience proves beyond doubt that children may be successfully begotten, ardently loved, and excellently brought up by their parents, though these latter should never have been in love with each other."[31] What Solovyev wants to demonstrate here is that love between parents is a most valuable thing; and its value is intrinsic, independent of its connection to giving birth to children. I appreciate this point and would like to go on to stress the other side of the equation, namely, that our love for children is independent of its connection to sexual love and even to biological inheritance.

3

Surrogate Motherhood:
An Ethical Puzzle

Nolite te bastardes carborundorum.
—Margaret Atwood[1]

What happens when we begin to separate genetic, gestational, and social parentage? What happens when we sever the tie between biological connection and childrearing? Severing these ties raises the ire of those who believe that marital sex and procreation are inseparable. The Vatican's Congregation for the Doctrine of the Faith, for example, condemns in vitro fertilization (IVF) and all forms of external fertilization because it "manifests a rupture between genetic parenthood, gestational parenthood and responsibility for upbringing."[2] On this premise the rejection of surrogate motherhood becomes categorical.

> Surrogate motherhood represents an objective failure to meet the obligations of maternal love, of conjugal fidelity and of responsible motherhood; it offends the dignity and the right of the child to be conceived, carried in the womb, brought into the world and brought up by his own parents; it sets up, to the detriment of families, a division between the physical, psychological, and moral elements which constitute those families.[3]

Without the uninterrupted tie between marital sex and the birth process, the Congregation for the Doctrine of the Faith assumes that attempts at maternal love, conjugal fidelity, or responsible motherhood will fail. Yet, we might ask, is this in fact true? Or, more specifically, does it apply accurately to the effect that new reproductive technologies will have on family life and childrearing? We are already quite used to some forms of separation between genetic parenthood and social parenthood—for example, adoption. Do the families of adopted children necessarily fail in their obligation to express maternal love, conjugal faithfulness, or responsible motherhood? This, of course, would be difficult to prove. Nevertheless, the Vatican lays before us the ethical burden of sizing up a reproductive practice such as surrogacy and honestly asking about its ethical dimensions.

As a background for the contemporary controversy, we will take a look, in this chapter, at an ancient low-tech example of surrogate motherhood—the biblical story of Abraham, Hagar, and Sarah. We will then turn to the more high-tech contemporary scene and list the problem areas of surrogacy—anxiety, relinquishment, the identity of the child, surrogate payment, class discrimination, traditional versus nontraditional families, birthing children for selfish ends, and, most important, the commodification of children and women. To illustrate these problems we will briefly review two dramatic and perhaps precedent-setting cases—"Baby M" in New Jersey and Chrispina Calvert in California. We will listen to arguments found in differing feminist positions and in procreative liberty in order to evaluate the surrogacy phenomenon. Even though the tide of ethical arguments seems to be flowing in the direction of prohibiting surrogacy entirely, my own position is less negative. Babies may be brought into this world through various arrangements, with surrogacy being one of them. I wish simply to register two concerns: First, arguments for or against this method of giving birth should not rely on the inheritance myth or parallel appeals to some sort of essential bond between mother and fetus; second, regardless of what arrangements are made to bring an infant into the light of day, our ethical mandate is to guard against commodification and make every effort to assure that the child will be loved.

Abraham, Sarah, and Hagar:
A Case of Surrogate Motherhood?

The story of Abraham and Sarah becoming parents is instructive on two counts: First, it is an account of surrogate motherhood; second, it reveals an unabashed biblical acceptance of sexual enjoyment, an issue that we will take up theologically in a later chapter.

Abraham and Sarah were childless and entering old age. Sad. Yet their sadness had little to do with their natural desire to propagate children so they could join the Canaanite PTA; rather, it had to do with the drama of God's providence. God had made a covenant with Abraham, promising—among other things—that his descendants would be like the stars in the heavens, uncountable (Gen.15:5). But with Sarah apparently unable to conceive, it was beginning to look like God's promise would go unfulfilled. Should Abraham and Sarah enter the cemetery with no heirs, God's plan would be thwarted.

So, to help things along, Sarah devised a plan: surrogate motherhood. She invited her husband to have intercourse with Hagar, her servant girl from Egypt. Abraham accepted the invitation, and soon Hagar was showing signs of pregnancy. Eventually Ishmael was born, and the line of Abraham's descendants was established. The genes of the grand patriarch of Israel could now be passed on to countless future generations.

Surrogate motherhood looked like a good idea at first, yet the plan failed to take into account an important ingredient in human nature, namely, jealousy. When Sarah saw how quickly Hagar had conceived, indicating that the servant girl was fertile, she could not repress her jealousy. Rather than seeing Hagar as her partner in child production, she began to see her as a rival. Hagar then returned the compliment, looking with contempt on the infertile Sarah (Gen.16:5). Now, with two women fighting in one household, what was Abraham to do? He chose between them, ceding authority to Sarah. "Your slave-girl is in your power," he told Sarah, "do with her as you please." So she "dealt harshly" with Hagar, and the disenfranchised Hagar fled to the wilderness (Gen.16:6–7). In time, at the Lord's request, Hagar returned to raise her son in Abraham's home and to suffer daily her subordination to the mistress of the household.[4]

Now, some might interpret the choice of surrogacy as evidence that Abraham and Sarah were losing faith in God's promise; that in their doubting, they could not trust God to find a way to give them children. Perhaps they should have simply sat by passively, waiting for God to do something. After all, isn't there something immoral about this? Isn't it irregular for a wife to give her husband over to a concubine? Could they not predict that a rivalry would occur between the two women? Would not the wiser thing have been to simply wait patiently, hoping that God would miraculously intervene?

Not necessarily. "The Hebrew Bible does not generally support an equation of faith with passivity," writes Harvard biblical scholar Jon D. Levenson.[5] There is a Jewish dictum: Do not rely upon miracles. If miracles come, then say "praise the Lord." But if they don't, then take action. So, says Levenson, "Sarai and Abram were in no sense faithless to the promise of progeny when, after more than ten years of unsuccessful attempts to conceive a child, they resorted to surrogate motherhood."[6] Be that as it may, an unpredictable miracle was in the offing. To this miracle we now turn.

Genesis 17—18 tells us that Abraham was approaching his hundredth birthday and Sarah her ninetieth when the God of Israel reiterated the covenant by which Abraham would become "the ancestor of many nations." Sarah's childlessness was just fine with Abraham, for he and Hagar already had a firstborn son, Ishmael, who could carry on the family line. This did not satisfy God, however. The heavenly covenant maker announced that Sarah, not Hagar, would cogenerate this family line. Furthermore, Sarah was about to become pregnant and start off the process. Abraham laughed. Then Sarah laughed. Pregnancy would be impossible, of course, because Sarah was beyond childbearing age. "After I have grown old, and my husband is old," remarks Sarah, "shall I have pleasure?" (Gen. 18:12). It is instructive that Sarah speaks here of pleasure. The assumption seems to be that sexual pleasure belongs naturally to conceiving a child. Perhaps the laugh was also a giggle, combining the absurdity of a barren woman conceiving with the prospect of a romp in the tent's master bedroom. I offer this as an observation regarding what the story may reveal about the assumed tie between sexual enjoyment and baby making. The central point of the story lies elsewhere, of course. The story explains the etymology of the name Isaac, the next ancestor of Israel, in terms of laughing. Isaac means laugh. Israel is born out of a humorous event. Though humorous, it is still serious. The story's point takes on additional depth as history unfolds; because this birth by a barren woman, as a prelude to Isaac's sacrifice, becomes the prototype for interpreting the virgin birth and the sacrifice of a later descendent of Abraham—Jesus of Nazareth.[7]

It is not easy to recommend that we at the beginning of the twenty-first century take ancient Hebrew family practices as models of our own. Ethicists Lisa Sowle Cahill and Thomas Shannon are both complimentary and critical of what is going on here. On the positive side, they compliment Sarah (and also Rachel who has a similar story) for offering surrogates to their husbands. Sarah and Rachel "sought to verify their own womanhood and to make their contribution as wives and mothers of sons to the continuation of the family and of the Chosen People." Yet, Cahill and Shannon do not believe that the definition of fulfilled womanhood should be restricted to motherhood, nor do they want us to emulate the jealousy depicted in the story. "On the negative side must be counted the competition and strife among wives, surrogates, and their offspring; and the assumption that the role of women (and of sexual intercourse) consists above all else in childbearing."[8]

Cahill and Shannon would have us turn to the New Testament where the apparently all-important function of family in determining religious identity is set aside, and with it the Israelite reliance on sex, marriage, and parenthood. The shift is particularly significant with regard to womanhood. Women are included in important ways in the ministry of Jesus and in the mission of the early church, and this importance is not tied to women's spousal or maternal roles. One consequence is to reduce the significance of parenthood in defining personal identity, especially for women.

Problem Areas
in Surrogate Motherhood

Married couples today who find themselves in a situation similar to that of Abraham and Sarah sometimes pray for a miracle. If a miracle occurs they say, "praise the Lord." If it does not occur, they frequently take action. One type of action is for a couple to contract with a woman who is willing to be a surrogate mother and give birth on behalf of the couple who plan to provide the child with a social family. Such arrangements are not problem free, however. A number of possible problem areas arise, some of which were anticipated in the story of Abraham, Sarah, and Hagar and are described below.[9]

Anxiety

The commissioning parents are liable to become anxious. Although the surrogate herself has volunteered to help them, she remains a threat. In most contemporary cases she is a stranger, someone brought into the arrangement by a lawyer or agency; she is an unknown. She may even live geographically remote, and she may have only minimum contact with the parents-to-be during the pregnancy. Imaginations may get out of control. Is the surrogate taking good care of her health? Is she having sexual intercourse during her fertile period? Will she demand more money, perhaps holding the child ransom? Will she develop an attachment to the child, and will she want to maintain a relationship after the child is born?

There are two ways to allay such anxieties: a binding legal contract or the development of a trust relationship between the commissioning parents and the surrogate. Contracts do help; yet no matter how airtight the legal contract, worries about unforeseen contingencies and images of possible court battles may continue to cause anxiety. Trust is the better method. In some cases, the commissioning mother accompanies the surrogate mother to her monthly ob-gyn checkup and then take in lunch. This helps establish a bond of mutual trust. The moment in which the baby is handed over frequently becomes somewhat of a ceremony in which the surrogate expresses her joy at having been able to provide happiness for the family and the parents express their gratitude. One could imagine a future liturgy of baptism in which the surrogate along with the commissioning parents and the godparents all participate.

Relinquishment

The surrogate mother is likely to find the whole adventure more difficult in executing than in planning. The various methods of implantation are complex and time consuming, usually requiring repeated procedures performed over many months at inconvenient locations. The pregnancy may include unforeseen side effects, and the childbearing itself may be quite painful. As the bond develops between the surrogate mother and the life growing in her womb, it may be difficult to think of the child as "theirs" and not "hers." The relinquishment of the baby may turn out to be much more difficult than anticipated, and for weeks afterward she might be burdened with a sense of loss. If the commissioning parents demand that further communication be cut off, then the surrogate might become angry or perhaps even feel guilty at having given up her responsibility to the child. As the cold reality of separation sets in, she might chastise herself for not having bargained harder for access to "her baby."

The best advice one can offer at this point is for the woman considering surrogacy to assess her own emotion, to try to anticipate how she might feel, and to plan ahead accordingly. If there is worry that a change of mind is in the offing, then perhaps the invitation to surrogacy should be turned down. Ethically, if she enters into a covenant relationship with the parents (what is at stake here goes way beyond what legal contracts usually cover, hence, my use of the word *covenant*), then she is bound to remain faithful to her initial commitment. Despite the physical and emotional challenges, her integrity will be found in her faithfulness.

It must be admitted, of course, that faithfulness is a rather difficult virtue to embody. A woman experiencing a growing bond with the life within her may ask: to what should I be faithful? The contract (covenant) or the baby? This is a genuine dilemma. Given current legislation, surrogacy contracts are almost unenforceable. They clarify the promises we make, but they have little legal effect when these promises are not kept.

Philosopher Bruce Reichenbach and geneticist Elving Anderson offer a sensitive plan for working through these difficulties. They suggest that perhaps surrogacy contracts could be written to include the possibility that the surrogate mother might wish to keep the child. The contract could specify up front that if she believes that bonding during pregnancy might occur and that she might be unable to relinquish the child, then she would have certain rights regarding the makeup of the child's social family. The final decision, made after birth, would parallel adoption procedures.[10] If the surrogate mother walks away with this child, perhaps the contracting family might try another. One could imagine a couple suffering through a series of surrogacy contracts and still ending up without a child of their own. Although the Reichenbach-Anderson plan shows appropriate sensitivity, it may generate a new set of problems.

The Identity of the Child

With the separation of genetic and gestational parentage from the child's rearing family, we have good reason to speculate about matters of identity. The child may question his or her roots. If the semen and egg come from anonymous donors, will the child wonder or fantasize about the biological parents? Will the child ponder the mysteries of growing in the surrogate mother's womb? We know from experience with adopted children that such questioning is normal. In extreme cases, an adopted child at age 18 or 21 may seek out the birth parents and, once having satisfied his or her curiosity, return to life as normal. This might happen with an artificial insemination with donor sperm (AID) and surrogate children as well, and should pose no special traumas or surprises.

Should the donor father or surrogate mother show up on the family doorstep unexpectedly, then what? What if they request opportunity to spend time with the child? Will this create a situation of competing parentage that undermines the family? Not necessarily. We already have considerable experience with parenting and childrearing beyond immediate family members such as wet nurses, nannies, baby-sitters, and day-care workers. This practice is widely accepted. Deep bonds of affection may develop between the children and such persons involved in rearing, yet the principles for family adjustment are no mystery. Unless the outsider becomes possessive or manipulative so that disciplinary action must be taken, family unity is not undermined.

My initial recommendation is that the rearing family inform the child from the onset of his or her origins. Whatever the parents know should be told, openly and honestly, as the child progressively asks for more and more detailed accounts. Any attempt to hide something only connotes a sense of embarassment or shame, and such embarassment or shame is totally uncalled for here. A sense of shame might arise if the parents themselves are victimized by thoughts that they had somehow gone against nature, that somehow genetic inheritance has something essential or sacred about it. They might, inadvertently, pass on this misleading myth of inheritance simply by behaving as if what they have is second best. Yet if each child is loved by God regardless of genetic inheritance, and if the parents can combine this knowledge with their own passion as demonstrated by the Herculean effort they exerted to bring this child into their family, all grounds for thinking in terms of second best evaporate. As the child grows the parents can explain the facts of his or her origin in the context of emphasizing the child's belovedness and dignity.

The principle here is openness and honesty in a context of love and dignity. It is not inconceivable that the family may want to include such persons as the donor father and the surrogate mother in their circle of acquaintances. Even in the extreme case where the child has three mothers and two fathers, the whole complex can be celebrated rather than secretized. Visiting time could be authorized by the rearing parents, should the other mothers or fathers request it. Undermining family unity or weakening parental authority is not likely to be a threat here, unless the semen donor or surrogate maliciously tries to do so. Even then a strong family will have the tensive strength to withstand some such pressure.

The key here is this: The child's worldview especially in the early years is formed almost totally by the intimate relations of the social family. In addition, the child works diligently to incorporate new experiences into that worldview, pressing for an integrated understanding of things. To tell the child he or she has two daddies and three mommies, or any such combination, will not create cognitive dissonance or identity confusion. The givenness of the child's identity with the family he or she knows is just that, a given; so it comes prior. New information about other identity factors is only added on, not substituted. Therefore, no identity confusion will arise unless the parents inject it. And even if the parents accidently inject it, the child's own press to integrate even this into a holistic world understanding will diminish the threat of irreparable damage.

The surrogate mother could become part of the child's world just as other affectionate members of the consanguine family such as grandparents, aunts, uncles, or close neighbors. For this option to be successful, the surrogate need not be a saint. Few of us are. She should be allowed the same latitude for personality strengths and weakness we all ask for. Simple realism in the tug-of-war that characterizes getting along with others socially is all that a child can ask for. The family parents can and should retain their proper authority so that the surrogate mother— just like the grandmother or other similar figures—will feel welcome to share her affection, but do so according to the policies set down within the child's home.

Surrogate Payment

Should surrogate mothers be paid? Currently many are. But as we will see when we review the landmark cases described later in this chapter, many states are outlawing paid surrogacy.

University of Chicago social theorist Leon R. Kass takes a stand against payment; in fact, he opposes surrogacy itself. His opposition begins with the assumption that a child's identity is of chief importance, and the problem with all forms of ectogenesis is that they fail to maintain genetic identity with family identity. "Clarity about your origins is crucial for self-identity," he writes, "this means, concretely, no encouragement of embryo adoption or especially surrogate pregnancy."[11] Addressing the issue of surrogate payment, he says:

> To bear another's child for pay is in some sense a degradation of oneself—in the same sense that prostitution is a degradation *primarily* because it entails the loveless surrender of one's body to serve another's lust, and only *derivatively* because the woman is paid. It is to deny the meaning and worth of one's body, to treat it as a mere incubator, divested of its human meaning. It is also to deny the meaning of the bond among sexuality, love, and procreation.[12]

Paul Lauritzen's argument against paying surrogates is based on somewhat different reasoning. According to Lauritzen, a Roman Catholic ethicist, a woman's body has integrity and pregnancy involves her entire person; she cannot simply rent out her womb and go on living unaffected by the relationship with the unborn child. He believes that financial compensation dehumanizes the woman because it tries to sell what cannot be sold: a caring relationship. "The problem with commercial surrogacy," he writes, "is thus not simply that it requires a woman to treat her bodily integrity as owned property available for sale to a buyer, but also that it places human relationships, indeed, one of the most intimate human relationships, in the marketplace. And the problem with commercializing relationships is that truly committed, caring relationships are not something we can simply buy and sell."[13]

Legal theorist and bioethicist John A. Robertson, in contrast, advocates surrogate payment. "Without payment, it is likely that too few surrogate mothers will be available to meet the needs of infertile couples. Paying surrogates (though perhaps not gamete donors) is probably necessary if infertile couples are to obtain surrogacy services."[14] In addition, he notes that the doctors and lawyers who make the arrangements are well paid; so fairness would require that the women undergoing pregnancy also be paid.

After considering questions surrounding the patriarchal exploitation of surrogate mothers, Sharon Elizabeth Rush, a woman's rights specialist at the University of Florida College of Law, argues that surrogates should be paid. "As a woman and a feminist," she writes, "I share the skepticism surrounding surrogacy." She notes how easy it is to ignore the surrogate-contract mother's feelings, which might range from depression because of her loss, on the one hand, to sincere altruistic happiness at being able to provide a family with a child, on the other hand. Once her role in the birth process is completed, she could easily be forgotten while the father in the rearing family enjoys mutuality with the child he is raising. This sequence reaffirms the perceived utility of women who are limited to childbearers, a cultural restriction imposed by patriarchy. Even though Rush believes that these "concerns are troubling," she feels that a legal ban on paid surrogacy is not the appropriate response. Paying a woman to bear a child enhances a woman's financial independence, and to deny this opportunity by law would be paternalist.

> Outlawing surrogacy, as a practical matter, would do little if anything to promote the demise of patriarchy. Allowing a woman to become a surrogate contract mother arguably could do more to promote women than would a ban. . . . Allowing fee-paid surrogacy enhances a woman's economic power. The surrogate contract also could be structured to protect and promote the mother's right to privacy and personhood.[15]

After considering the pros and cons, Rush believes that legally defending choice regarding surrogacy will better promote the interests of women than banning it. I think I agree with Rush.

We should note here that these positions in the payment debate tend to revolve around the interests of women. What about the children? Does payment risk commodification of the children? This is the worry of Reichenbach and Anderson.

> In introducing financial considerations, there must be no hint of the exchange of money for the child. What makes surrogacy questionable is not that the woman consents to use her reproductive system for another's benefit, nor that she is reimbursed for her labors, but rather that the product of the process, who is a human being, might be treated as a mere product to be traded away or bought or sold.[16]

The question is this: Can paying surrogates be considered baby buying?

Class Discrimination

Relevant to the payment and patriarchy issues is the question of social or economic class. Is it likely that the commissioning parents will come from the professional or wealthier classes and that the surrogate mothers will come from the working class or even from among the poor? Yes. Should we consider this exploitation? Is this just another example of the bourgeoise exploiting the proletariat, or an example of patriarchal exploitation of women? Yes, probably so. Do these acknowledgments, then, provide sufficient warrant for prohibiting surrogacy? No, not necessarily. In a liberal society we must distinguish between exploitation and coercion. Surrogate mothers are not coerced into offering their services; they volunteer. They may even compete for the opportunity. Even if a woman has need for the money yet still turns down an opportunity to sign a surrogate agreement, she would not be deprived of anything she is otherwise entitled to.

The possibility of abuse lurks close by the enterprise of soliciting and paying woman for gestational surrogacy, but this is an insufficient reason to deny all compensation. At least this is how the argument goes. Robertson writes,

> There is a danger that class bias and financial need will determine the supply of surrogates. Carried to extremes, a breeder class of poor, minority women whose reproductive capacity is exploited by wealthier people could emerge.

> But what is to be done about this practice? . . . Whatever our
> qualms about such a practice, it may have to be tolerated because
> the procreative liberty of all the parties is so intimately involved.[17]

For Robertson the undesirability of class bias is insufficient cause to
compromise the freedom to enter noncoercively into a surrogate contract, a freedom enjoyed by both the lower-class surrogate and the
wealthier social parents who write the check.

This question of class exploitation can cut more than one way. On the
one hand, we can easily accuse those with money for exploiting lower-
class women by hiring them as surrogates. On the other hand, we can accuse those with money of class bias if they choose surrogates within the
same social or economic status. Feminist Barbara Katz Rothman, for example, writes vituperatively, "Because women are genetically related to
the babies they produce, the father-purchasers want only certain kinds of
women: intelligent, attractive, and most assuredly of the same race as the
couple."[18] Because so many of the couples seeking this service are white
professionals, she fears, this will limit the marketing of surrogates to
healthy white women and leave out those who are already racially or otherwise marginalized. This would result in the wealthy keeping the money
within their economic class without any trickle down.

There is a problem with the accuracy of Rothman's complaint, however, because she limits herself to only genetic-gestational surrogacy
and ignores the practice of IVF-gestational surrogacy wherein the race
and class of the surrogate mother would be biologically irrelevant. Be
that as it may, the relatively small number of expected surrogate
arrangements is not likely to become a noticeable factor in the economic
structure of our society. The importance of raising the class issue has
more to do with the moral tenor of the surrogacy phenomenon than it
does with actual financial impact.

Traditional versus Nontraditional Families

Surrogacy agreements are one of the ways that infertile married couples can expand their families. What is seemingly nontraditional is the
genetic origin of the children—that is, they may not inherit the specific
genes of the two social parents who are raising them. On a daily basis,
this difference from a biologically homologous family is virtually indis-
cernible. And, if what we think of as the traditional family can spread
its apron to enclose families with adopted children, families with surrogate children should also be considered traditional.

What about families with two homosexual parents? A home with two lesbian women can relatively easily arrange for a birth that will lead to a child bearing the genes of one of the partners—for example, AID. For gay men, however, surrogacy may offer a method of bringing children into the home, again with the child bearing the genes of one of them. "Homosexuals should be entitled to parental rights, just as heterosexuals are," contends Elizabeth Rush. And "surrogacy may be one of the best ways for a homosexual man to fulfill his needs or desires to have children."[19] She proceeds to spell out some of the conditions. If a homosexual couple decides to have children through a surrogacy arrangement, the biological father's partner should be treated as if he were the adoptive parent. Because so many states do not recognize homosexual marriages, Rush recommends that in these instances a separate agreement be drawn up specifying the adoptive relationship.

Rush believes that the state must put the welfare of the child first, regardless of the sexual orientation of the social parents. This means careful planning in advance so as to reduce to a minimum the possibility of a custody dispute ensuing after the child is born. If the surrogate mother shows signs that she might be reluctant to follow through on her commitment, she should be prohibited from entering the agreement. "Laws should prevent parties from making surrogate contracts when there is a known possibility of failure. Correspondingly, a person's marital status or sexual orientation should be irrelevant to the person's ability and capacity to enter into the contract."[20]

Commodification

It is the tone of commercialism, the tone of commodifying women that has rightly raised many of the objections thus far in the debate. The developing bond between the surrogate mother and the new life growing in her womb is an emotional bond, which we in the rest of society hope will be characterized by tenderness and love. Yet the contract she must sign includes an agreement to break that bond when the child is to be relinquished. Conflicts within the gestating woman ought to be expected under these circumstances. This leads Elizabeth S. Anderson to contend that "treating women's labor as just another kind of commercial production process violates the precious emotional ties which the mother might rightly and properly establish with her 'product,' the child."[21] The fundamental problem with surrogacy is that the contracts are "inherently manipulative," she argues, "since the very form of the contract invokes commercial norms which, whether upheld by the law or by social custom only, imply that the mother should feel guilty and irresponsible for loving her own child."[22]

Not only are women at risk of becoming "commodified," so are the children. Does surrogacy constitute baby selling? Does surrogacy violate the human dignity of the infant? This is a delicate yet decisive issue. It seems to me that a clear distinction must be made between the sale of a child, on the one hand, and rewarding the surrogate mother for her contributions to the birthing process, on the other hand. Under no circumstances ought a child be put up for sale.

Rothman says that "surrogacy is baby selling," pure and simple.[23] Rush, however, disagrees. "In my opinion," she writes, "surrogacy is significantly different from baby selling. First, one of the 'buyers' of the baby is the child's biological father. How does a father buy his own child? Second, in the typical surrogacy arrangement, the biological father's wife becomes the baby's adoptive mother. Her economic interest in obtaining the child through the surrogate contract is similar to the economic interest of any adoptive parent who pays a fee for the adoption process."[24]

Less significant than the technical question regarding payment for a baby versus payment for services, I think, is the question regarding the social parents' attitude toward the child that comes into the family home. The commodification question leads to the next issue: What about the self-interest of parents-to-be in planning and executing the reproductive process?

Birthing Children
for Selfish Ends

The simple task of giving birth to a child, whether through a surrogate or through sexual intercourse, cannot be dubbed immoral merely on the grounds that self-fulfilling or even selfish motives are present. Parents planning to have children always have some form of selfish motive or another, even if it is to fulfill their own dreams of becoming parents. If we demand that all selfish components be eliminated before conception, then all our maternity wards could be eliminated and no one would miss them. The issue here is this: Has someone made a commitment to the interests and welfare of the child? Society places its children in the care of rearing parents as a trust, and the child's basic subsistence, along with intangible benefits from living in a loving family, are not defined independently from this family.

Our great fear, as we flirt with commercial surrogacy, is that a child may be born genetically defective or in some way undesirable and no one will want to take it home and offer care "until death us do part." Many remember the surrogacy case in which a child was born with microcephaly. No one wanted to claim parental responsibility. The commissioning father, on the basis of a blood test, claimed the baby was not his; therefore, he was not obligated to take it nor was he obligated to pay the surrogate's fee. Tests eventually showed that the surrogate had unwittingly become pregnant by her own husband before becoming artificially inseminated by the contracting man. Eventually the surrogate and her husband assumed responsibility for the child.[25]

Herbert Krimmel raises the challenge of means and ends. He sees no insurmountable objections to the surrogate playing host to a child that will be reared in someone else's family. In this case, her actions are similar to those of a foster mother or wet nurse who cares for the child. Rather, the moral issue has to do with means and ends—that is, the motive for creating children for a purpose other than the traditional one. "Surrogate mother arrangements involve a change in motive for creating children: from a desire to have them for their own sake, to a desire to have them because they can provide some other benefit. The surrogate mother creates a child with the intention to abdicate parental responsibilities. Can we view this as ethical? My answer is no."[26]

What really bothers Krimmel is not the surrogate whose womb plays host to someone else's fertilized egg, but rather the woman who allows herself to be artificially inseminated using her own egg and then giving the child away. Here surrogacy becomes a form of adoption. Krimmel finds the practice of providing both genes and gestation to a child that will be delivered to another family for rearing intolerable. It is the inheritance myth that is at work here, for he finds no objection in principle to renting a womb via IVF. Yet the issue as he formulates it is that it turns children into commodities to be bought and sold. "Creating a child without desiring it fundamentally changes the way we look at children—instead of viewing them as unique individual personalities to be desired in their own right, we may come to view them as commodities or items of manufacture to be desired because of their utility."[27]

The commodifying of children could lead to tragedy. What will happen if the baby is born deformed? It is only natural to think that if one pays money, one expects value. If the paying parents do not believe they are getting their money's worth, they may reject the product.

A Case of Genetic-Gestational
Surrogate Bonding: Baby M

Perhaps the most widely publicized dispute over genetic-gestational surrogacy is that of Baby M, born March 27, 1986. William and Elizabeth Stern wanted a baby, but because Mrs. Stern had multiple sclerosis, they were unable to do so through sexual intercourse. A surrogate contract for a $10,000 fee was signed with Mary Beth Whitehead, who was already a mother of two, after the parties had been brought together by the Infertility Center of New York. Mrs. Whitehead, who had contributed her own egg, was artificially inseminated with William's sperm. The pregnancy was successful, and three days after the birth, the surrogate handed the newborn over to the commissioning parents. All seemed to be going according to plan.

The next day, Mary Beth paid a visit to the Stern family at their New Jersey residence and took the baby home with her—an action the Sterns believed to be temporary. Mrs. Whitehead then informed the Sterns that she had decided to keep the child permanently, and threatened to leave the country should William and Elizabeth try to retrieve the baby. Mr. Stern obtained court-ordered custody, so Mrs. Whitehead took the baby and fled to Florida where she remained in hiding. Telephoning Mr. Stern she said, "I'd rather see me and her dead before you get her. . . . I gave her life, I can take her life away." Unless Mr. Stern dropped his pursuit, Mrs. Whitehead threatened to accuse him of molesting her ten-year-old daughter. Florida police eventually raided the house where Mrs. Whitehead had been staying, and returned the infant to the Stern family in New Jersey.

The case went to the New Jersey Superior Court where the little girl was referred to as "Baby M" because of a name dispute during the trial. In the Stern family she was named Melissa; in the Whitehead family, Sara. (Now, as a ten year old, she calls herself Sassy.) Finally, the presiding Judge Harvey R. Sorkow turned Baby M over to the Stern family, extending visiting privileges to the Whitehead family. Judge Sorkow's decision declared that Mr. Stern did not, in actuality, buy the baby from Mrs. Whitehead because Baby M was already his.[28] He became both the social and genetic father because his sperm was used.

However, a closer look at the surrogacy contract raises questions about baby buying and selling. According to the stipulations of the contract, Mrs. Whitehead was not to receive any compensation in the event of miscarriage prior to the fifth month pregnancy. A later miscarriage or stillbirth would result in a payment of only $1,000. Since payment was scaled according to relative success, it appears that Mr. Stern was not compensating Mrs. Whitehead for her discomfort or suffering during pregnancy; rather, he was paying for a product. In addition, by declaring that the "child is already his [Mr. Stern's]" the judge seemed to be overlooking one quite obvious fact, namely, it is also Mrs. Whitehead's.[29] A strictly biological or genetic criterion makes Mr. Stern and Mrs. Whitehead the genetic parents. However, where does this leave Mrs. Stern? In 1988, the New Jersey Supreme Court declared that Mrs. Whitehead had in fact sold her own half of the baby for $10,000. The court also found Mrs. Stern ineligible to adopt Baby M.[30]

Quite relevant to the theme of this book is the interest Judge Sorkow took regarding the "best interests" of the child. Although the enforceability of the contract was of considerable concern, Sorkow himself thought that the welfare of the child took priority. "The sole legal concepts that control are *parens patriae* and the best interest of the child."[31] He stated that the parents could not enact a contract that would override Baby M's welfare; the child's best interests were paramount. However, in this instance the judge was also unwilling to abandon the contract's validity; the surrogate-parenting agreement of February 6, 1985 would be specifically enforced. The logic is this: Enforcing the surrogate agreement serves the best interests of the child, since Baby M would be placed in a loving two-parent home with financial security. However, we might observe that this was an unclear decision that only *seemed* to favor social welfare over what some might construe as biological welfare.[32] Does living with one's genetic parents contribute to one's best interests? Judge Sorkow was less than fully clear. In defending Mr. Stern, he recognized "the social and psychological importance" for parents to "reproduce blood lines" by children who are "genetically theirs." According to this criterion, both Mrs. Whitehead and Mr. Stern would qualify. The biological connection alone could not discriminate which parent would best serve the child's interest.

Perhaps the right to enter into a contractual agreement, with its underlying Enlightenment commitment to freedom understood as choice, in fact played the decisive role in Judge Sorkow's decision. "If one has the right to procreate coitally, then one has the right to reproduce noncoitally," he said, "this court holds that the protected means extends to the use of surrogates. The contract cannot fail because of the use of a third party."[33] Judge Sorkow felt he could withdraw parental custody from Mrs. Whitehead partially on the grounds that she had signed a contract, which gave her informed consent. But, we might ask, what does *informed* mean prior to the actual experience of going through a pregnancy and bonding with the child that is living within? The New Jersey Supreme Court asked this question. It observed that a natural mother never makes a totally voluntary, informed decision. Any decision prior to the baby's birth is by definition uninformed, that is, truly uninformed by the experience. So, any pre-existing contractual commitment makes the decision to give a baby away or to sell a baby less than totally voluntary. The New Jersey Supreme Court seemed to presume an essentialist understanding of the mother-child bond that went deeper than choice, a position the Court also shares with Lisa Sowle Cahill and the Vatican.

A California Case of
In vitro Fertilization-Gestational
Surrogate Bonding

Anna Johnson might provide us with an example of IVF surrogate–child bonding. She was a coworker of Chrispina Calvert who had undergone a hysterectomy. Chris, along with her husband Mark, asked Anna to bear their child. All parties agreed and a contract was signed on January 15, 1990. The embryo implanted in Anna Johnson's womb consisted of Chris's egg, which was fertilized by Mark's sperm. At approximately seven months, Anna announced that she and the fetus had bonded and that she believed Mark and Chris were losing interest in the baby-to-be. She claimed mother's rights and sought possession of the fetus. The Calverts became angry and complained that Anna was making repeated demands for advance payments on the agreed-upon $10,000 fee. They even accused Anna of kidnapping their child.

After a court battle, parental rights were granted to the Calverts for the child born September 19, 1990. Orange County Superior Court Judge Richard N. Parslow ruled that "a surrogate carrying a genetic child for a couple does not acquire parental rights."[34] He stated that Anna Johnson and the child are "genetic hereditary strangers" and likened her surrogacy to that of a "foster parent providing care."[35] The judge waxed philosophical: "Genetics and what happens to you after you're born are the primary factors, as I understand it, of who we are, what we become."[36] He went on to say that such a surrogacy agreement is not against public policy, and is valid and enforceable. The $10,000 payment covers discomfort or suffering on the part of the surrogate woman; it is not a purchase price for the child itself. And he rightly confined his remarks to nongenetic surrogacy—that is, his decision could not apply to a case such as Baby M where the surrogate contributes her egg, placing genetic parents on both sides of the litigation.

In May 1993, the California Supreme Court sided with the Calverts, declaring them the "natural parents." But the argument was nuanced. Rather than brute genetic inheritance, the Supreme Court inquired into motive. It found that Mark and Chris had begun with the intention of bringing a child into the world to rear in their own family, and that Chris had from the outset intended to be the child's mother. This could not be said of Anna, of course. What I find significant here is that the argument went beyond mere genetic heritage to psychological and social criteria for rendering its decision.

Who Is the So-called Real Mother?

Baby M and similar cases have stimulated discussions in state legislatures, and the resulting laws tend toward prohibition of payment for surrogacy. The New York Task Force on Life and the Law declared that paying women to bear children "has the potential to undermine the dignity of women, children, and human reproduction." On this advice New York passed legislation in 1993 outrightly banning paid surrogacy. Arizona, Indiana, Kentucky, Louisiana, and Utah have declared surrogacy contracts invalid. In New Hampshire, Virginia, and Washington some surrogacy contracts are recognized but compensated surrogacy is not. In other states the matter is murky. Because of the murkiness, perhaps it is time that our legislators take a look at the bigger question: Just what is a family? What is a parent-child relationship in the larger philosophical sense? What laws would best help to guarantee each child a caring and nurturing home in which to grow up?

The pressure to develop new laws in the medium-range future should provide the occasion for some fundamental thinking and the cultivation of general legal rules and principles that could guide the specific laws being called for.[37] Courts are beginning to accord greater rights to persons with psychological or social responsibilities other than merely biological ties of parenthood, particularly in areas of custody.[38]

In the public debate much attention is given to bonding, perhaps even more attention than is given to genetic inheritance. The National Coalition Against Surrogacy, co-chaired by Jeremy Rifkin, contends that the real mother is the gestation mother, a position common to bioethics in the Jewish tradition. The coalition believes that the woman who carries the pregnancy—with or without a contract—is "the biological, true mother of the child."[39] Therefore it opposes the use of the term *surrogate,* which means substitute. Their reasoning is based on the observation that during pregnancy the woman develops a deep relationship with her child, one that she might not have anticipated before becoming pregnant. A surrogacy contract could then lead to devastating emotional pain by explicitly and implicitly forbidding gestation mothers from forming a parent-child relationship. Hence, the coalition lobbies legislatures to pass antisurrogacy laws.

The bonding issue has drawn the attention of feminists and others concerned about the exploitation of women. This is the fear registered by Rifkin's colleague, Andrew Kimbrell.

> The practice of surrogacy represents a new and unique form of slavery over women. Once women, enticed by a fee, sign these contracts to produce babies for clients, they are physically exploited. They are placed in commercial servitude twenty-four hours a day for 270 days. . . . These contracts also contain written provisions placing liability on the mother for all risks, including death, which are incidental to conception, pregnancy, and childbirth, including all pregnancy-induced diseases and any postpartum complications.[40]

Kimbrell also fears that one repercussion of surrogacy might be couples shopping around for just the right genetic-gestational surrogate, the one with the superior traits. The choice of one surrogate over another, then, would be based on eugenic grounds.[41]

What Is the Feminist Stake
in the Surrogacy Debate?

When we inquire about the feminist stake in the issue of third-party parenting—which includes surrogacy as well as AID—two irreconcilable positions make their appearance, both classified as feminist. A closer look will show that something like the basic conflict between libertarian individualism and the egalitarian spirit is surfacing within feminist thought. On the issue of surrogacy, the conflict takes the form of a dispute between libertarian feminists and essentialist feminists.

The clear thrust of the women's liberation movement of the 1960s that led to the pro-choice position on abortion represents one more application of the Enlightenment commitment to individual liberty over against the demands of culture, tradition, society, and government. A woman's choice became both the goal and the evidence of her freedom. The key obstacle that had to be overcome was the competition between the woman's right and the right of the child in the womb, which was accomplished by *Roe v. Wade*. The goal here was not to eliminate babies per se; rather, it was to cede to women the right to determine what happens to their own bodies. This decision, declaring that no woman would have to bring a conceptus to term but could either abort or give birth according to her own decision, marked a triumph in the history of freedom—at least freedom understood as choice. The power of choice lies in the choosing self.

It would seem that surrogacy and other reproductive technologies would increase the range of choice and the degree of control that the choosing woman has over the use of her body. The woman who contracts with a surrogate to carry her fetus now has an opportunity to become a mother, an opportunity that would be denied her if this reproductive technique were not available. The commissioning woman in this case does not become a mother by accident but rather as a clear result of her own choice. The surrogate similarly enters into the contract as the result of a personal decision. The formal recognition of rights in our liberal society is accomplished through agreements and contracts freely entered into by the parties involved. A surrogate contract, like abortion on request, is clear evidence that the woman in question has the power to determine what happens to her body. I will refer to this as the libertarian feminist position.

Juliette Zipper and Selma Svenhuijsen, who formulate the interests of feminists in the surrogacy debate in the Netherlands, distinguish between the broad political strategies for feminism and the individual choices women make. They make their point forcefully: "The mother-child bond is not sacrosanct. This implies that children can grow up happily with parents who are not their biological parents. It also means that women who give birth to a child and give it away can have sound motives: we should respect their choice."[42]

Yet there is more than just this one feminist perspective on the issue of third-party parenting. Many other feminists oppose third-party parenting, especially surrogate motherhood, and do so for different but overlapping reasons. At least three such reasons are appropriate here: First, what appears to be choice is in fact victimage at an unrecognizable level; second, the ideology of reproductive choice that drives the marketing of surrogacy is excessively libertarian and individualist, whereas many feminists are egalitarian and press for social considerations in procreative choice; third, some feminists embrace a form of essentialism, arguing that the biological relation of mother and child (or in some cases parents and child) is so essential that it is immoral to break it.

The first reason for opposing surrogacy—the argument that increased choice may mask unrecognizable victimage—applies to reproductive technology in general. Michelle Stanworth, for example, identifies "the centre of feminist concern: that, on the one hand, medical and scientific advances have offered women a greater chance to decide if, when, and under what conditions to mother, while on the other, they have increased the potential for others to exercise an even greater control over women's lives."[43] Who are the others taking control? The medical profession and the state.[44]

Lisa Sowle Cahill offers another version of the first reason: When choice is purveyed in the free marketplace it becomes subject to powerful social forces that shape choice. The options for women are defined by the patriarchal culture that structures our perceptions of the world and influences our values. What appears to be freedom is in fact co-optation. It is self-delusory to think that we can establish a morality rooted in choice.[45] Cahill seems to be assuming that an individual woman in the act of choice may feel free but is in fact the victim of supraindividual cultural and economic interests. Cahill adds that to think of institutionalizing personal choice regarding such technologies as gamete donation or surrogacy conveys the priority of privacy and liberty over sociality and the common good.[46] This criticism of choice as illusory leads to the second criticism, namely, the choice ideology on which the practice of surrogacy relies is too individualist.

As we have seen, feminists such as Lisa Cahill work out of a more egalitarian social philosophy that gives priority to the common good as a criterion for measuring choice. Some values are more important than choice. Jean Bethke Elshtain, a University of Chicago ethicist, is impatient with pro-choice feminism because "the atomistic, contractual frame exudes a politics of self-interest undertaken by a freely choosing, rational agent who, within the present order, is reborn as a sovereign consumer."[47] Elshtain fears that this position reduces the family to a mere "nonbinding commitment" (the modern oxymoron). The atomism of the pro-choice party fails to take into account a woman's relationship to the human life cycle, to her role in social regenesis. What feminism should deliver to women is not merely the freedom to control but also the responsibility for caring. Elshtain wants to draw on the wisdom of the early Christian church that projected a future human community patterned after the family that embraces rich and poor, male and female, and puts on the rich the duty to support the poor.[48] According to Elshtain, this does not rule out abortion under all circumstances, but certainly "abortion-on-demand would represent an anomaly within this world."[49]

This leads to the third reason for rejecting a thoroughgoing ideology of reproductive freedom. The more relational and egalitarian disposition of many feminists leads them to affirm something essential about the biological relationship of parent to child, so essential that it cannot be subject to choice. The bonding of mother and fetus is decisive here. The physical communal tie between the mother-to-be and the child-to-be is so important that it takes priority over the freedom to choose an abortion, or correlatively to choose to rent out a womb for someone else's child. The philosophical appeal here is to some essential dimension of womanhood that simply cannot be given away even if the woman in question freely decides she wants to. The physical or biological dimension of being a woman is thought to be essential to her selfhood and is an expression of that selfhood. Her self is inextricably tied to the baby she bears. I will refer to this as the essentialist feminist position. I submit the title *essentialist feminist* rather than *pro-life feminist,* because—despite the apparent incoherence—some pro-choice feminists also emphasize communitarian or relational ethics and are sympathetic to the gestational-bond argument.

Maura Ryan is a feminist concerned about the social dimension of procreative decision making, and who emphasizes not simply individual autonomy but a communal understanding of responsibility. She argues,

> Thus it is not enough to assert that providing genetically related children to infertile individuals is a good to be promoted. . . . Interest in a genetically related child cannot be seen as an independent end, the value of which automatically discounts concerns for the present and future state of the offspring, for the physical and emotional safety of the collaborators, or for the place of the experience of reproduction in our collective value system.[50]

The net result is a defense of the child as an end, not a means for a further end, even if that end be the procreative experience of the parents.

When it comes to the surrogacy debate, the essentialist feminist position usually gives first priority to the gestational mother on the grounds of her unbreakable bond with the child. This position takes a stand both against surrogate motherhood and against AID. Hilde Lindemann Nelson and James Lindemann Nelson at the Hastings Center, for example, use a causal ethical argument: Since the mother is the biological cause of the child, she cannot surrender her personal responsibility to raise that child. The Nelsons apply this ethical argument to both father and mother, contending that if they cause—biologically cause—a child to come into existence, then their lifelong responsibility to that child is irrevocable. They cannot sign it away in a contract. "Parents' causal role in procreation grounds their obligation to their children more firmly than does the notion of consent."[51] The ethical bond is biologically determined, not socially determined.

> It is, we think, not the *decision* to have children but rather the *fact* of having done so, which primarily creates responsibilities. The leading idea of our view is that in bringing a child into the world, the parents have put it at risk of harm; it is extremely needy and highly vulnerable to a vast assortment of physical and psychological damage. Because they have exposed it to that risk, they have at least a prima facie obligation to defend it; further, they may not transfer their parental duties to another caretaker simply as a matter of choice, for it is the child who holds the claim against both mother and father, and it cannot release them.[52]

As the Nelsons work out the implications of this position, they emphasize that the lifelong responsibility of raising a biologically caused child cannot be relinquished by contract. "The surrogate mother may not relinquish this control."[53] Nor can the father who donates semen. The very practice of AID is ethically dubious, they say.

What I find curious here is that the term *cause* is applied both to the gestating mother and to the genetic father. If the fundamental point of departure is the physical bond between mother and child that develops during pregnancy, then the term *cause* should apply to the mother regardless of whether she uses her own egg or a donor egg. Gestation, not genetics, seems to determine the causal ethic here. So, how does it follow that the father—who never gets pregnant—shares the same responsibility? How does it follow that AID is ethically dubious? The father does not gestate. The father may contribute genes to his own child knowingly or, if he is an anonymous semen donor, contribute genes to children he will never meet. How is it that his responsibility is similarly irrevocable?

Rothman argues vehemently: "Any pregnant woman is the mother of the child she bears, regardless of the source of the egg or the sperm."[54] Rothman presents this argument not for the purpose of supporting the practice of surrogacy but rather in opposition to it.

> The time to stop such nightmare visions is now. We stop it by not acknowledging the underlying principle of surrogate contracts, by not accepting the very concept of "surrogacy" for motherhood. A surrogate is a substitute. In some human relations, we can accept no substitutes. Any pregnant woman is the mother of the child she bears. Her gestational relationship establishes her motherhood.[55]

Although siding with the essentialist feminists on surrogacy, Rothman does not appeal to the same first principles. She does not appeal to some sort of "maternal instincts" argument.[56] Rather, she appeals to the principle of relationship, especially a freely chosen relationship. As a pro-choice feminist, she affirms a woman's right to abortion, the right to refuse entering into a relationship with the child. Conversely, a woman who has chosen to relate to a fetus through pregnancy-to-term has a right—apparently also an obligation!—to maintain that relationship indefinitely. The bond between gestational mother and child is the definitive bond for Rothman, a bond that trumps any genetic or contractual bond. By emphasizing the element of choice in relationship, Rothman seems to side with the libertarian feminists; but by focusing solely on the gestational relationship, she ends up keeping company with the essentialist feminists, many of whom are pro-life on abortion.

John A. Robertson responds to the essentialist feminists by defending his own version of libertarianism which maximizes choice and permits surrogacy. Robertson believes that the above-mentioned disputes can best be solved with clearly binding prepregnancy contracts. He objects to critics who attempt to nullify such contracts on the basis of an appeal to some vague principle of essential womanhood that is allegedly expressed during pregnancy, seeing this kind of feminism as paternalist toward women. According to Robertson the essentialist rejection of preconception agreements to fix rights and duties for the rearing family

> seems to be based on paternalistic attitudes toward women or on a symbolic view of maternal gestation. Privileging the surrogate's wishes over the reliance interests of the couple assumes that women cannot make rational decisions about reproduction and child rearing prior to conception. It also treats gestational motherhood as a near sacred endeavor, which preconception contracts that separate gestational and social parentage violate. However, paternalistic and symbolic attitudes over which reasonable persons

differ do not justify trumping the fundamental right to use collaborative means of procreation.[57]

Cahill on Surrogacy

Of the voices raised in alarm over the practice of surrogate motherhood, the one I find most worth listening to is that of Lisa Sowle Cahill.[58] Although Cahill gives much more weight to the inheritance myth than I do, she is clear in setting priorities that serve the love of children. "The deciding factor in surrogate arrangements," she writes, "should be the best interests of the child. An important but secondary and modifying consideration should be the rights and duties of parents in regard to their biological offspring."[59] In cases of babies born through surrogate arrangements, Cahill would give priority to a loving home over a wealthy home, to an atmosphere of trust and cooperation over financial security. The most important criterion is the firm and reliable determination on the part of the parents to whom the raising of the child will be entrusted. Permanent care and love to the child are paramount. Second to this psychospiritual parental context is the family's financial ability to meet the child's basic physical needs and, when possible, to provide affluence.

Having said this, two corollaries follow. First, the interests of the parents should be seen as distinct from, and secondary to, the child's interests. Second, biological connection with the parents helps ground psychospiritual flourishing and must be considered a factor in determining a child's true best interests.

The philosophical problem Cahill has with surrogacy is that its advocates operate out of an individual choice libertarianism that expresses itself through contractual arrangements. She finds surrogate contracts morally objectionable because they insist on free choice in human relations where free choice ought not exist. The libertarian approach denies the important physical aspects of both the relations of spousehood and of parenthood, and also of moral obligation in general. We as individuals simply cannot choose in all circumstances whether or not we have a moral obligation; some mutual obligations come with our biology. "The mutual obligations of biological family members—children, parents, siblings—are a paradigmatic case of obligations that one cannot simply decide do not exist."[60]

Cahill advocates that we tolerate but discourage the practice and legality of surrogate motherhood. "Surrogate motherhood should not be outlawed, but neither should it be given the legal protection that would encourage it as a social practice."[61] Consistent with her larger agenda in sexual ethics to affirm the equal interaction of love, sexuality, and parenthood, she says, "The Church has given us an important message by insisting that having children belongs in a loving marriage; hence, third-party reproductive methods are excluded."[62]

The Limited Scope of Concern

The conversants we have noted thus far in the ethical controversies over surrogate motherhood are too limited in the scope of their concerns to be of much help on the issue of children. Procreative libertarians and pro-choice feminists are limited by focusing only on the interests of the parents or, in the feminist instance, only on the woman's interests. The essentialist feminist position, despite its reverence for the mother-fetus bond, still centers its concern primarily on the interests of the mother as a woman. Although the two perspectives conflict with one another at certain points, their net effect is that the fetus becomes a commodity to be accepted or discarded by those with the power of choice. With exceptions such as Lisa Sowle Cahill, relatively few in the reproductive conversation, it seems, are willing to speak up for the child. As long as our antennae are tuned only to the issue of maximizing or restricting choice, concern for the welfare of the child drifts right off the ethical radar screen.

If we start with the need of the newborn for care and nurturing and then work backward to his or her procreative origin, the form of genetic and gestational origin matters less than the quality of family life the child will enjoy during the rearing years. Could we argue that the family's intentions of bringing the child into the world count as partial evidence of that family's commitment to love that child when it arrives? Could we argue that a family willing to spend its resources—financial resources as well as inconvenience and, perhaps, even physical discomfort—is demonstrating its potential to love that child? Would this not also apply to baby making both through sexual intercourse and perhaps even more to the employment of reproductive technology? All things being equal, shouldn't the family who demonstrates commitment to establishing a home where a child would be loved unconditionally trump genetic or gestational or other biotechnical bonds? It is in this direction, I believe, that we should swim in this stream of reproductive choice.

4

Designer Genes
and Selective Abortion

Even if a child is unattractive when it is born,
we nevertheless love it.
—Martin Luther[1]

A new form of discrimination looms on the horizon, one that could lead to a rerun of the now defunct eugenics movement. During the first quarter of the twentieth century, political activity in England and in the United States included advocates of eugenics—that is, a movement that used family planning to improve the health, intelligence, and productivity of the human race. By encouraging the proper people to breed and by discouraging the wrong people from making babies, eugenicists sought to prepare the way for future generations of superior people. The positive eugenic platform encouraged intelligent men and women to meet, marry, and propagate in order to provide civic leaders for the future; the negative eugenic platform lobbied for legislation to discourage baby making among the mentally retarded, feebleminded, physically disabled, alcoholics, and petty thieves. This led to the forced sterilization of thousands of inmates in America's prisons, on the grounds that convicted felons might propagate children who would also become felons and cost the state corrections system further expenses. The idea of eugenics was abandoned in the 1930s because it was based on faulty genetic theory. When it became clear that two mentally retarded persons could give birth to a child with normal intelligence, the assumptions on which eugenics were based dissolved.

This realization was too late to stop the Nazis, however. By the mid-1920s the National Socialist Party in Germany had brought together eugenics with anti-Semitism, and "racial hygiene" became party policy. Nazis sought and received advice from California officials as to how to implement eugenic measures in state-run institutions. Eugenics became the means for enhancing the interests of the so-called Aryan race. This led to the development of the Superman (*Übermensch*). Adolf Hitler's SS was charged with the mission of racial hygiene that led to using gas chambers and other extermination procedures on children who were physically disabled or mentally handicapped. Eventually gas chambers were used on political dissidents and Jews.

Nazi Germany was a fascist dictatorship and eugenics was imposed from the top down. This top-down approach is not likely to repeat itself in the near or medium-range future, since the political climate has changed. However, the idea of neo-eugenics may sweep over us quite soon; and if it comes, it will blow in on the winds of a free market economy.[2]

Like a single leaf from an oak tree in October, the Herman J. Muller Repository for Germinal Choice floats on the winds of the times. This sperm bank, which was established by Robert K. Graham in the late 1970s, collects sperm from Nobel prize winners and offers insemination to women under thirty-five with high IQs. The goal is to help guide nature into producing more intelligent children. This overt eugenic program is singular and small, hardly worth including in a weather report about things to come.

Still, I forecast that a new form of eugenics may eventually come on us at gale-like speed. Since moving air is invisible to the eye, at first we will feel but not see the eugenic winds blowing from two directions: discrimination in health insurance and personal tastes for designer children. I forecast that these winds will advance to gale-like or hurricane-like force, and future children will walk in the debris of the coming storm over selective abortion.[3]

Let us measure the speed of these two winds in turn. I will try to outline briefly the controversy that is brewing regarding possible discrimination in employment and insurance due to presymptomatic genetic testing, and then I will show how this will add oxygen to the already burning fires in the abortion debate.

Discrimination in the
Employment Insurance Healthcare Loop

The advance of genetic research is leading to the advance of medical diagnosis, and this in turn is leading toward possible discrimination against people diagnosed with bad genes. Why? Because bad genes are thought to be expensive, and private insurance carriers would like to save the money.

The triumphs of the Human Genome Project thus far can be measured in part by the discoveries of disease-related genes: The gene for cystic fibrosis has been found on chromosome 7; Huntington's chorea was discovered lurking on the end of chromosome 4; in 1994, the first of two defective genes for inherited breast cancer was found on chromosome 17; in 1995, scientists found that early onset Alzheimer's disease is caused by a gene mutation on chromosome 14; colon cancer has been associated with a gene on chromosome 2; and disposition to muscular dystrophy, sickle cell anemia, Tay-Sachs disease, late onset diabetes, certain cancers, and numerous other diseases are being tracked to locatable genetic origins. The search goes on for disease-causing alleles leading to 5,000 or more genetically based diseases. The search goes on as well to find the DNA switches that turn such genes on and off. Researchers are also trying to search for genetic therapies that will turn the bad genes off and keep the good genes on.

Such discoveries should fill us with cheer and hope, because this new knowledge could be used in medical care for diagnosis, prevention, and therapy. It could also advance the quality of health for everyone. Yet this apparent good news comes as bad news to those who are born with genetic susceptibilities to disease, when medical care is funded by private insurance companies or when medical insurance is tied to employment. An identifiable genetic predisposition to disease counts as a pre-existing condition, and insurance companies are pressured to deny coverage. Just as new techniques for prevention and therapy become available, the very people who could benefit may be denied access to these medical services.

Paul Billings, a genetics researcher and ethicist at the Stanford University Medical School, has begun collecting anecdotal evidence which shows that genetic discrimination has already begun. Testifying before Congress, Billings said he found one woman who, during a routine gynecological check, spoke to her physician about the possibility of her mother having Huntington's disease. When she applied for life insurance, she subsequently lost all insurance when her medical records were reviewed.

Phenylketonuria (PKU) experiences today may become routine genetic experiences tomorrow. Billings reports on an eight-year-old girl who had been diagnosed with PKU fourteen days after her birth through a newborn-screening program. A low-phenylalanine diet was prescribed at the time, and her parents effectively followed the diet's rules. The child has grown to be a normal and healthy person. Her healthcare at birth was covered by her father's group insurance policy that was associated with his employment. When he changed jobs, however, the carrier associated with his new employer declared her ineligible for coverage.[4] Once a genetic predisposition for an expensive disease becomes part of one's medical record, insurance carriers and employers that are connected to them will find it in their best financial interest to minimize or outrightly deny healthcare coverage.

Loss of healthcare and perhaps loss of employment opportunities may, if left unchecked, create a whole new underclass. After hearing from Paul Billings and others, Congressman John Conyers said,

> Like discrimination based on race, genetic discrimination is wrong because it is based on hereditary characteristics we are powerless to change.
>
> The fear in the minds of many people is that genetic information will be used to identify those with "weak" or "inferior" genes, who will then be treated as a "biological underclass."[5]

For the most part, the government has not been willing to listen to the prophetic voices raised in behalf of the genetically poor and oppressed who may appear in the next generation. In order to make the point that this is a serious matter, researchers in the Working Group on Ethical, Legal, and Social Implications of the Human Genome Project at the National Institutes of Health and at the Department of Energy created a task force that, in 1993, produced a report calling for action. The task force included geneticists, ethicists, and representatives from the insurance industry. The central message here was this: Information about past, present, or future health status—especially health status due to genetic predispositions—should not be used to deny healthcare coverage or services to anyone.[6] In 1996 the New Jersey General Assembly passed legislation banning health insurance companies from denying access or setting higher rates for persons genetically predisposed to certain diseases.

In December 1994, the Genetic Privacy Act was introduced in the federal legislature as well as six state legislatures. This act would govern the collection, analysis, storage, and use of DNA samples, requiring explicit authorization for the collection of these samples for genetic analysis and limiting the use of information that is gained from them. The aim here was to protect individual privacy by giving the individual the right to authorize who may have access to his or her genetic information.

The Genetic Privacy Act is a good start, but in my judgment it is not enough. Laws to protect genetic privacy would appeal to our sense of autonomy, to our desire to take control of what appears to be our own possession, our genome. But privacy protection will not in itself eliminate the threat of genetic discrimination for two reasons: First, it probably will not work. Genetic information as well as medical records are computerized. Computers are linked. In the world of computech, if someone really wants to gain information, he or she will eventually find a way to do so. An attempt to maintain control over genetic information is likely to fail. Second, privacy regarding one's genome is undesirable since knowledge of one's genome could be of enormous value in preventative healthcare. The more our physicians know about our genetic predispositions, the more they can plan to head off difficulties before they arise. Rather than privacy, it seems to me that we want *genetic information without discrimination.*

A few years ago our twenty-three-year-old godson, Matthew Hunneshagen, was rushed to the hospital for an emergency surgery. Without warning he was suddenly diagnosed as suffering from familial intestinal polyposis, an advanced-stage colon cancer. The surgeon's team worked for a number of hours in a heroic effort to remove all signs of malignancy. The operation was successful. The surgeon, fatigued after his Herculean achievement, flopped down in a chair next to Matthew's nervously waiting parents. "Are there any cases of colon cancer in Matthew's grandparents?" asked the doctor.

"We don't know," answered Matthew's mother and father. They went on to explain that Matthew had been adopted as an infant and that the records were closed. My wife, Jenny, and I had been present at Matthew's baptism two decades prior.

"Well," said the doctor, "on the day Matthew was admitted to the hospital I read in a British Medical journal that a marker has been found for this kind of cancer. It's genetic. It runs in families. Had we known that Matthew had a predisposition, we could have been monitoring him from age ten or so on, removing pre-cancerous polyps, and he never would have come to this crisis situation."

This case shows the potential value of computerized and accessible genomic information. At some point in the future, a simple blood test could reveal each of our individual genomes, and this knowledge could be used to great benefit. I advocate laws to promote *genetic information without discrimination* so what we learn about our genomes will contribute to better healthcare rather than deny it.

A number of states currently have laws requiring that genetic information be secured from birth parents and made available to adopting parents. This genetic information has been obtained from family histories—that is, learning the frequency of a disorder in a family without revealing the identity of the family. As genetic testing becomes more sophisticated, DNA tests themselves will likely be sufficient.

If children who are to be adopted become viewed as commodities to be consumed by prospective parents, however, such genetic testing could inadvertently lead to discrimination. If the child tests positively for a genetic defect, the adopting parents may think of the child as defective and refuse to adopt the child. This refusal could be due to two reasons: First, the adoptive parents may simply be engaged in the *perfect child syndrome* and will not accept anything less than a perfectly healthy infant or toddler; second, they may refuse to adopt, fearing that they might lose their family healthcare insurance and become stuck with high medical bills.[7] The first reason is cultural or ethical; the second is economic. Commending our principle—God loves each of us regardless of our genetic makeup, and we should do likewise—to adoptive parents aims at encouraging families to make homes for children who are going to need them. Commending such a principle to public policymakers regarding the funding of medical care reasserts that we want information without discrimination.

From Healthcare Discrimination
to Selective Abortion

Now, just what is the connection between genetic discrimination and selective abortion? The following case will serve to make the connection. A couple living in Louisiana had a child with cystic fibrosis, a genetic disorder leading to chronic lung infections and excruciating discomfort. When the wife became pregnant with the second child, a prenatal genetic test revealed that the fetus carried the mutant gene for cystic fibrosis. The couple's health maintenance organization (HMO) demanded that they abort. If they refused to abort, the HMO threatened to withdraw coverage for both the newborn and the first child. The HMO only granted coverage for the newborn when the couple threatened to sue.[8]

This incident may be a harbinger of things to come. With the advance of prenatal genetic testing, both parents and insurance carriers can tell in advance that a given child might be prone to having a debilitating and expensive disease. The insurance industry may apply pressure to couples to have abortions because of financial interests. It would not be too unrealistic to imagine the following scenario occuring a decade from now: A published list of genetic predispositions that, if found in a fetus, would mandate an abortion under penalty of loss of coverage. This policy would surely outrage pro-life parents. Even those who may have taken a pro-choice position on abortion, however, would find this financial pressure to be the equivalent of a compromise on choice.

We are moving step by step toward the selective abortion scenario. In addition to pressure from the privately funded insurance industry, parents themselves will likely develop criteria for deciding which fetuses will be brought to term and which will be aborted. Genetic criteria will play a major role. Prenatal testing to identify disease-related genes will likely become routine, and eventually tests for perhaps hundreds of deleterious genes may become part of the prenatal arsenal. Parents, wanting what they believe to be a perfectly healthy child, may abort repeatedly at each hint of a genetic disorder. Parents who are willing to accept some degree of malady, however, may abort only the most ominous cases. What we can fully expect is that choice and selection will enter the enterprise of baby making at a magnitude unheard of in previous history.

The point at which most families will confront the issue we are identifying here is when they seek genetic counseling. A genetic analysis of heritable family traits, preferably before pregnancy or even before marriage, can help immensely in planning for future children. However, talking with the genetic counselor, too, often begins with a pregnancy already in progress. The task of the genetic counselor is quite specific: to provide information regarding the degree of risk that a given child might be born with a genetic disorder, and to impart this information objectively, impartially, and confidentially (when possible) so that the autonomy of the parents is protected. What is surprising and disconcerting to mothers, or couples in this situation, is that genetic risk is usually given statistically. The assumption that medical science is an exact science is immediately challenged, and the parents find themselves confronted with difficult-to-interpret information while facing an unknown future. Conflicting values between marital partners, or even within themselves, increase the difficulty, as well as the anxiety.

The statistical unknown comes in two forms: First, for an autosomal recessive defective gene such as that for cystic fibrosis, if both parents are carriers, the risk that their child will also be a carrier is 50 percent and the risk that the child will actually contract the disease is 25 percent. The parents decide whether to proceed with the birth or to terminate the pregnancy once they receive this information. Second, via amniocentesis and other testing procedures being developed, the specific genetic makeup of a fetus can be discerned. In cases of Down's syndrome, for example, which is associated with trisomy (three copies of chromosome 21), we know from experience that eight out of every ten negative prenatal diagnoses lead to the decision to abort. Even though the genetic predisposition can be clearly identified in this way, what remains unknown is the degree of mental retardation that will result. Mild cases mean near-average intelligence, and such individuals are pleasant members of families. Yet the choice to abort has become the virtual norm. The population rate of people with Down's syndrome in our society is declining, making this a form of eugenics by popular choice.

In only 3 percent to 5 percent of the cases does a positive prenatal diagnosis reveal the presence of a severe genetic disorder, so severe that the probable level of suffering on the part of the child warrants consideration of abortion. In making this judgment, I am invoking a principle of compassion, what bioethicists dub as *the principle of nonmaleficence,* which is aimed at reducing human suffering whenever possible. In situations where such a diagnosis is rendered and where the prospective parents strongly desire to bring a child into the world as an expression of their love, a number of things are observable. First, without thinking about it, the parents refer to the child as a "baby," never a "fetus."[9] They clearly think of the life growing in the womb as a person. Second, when confronted with the bad news, they experience turmoil. The turmoil leads more often than not to a decision to terminate the pregnancy, but certainly not always.[10] It is not the job of the genetic counselor to encourage abortion, and advocates of procreative liberty stand firm in protecting the right of parents to decide to bring such a child to birth. Third, even when the decision to terminate is made, these grieving parents see their decision as an expression of their love, not a denial of love. It is an act of compassion.

Ethically significant here is the distinction between convenience and compassion.[11] As the practice of prenatal genetic testing expands and the principle of autonomy—that is, the responsibility for choice—is applied to the parents and not to the unborn child, we can forecast that the total number of abortions will increase, perhaps even dramatically.[12] Each pregnancy will be thought to be tentative until the fetus has taken and passed dozens, perhaps hundreds, of genetic tests. A culturally reinforced image of the desirable child—*the perfect child syndrome*—may eventually lead couples to try repeated pregnancies, terminating the undesirables, and giving birth to only the best test passers. Those finally born in this fashion risk being "commodified" by their parents. In addition, those who might be born with a disability, but still with the potential for leading a productive and fulfilling life, might never see the light of day.

A social by-product of embracing selective abortion might be increased discrimination against people who have disabilities, with the assumption that to live with a disability is to have a life not worth living. Persons with disabilities find this prospect fearsome. They fear that the medical establishment and its supportive social policies will seek to prevent "future people like me" from ever being born. This translates to "I am worth less to society." The imputation of dignity to handicapped persons may be quietly withdrawn as they are increasingly viewed as unnecessary and perhaps expensive appendages to an otherwise healthy society. This would be a tragedy of the first order. Disabled persons are persons who deserve dignity and, furthermore, deserve encouragement. Marsha Saxton, a disabled rights advocate who herself suffers from spina bifida, reports that such people can gain victory in their difficult life struggles. "Most disabled people have told me with no uncertainty that the disability, the pain, the need for compensatory devices and assistance can produce considerable inconvenience, but that very often these become minimal or are forgotten once individuals make the transition to living their everyday lives."[13] Given the precedent set by Jesus who spent so much of his time with the disabled—whether born blind or having contracted diseases such as leprosy—it seems that no disciple of Jesus could lightly acquiesce to the wholesale aborting of this group of people. One could easily imagine that Jesus' disciples, if alive today, would organize social services and advertise: "Don't abort! Send us your genetically defective babies."[14] No medical insurance company is likely to cover such an enterprise, of course.

Whether we asked for it or not, the advancing frontier of genetics and its impact on reproductive technology thrusts us back once again into the abortion debate. We can reasonably predict that the number of abortions performed will skyrocket as prenatal genetic testing expands and becomes more commonplace. Before speaking directly to the issue of selective abortion, the question of abortion per se needs to be reviewed and theologically assessed.

Questions *Roe v. Wade*
Did Not Answer

The pro-choice position permits a pregnant woman to choose either to abort or not to abort. The motive for taking this position is not to sponsor a wholesale elimination of future children for the purposes of population control or genocide but rather to extend to each woman the right to control her own body. The power to determine whether or not to bring a fetus to term is just that, a power that had been denied to American women prior to 1973 but then granted by the U.S. Supreme Court in *Roe v. Wade*. This event of women's empowerment required making two intellectual moves: first, to place the unborn fetus within the province of the woman's body; and, second, to deny the status of personhood to the unborn fetus. The first move seemed axiomatic, especially if the second move held; the second, however, was crucial.

The public atmosphere had been charged with the question: When does life begin? If we assert that life—life understood as human personhood with dignity that should be granted equal protection under law—begins with conception, then the state would have to defend the rights of the embryo in the mother-to-be. On the other hand, if we assert that life begins later, such as at birth, or if we assert that the "quality of life" matters more than the mere fact of life, then the unborn fetus could be considered as strictly part of the woman's body and subject to the woman's decision making. The latter position prevailed. The court rejected the claim that the fetus is juridically a person, and so denied any entitlement to Fourteenth Amendment rights to equal protection under the law and due process. The court acknowledged that this was the crucial move in rendering its decision: "If this suggestion of personhood is established, the [pregnant woman's] case, of course, collapses, for the fetus' right to life would then be guaranteed specifically by the Amendment." The court established "viability" as the point where the state would take an "important and legitimate interest in potential life," but it eschewed the question of when human life begins. By not stipulating the point at which a legally protectable life begins, the court deliberately opened the door to the practice of abortion by choice.

Such choice is not absolute, however. It is nuanced by the trimester scheme, wherein the state takes increasing interest as the fetus develops over time. The woman gains total authority to decide on whether or not to have an abortion during the first three months of pregnancy. She is subject to reasonable regulation for health reasons during the second trimester. Her decision to abort can be overridden by the state, however, in the third trimester. The focus of *Roe v. Wade* here is not on fetal rights per se, but rather on the state's power to act on behalf of the fetus' interests at different stages.[15]

Stephen L. Carter, a law professor at Yale University, favors the pro-choice result but dislikes the reasoning. Carter believes that the focus should not be on the question of when life begins; but rather the focus should be on the right of the state to defend or take human life. If the state has the power to terminate life, as in the death penalty, it could in principle invoke that power with regard to the unborn. "The Fourteenth Amendment does not guarantee a right to life—it guarantees only that life cannot be taken *by the state* without due process of law. The distinction matters. . . . Consequently, even were the fetus deemed a person, the state would still have the power to allow it, under some circumstances, to be killed."[16] Carter's point is that the public debate need not focus as heavily as it does on when a person's life begins. The only reason we do, is because the Supreme Court did. Carter's assessment is not accurate, in my judgment, because the very question of when legally protectable life begins was the burning question of the era, which was tested in *Roe v. Wade*. That the court did not answer it completely does not mean that the question was nonsensical or that the public discussion is merely a product of the court's decision.

For us today the matter of abortion on demand (or request) appears to have been decided. Juridically speaking, the unborn—whether at the zygote, embryo, or fetus stage of development—at least during the first trimester, has no personhood and can make no legal claim vis à vis the mother. Judged as being part of the pregnant woman's body, the decision to abort or to not abort belongs to the woman in question. The sole agenda of the women's liberation movement prior to *Roe v. Wade* and of subsequent feminist activism has been the empowerment of women. The agenda has not been mean spirited with regard to children. Rather, the pro-choice movement has argued that children who are wanted will be loved, that to be a wanted child will increase the "quality of life" for that child. The reason our society posed the question, "When does life begin?" was to provide an answer to another question, "How much power does a woman have over her own body?" It is this question that *Roe v. Wade* answered.[17]

But is this enough of an answer to meet the new questions arising from the genetic revolution? What if new questions seem less tied to the issue of women's empowerment? For example, what are the rights of the fertilized egg—the conceptus—in a petri dish? If it has not yet been placed into the mother's fallopian tube or uterus, does *Roe v. Wade* still apply?

Signposts of new directions are readable. In the context of debating postcoital contraception—that is, flushing out a fertilized zygote after conception but prior to attachment to the womb wall—the question arises: Is this an abortion? Is the use of mifepristone within 72 hours of intercourse a form of contraception or abortion? If we invoke the criterion that the concept of abortion applies only to a fetus attached to the woman's uterus, then technically the destruction of a preimplanted zygote is not an abortion. This criterion was already used in 1962 by the British Council of Churches when it stated that "a woman cannot abort until the fertilized egg has nidated and thus become attached to her body."[18]

When Does the Fetus Gain Dignity?

The incompleteness of the answer to the question of when personhood and dignity begins is quite relevant to the study we are engaged in here, so retrieving some of the argumentation on the eve of that landmark court decision—*Roe v. Wade*—may prove to be worthwhile. In 1970 bioethicist Daniel Callahan distinguished three schools of thought on this issue: the genetic school, the developmental school, and the social consequences school. Although the political climate has changed considerably over the last three decades, conversants in the contemporary discussion still fall roughly into these schools of thought. Let us look briefly at each in turn.

The genetic school locates the beginning of human personhood at the genetic beginning—that is, at conception, the point at which one's individual genome is set. Defending the classic Roman Catholic position on abortion, judge and legal theorist John T. Noonan gives voice to the genetic school by arguing that there is "only one test for humanity: a being who was conceived by human parents and is potentially capable of human acts is human."[19] Or, "a being with the human genetic code is *Homo sapiens* in potency."[20] Similarly, Reformed theologian and ethicist Paul Ramsey argues that whoever the individual person will become is determined "from the moment of impregnation." What happens thereafter may be described as a process of becoming what the person already is. "Genetics teaches that we were from the beginning what we essentially still are in every cell and in every human attribute."[21]

The problem with the genetic position, says Callahan, is that it does not take into account the cleavage between genotype and phenotype, between our DNA blueprint and the actual body that develops. Yes of course the composition of our individual DNA is set at the moment of conception. Yet who we become physically is actually determined by the influence of our environment—stimulating some genes to expression while keeping other genes turned off—so that the actual bodies we end up with are the result of an interaction between nature and nurture. To say it another way, some but not all of our individual personhood is found in our genotype. "That is the whole point of distinguishing between genotype and phenotype," argues Callahan, "it makes clear that an individual is something other than (though it includes) his genetic potential. Neither Noonan nor Ramsey give a sufficient place to the importance of development as part of the process of becoming human."[22] Another problem with this position, according to Callahan, is that the unborn is the only person given moral attention. The pregnant mother-to-be is ignored.

We can divide the genetic school into two grade levels, the strong and the weak. The strong genetic claim is that actual personhood is achieved at fertilization. The conceptus is a genetically unique human being and, though yet unborn, should be granted all the rights of someone already born. Abortion, then, consists of the destruction of a human person—that is, abortion is murder. The Vatican's Congregation for the Doctrine of the Faith articulates for us today the position of the strong genetic school.

> The human being is to be respected and treated as a person from the moment of conception; and therefore from that same moment his rights as a person must be recognized, among which in the first place is the inviolable right of every innocent human being to life. . . . [This position] reaffirms the moral condemnation of any kind of procured abortion. This teaching has not changed and is unchangeable.[23]

Virtually the same position is taken by James Dobson's *Focus on the Family* program. "The pre-born child is, from the moment of conception, a human being endowed by his or her Creator with a divine dignity and inviolable rights. Every human life is of infinite value to God."[24]

This strong genetic position is the one assumed by the American pro-life movement. In 1995, when two new prescription drugs appeared on the market that would allow a woman to end her pregnancy at home, antiabortion activist Randal Terry faxed his outrage to the *New England Journal of Medicine* that had reported it. He said, "When abortion is made illegal again, you will be hunted down and tried for genocide."[25]

In contrast to the view that the conceptus is already a person in the full sense, the weak genetic claim is that the fertilized egg is a potential person, not an actual person. The conceptus is genetically unique and will, barring any external interruption, become a full human person at birth. Even though abortion is not the equivalent of murder, according to advocates of the weak genetic school, the current abortion policy still represents a denial of dignity because it ranks the interests of the early fetus lower on a relative scale than the interests of the woman in whose body it resides. Abortion symbolizes a lowered level of respect for the life of the unborn.

In a fashion similar to Callahan, John A. Robertson argues against the strong genetic school by defending the developmentalist position. Granting genetic uniqueness at conception, Robertson denies that personhood—in the sense of a person being a moral subject in his or her own right—can occur before it becomes sentient, which is at twenty-six weeks. The strong view confuses potential and actual personhood, he says. Yet he goes on to criticize the weak view as well, this time from a social consequences position. He suggests that, symbolically speaking, an early abortion should be more acceptable than a later one, because the loss of an early embryo or fetus shows less disrespect for life than an abortion of a fully developed one. Furthermore, he argues, circumstances regarding the pregnant mother-to-be should be relevant: We should distinguish between a mother making sex selection in the second trimester from a teen mother of three children under age five whose birth control failed.[26] In short, Callahan and Robertson respectively try to relativize the absolutist determination of the rights of personhood at conception as proposed by the genetic school.

The developmental school, like the weak genetic school, grants that conception determines the genetic basis of human individuality, but it goes on to add that some degree of development is required before an individual human being can claim moral or legal rights in the face of abortion decisions. The question is when? All biological development is on a continuum. Landmarks can be identified, of course, such as the following: conception, the fall of the zygote from the fallopian tube and its implantation in the uterine wall, development of the placenta, spontaneous movement or quickening, viability, and finally birth.

Biological development is important, though in itself does not answer the "when" question completely. The developmentalists grant that human life begins at conception, but human personhood comes later, and it is personhood that is really at stake in abortion decisions. This leads some members of the developmental school to argue that biological science cannot in itself determine the precise place at which human personhood begins, so we must intervene with arbitrary theological or ethical criteria. Others, such as Malcolm Potts, employ biological data and then introduce the viability criterion, asserting that the fetus is viable at twenty-eight weeks and at that point should be granted the same rights as a newborn child.[27] Robertson articulates the logic of the position.

> The case for previability abortions rests on the view that a previable fetus has not yet reached a stage of development at which it has interests in itself. Prior to viability, it lacks the neurological capability for sentience. Despite its potential, it thus is not owed any moral duties in itself. Continuing a pregnancy is thus a matter of personal choice, and not a moral duty owed the fetus.[28]

Along with biological development comes developing moral status. Bioethicist John C. Fletcher observes that "the more the implanted embryo and developing fetus grows and possesses some recognizable human features and crucial biological capacities, the more the moral status of the fetus approximates that of a living person."[29] The time at which most selective abortions currently occur is during the mid-trimester, between eighteen and twenty-four weeks following diagnosis by amniocentesis. At this point the fetus has a clearly recognizable human form with a central nervous system and other organs, and it is nearing viability. Hospital policies typically prohibit abortions after twenty-four weeks, some after twenty weeks.

The obvious strength of the developmental school, says Callahan, is that it gives significant weight to the development process. In addition, Callahan applauds the distinction between the general class "human life" and individual "persons," because this makes possible some biologically identified norms for decision making. Such a norm might be the existence of brain function, for example, a single norm applicable throughout the life span because it determines personhood both at the time of death and at the beginning in the womb. If we lose our brain function at the end of our life we may be declared dead; similarly, prior to the appearance of embryonic brain waves in the womb, we can be declared a nonperson.

However, argues Callahan, there is a limit to the developmental position, namely, it gives insufficient range to the idea of potentiality. The zygote or embryo no matter how early—even prior to the onset of brain waves—still has the potential for becoming a person. Finally, once one adds any degree of actualization through development to the potential given at conception, any norm that says just how much actualization is required for personhood must appear arbitrary.[30]

The social consequences school holds that life is continuous, so that the real question is when truly "human life" begins. The social consequentialists deny that there is any such thing as a moment that establishes personhood because the establishment of truly human life is a process that takes time. Granting that the genetic uniqueness of the individual is established when sperm and ovum meet to form the zygote, Garrett Hardin holds that such genetic uniqueness is without moral significance. "Whether the fetus is or is not a human being is a matter of definition, not fact; and we can define any way we wish."[31] Now, how do we wish to define? That is the question. In the late 1960s and early 1970s, the phrase "quality of life" was proposed as a way to establish a socially constructed norm that expressed just how we wished to define "human life."[32] This only exacerbated the problem, of course, because no agreement could be reached as to just what constitutes "quality of life," let alone agreement on how to justify it.

Callahan, after applauding the social consequentialists for admitting that the science underdetermines the ethics, goes on to criticize them for ignoring science completely. Although biology cannot all by itself determine our ethical norm, Callahan believes we must still take the biological data into consideration, which includes the embryo's potential for true human life. He criticizes the social school also for its transparent agenda in which the freedom to define human life according to our wish is merely a justification for a previous decision to approve abortion. "Define as you wish" is a dangerous moral principle.[33] Callahan argues that an important factor in deciding the point at which morally and legally defined human life is determined is that the norm should not be arbitrary. Callahan believes that the social consequentialists are no help in establishing this norm.

Callahan dubs his own criterion as "biomoral," and with this criterion he judges the developmental approach to be the best of the three schools of thought since it takes into account the biological evidence as well as other factors in formulating moral policy; allows sensitivity to the greatest range of values when making abortion decisions; and provides a way of weighing the comparative values of the various lives at stake, the lives of both the unborn and the pregnant woman. "By allowing development to count in the assigning of value, the developmental school thus argues for a moderate policy, one which allows flexibility when hard choices must be made but which does not, in the process, deny that even a zygote is individual human life."[34] In the two plus decades since *Roe v. Wade*, Callahan has identified himself with the pro-choice movement, which includes many in the feminist movement but certainly includes other choice advocates as well. Callahan, a most thoughtful ethicist, makes it clear that the political achievement of choice is by no means the end of the matter. What remains is the morality intrinsic to choosing. Some choices are better than others, and the task of ethics is to help identify criteria for identifying good choices. The assumption that all that matters is that women have choice regarding abortion is to consign the decision to private subjective desire alone. This is not ethical. Callahan's position is that women should be granted the opportunity for choice, but that in making a choice they should understand that their decision is morally serious and worthy of public ethical discussion.

Callahan is impatient with his pro-choice colleagues who are satisfied with this proposition: It does not matter what choice women make as long as they have the freedom to make their own choice. This is an amoral or nonethical defense of freedom. According to Callahan, such a position is difficult to sustain, especially in the face of how abortion choices in fact are being made. An egregious number—1.6 million abortions—are performed every year, 40 percent of which are repeated procedures. This shows that rather than a back up for failed birth control, abortion for many has become the first line of defense against pregnancy.[35] Motives, however, can differ. Callahan notes that many women abort just to please or spite the man who impregnated them; 30 percent of women who seek abortions report that they pursued an abortion because someone else, not themselves, wanted it; selective abortion practices reveal that many fetuses are eliminated simply because they are female; and finally, some fetuses are deliberately conceived and aborted for use in experimental research or for organ donation at a profit. Now, all of these are moral issues, says Callahan, and they should not be exempt from public discussion just because they fall under the umbrella of woman's legal choice.[36]

The abortion decision an individual woman makes is frequently described as difficult or tragic or the last resort following much anguish. We need to distinguish, however, psychological anguish from moral deliberation. We ought not assume that, just because there is psychological anguish or ambivalence regarding a decision to abort, there is moral seriousness present. These two are not necessarily the same. Anguish or ambivalence can arise from various factors: trying to decide just what one wants to do, whom else should be pleased, fear of the procedure it-self, and worry about the reaction of others. Serious ethical reflection goes beyond such worries. It entails thinking carefully about the moral status of the fetus in light of ethical values and ideals.

As a member of the developmental school, Callahan thinks that an early abortion is morally better than one that is later. He pleads with pro-choice advocates to consider compromises with the pro-life camp that would reduce the overall number of abortions. He suggests that the policy adopted by many hospitals to establish a cut-off point at twenty weeks into the pregnancy would help here, and it would do so without compromising the basic pro-choice stance. Most abortions are carried out for personal or private reasons, and Callahan asks that at least in government-sponsored facilities such procedures be limited to those done for health or medical reasons. He thinks the proposals in many states for a mandatory waiting period of a few days for a woman to think over her decision is a reasonable accommodation to make and also fa-vors parental notification for pregnant teenagers seeking an abortion.

These are compromises, wherein public policy discussion influences the range and nature of the choices that pregnant women will make. Such arguments in favor of compromise sound to me more consequen-tialist than developmentalist, for Callahan believes that these compro-mises may help find middle ground with the strong pro-life movement and keep abortion choice alive in this society. He fears that if the pro-choice party tries to grab all the spoils—tries to maintain choice with-out moral responsibility—then it may lose its foothold in legislatures and in the courts, and the choice option itself would disappear.

The Callahan analysis is significant for two reasons. First, it recog-nizes, accepts, and even celebrates the era of politically protected choice in which we now find ourselves. Once the freedom to choose has been granted to individuals by society, it is difficult to rescind without the grave feeling that rights would be taken away. One of the weaknesses I see in so many conservative or reactionary treatments of reproductive technology is that they try to solve the moral problem by appealing to some normative source that would obviate choice. In our modern post-Enlightenment culture, I do not believe we can simply wish choice away. Rather, we need to see choice as the point at which individuals and society engage in ethical analysis and decision making.

Second, Callahan reminds us that there is a difference between per-sonal desire and ethical criteria. Granting the freedom to choose can be experienced as a liberation of desire, to be sure, but it can also be understood as a prerequisite for a higher level of ethical responsibility. The decision to pursue the good, the right, or the true over against the bad, the wrong, or the false is becoming lodged ever more in the subjectivity of the individual rather than the tradition of one's culture. Whether we unthinkingly act according to social convention or out of personal commitment and deliberation, the pursuit of the good remains a noble goal.

One residual question remains, however. Is it consistent to defend choice in the public realm and then appeal to an ethical standard that might deny choice at the personal level? Callahan has issued a call for public ethical discussion. Pope John Paul II engages in such public ethical discussion, as we will see in the next section. His antiabortion stand is clearly ethical, but the way it is ethical repudiates the very right to choose between aborting or not aborting. Callahan's own ethical position would permit abortion under some circumstances, and in this regard he does not side completely with the pope. So, just what is Callahan saying? Does he believe that only ethical discussion that is consistent with the choice assumption counts as serious moral deliberation? Does anti-choice discussion count as ethical? Is choice a good but not an absolute good? What if choice itself is considered the issue on which ethical deliberation is focused?

The Strong Genetic School, Murder, and the Beginning of Life

"Keep your rosaries off my ovaries" is a defense cry of pro-choice forces when faced with their able adversary, Pope John Paul II. The Roman Pontiff is perhaps the most aggressive advocate of the strong genetic position. Like a general leading an army, the Holy Father is leading his church and all others of sympathetic persuasion in a crusade against the "culture of death" and in defense of the "culture of life." Everywhere in the world the pope sees a catastrophic loss of sensitivity on the part of cultures and governments toward the needs of persons who cannot help themselves, toward weak persons such as infirm elderly and unborn children. The growing practices of euthanasia at the final edge of life and abortion at the front edge of life betray a widespread loss of regard for human dignity, a loss of reverence for the sacredness of human life.

Abortion on request is a form of murder, says the pope, and the obligation of everyone who believes in God is to protect innocent human life at every stage from murder. No argument, such as a mother's self-defense against an aggressor, could mitigate the charge that procured abortion constitutes the killing of an innocent human being. "He or she is *weak,* defenseless, even to the point of lacking that minimal form of defense consisting in the poignant power of a newborn baby's cries and tears. The unborn child is *totally entrusted* to the protection and care of the woman carrying him or her in the womb."[37] Deliberate abortion is a betrayal of parental trust and a wanton permission for the strong to oppress the weak.

The defense of the weak and helpless against the misuse of power by the strong is a point at which the Vatican makes common cause with many in the feminist camp. Sidney Callahan is a pro-life feminist, a Roman Catholic with a strong dose of Quaker pacifism. For some years now she has been likening the need of the unborn to the need of women in their respective struggles against patriarchal domination.

> The argument that the fetus is treated as women once were motivates the many feminists who are prolife. . . . From this feminist, prolife, pacifist viewpoint, all the arguments asserting the value of women's development in the face of male power and hostility to feminine equality can be made on behalf of the fetus. Immediate affirmative legal action is needed to protect women, the unborn, and all life on earth from violence.[38]

We have been entrusted with the divine mandate to protect those who cannot protect themselves, and now this applies to the conceived but yet unborn persons among us.

This doctrine of protection developed in the abortion controversy is applied by the pope to questions surrounding embryo research and reproductive technology. Experimentation on embryos, which is becoming increasingly widespread in the field of biomedical research, is to be encouraged when it does not involve disproportionate risks for the embryo's safety and when its purpose is the embryo's health or survival. But the discarding of unimplanted embryos created by in vitro fertilization (IVF), or the use of human embryos or fetuses as an object of experimentation, constitutes a "crime against their dignity as human beings who have a right to the same respect owed to a child once born."[39]

With regard to prenatal diagnosis of genetic diseases and other threats to the health of the fetus, the pope says such procedures are licit when they make possible early therapy and when they do not involve disproportionate risks for the child or for the mother. When prenatal diagnosis is employed for selective abortion—"with a eugenic intention which accepts selective abortion in order to prevent the birth of children affected by various types of anomalies"—then it is "shameful and utterly reprehensible." The pope condemns selective abortion because "it presumes to measure the value of human life only within the parameters of 'normality' and physical well-being, thus opening the way to legitimizing infanticide and euthanasia as well."[40]

This strong genetic position as taken by the Vatican requires assent to one fundamental belief: At the moment of fertilization a new and unique individual human being comes into existence who has claim to the same right to dignity and life that every other human being has—that is, at conception we have the moral equivalent of a person. This is the irreformable position that the church has always taken, argues John Paul II with considerable vehemence and force.

To support this position he marshals evidence from four sources: theology, natural science, scripture, and tradition. Theologically, he upholds the view that at the moment of fertilization the conceptus receives from God a soul, a soul which along with the body constitutes the *imago dei*. Scientifically, the DNA in the zygote determines that the genetic program to become this person, and not some other person, is fixed. Like special and natural revelation or like faith and reason, these two ethical sources support one another. "Even if the presence of a spiritual soul cannot be ascertained by empirical data," writes the pope, "the results themselves of scientific research on the human embryo provide a valuable indication for discerning by the use of reason a personal presence at the moment of the first appearance of a human life."[41]

The pope's scriptural argument is not exegetical; rather, it is a deduction. He acknowledges that the Bible itself says nothing about abortion. So, he deduces from the commandment against murder that our responsibility is to protect the unborn. "The texts of *Sacred Scripture* never address the question of deliberate abortion and so do not directly and specifically condemn it. . . . A logical consequence that God's commandment 'you shall not kill' [is that it] be extended to the unborn child as well."[42]

The troops of tradition provide force for the final argument. John Paul II cites the first-century document, *Didache*, "you shall not put a child to death by abortion nor kill it once it is born."[43] He then rallies support from Athenagoras, Tertullian, Pius XI, Pius XII, John XXIII, Vatican II, and his own papacy. Finally he launches one grand offensive which culminates in the raising of the flag of papal authority—granted to him by the see of Peter, by his office as the Vicar of Christ.

> Therefore, by the authority which Christ conferred upon Peter and
> his Successors, in communion with the Bishops—who on various
> occasions have condemned abortion . . . have shown unanimous
> agreement concerning this doctrine—*I declare that direct abortion,*
> *that is, abortion willed as an end or as a means, always constitutes a*
> *grave moral disorder,* since it is the deliberate killing of an innocent
> human being. This doctrine is based upon the natural law and
> upon the written Word of God, is transmitted by the Church's Tra-
> dition and taught by the ordinary and universal Magisterium.[44]

That this triumphant commitment is absolute and not subject to miti-
gation by extenuating circumstances is made clear by what follows: "No
circumstance, no purpose, no law whatsoever can ever make licit an act
which is intrinsically illicit, since it is contrary to the law of God which
is written in every human heart, knowable by reason itself, and pro-
claimed by the Church."[45]

Now the pope may be satisfied by making appeal to the authority of
Christ our Savior in making such a pronouncement, but this should not
stop others faithful to the same Christ from reexamining his argument
to see if it exemplifies wisdom and sound judgment. It appears to me
that the Holy Father's argument depends fundamentally on the coincidence of three things: fertilization with the establishment of an individual's DNA, the divine infusion of a spiritual soul, and the immediate
establishment of a person who deserves dignity.

Combining Genetic
and Developmental Views

A sympathetic, yet discernibly different, approach is taken by Lisa
Sowle Cahill. The key questions at this point are the following: Does the
conceptus have any right to be considered a human person and be
treated with dignity? Does the fertilized egg exert a moral claim on society so as to warrant protection? Cahill's answers creatively combine
the genetic and developmentalist views.

We note that the pope along with The Vatican's Congregation for the
Doctrine of the Faith answer with confidence: "The human being must
be respected—as a person—from the very first instant of his existence
[that is, from conception]."[46] All procured abortions are declared illicit.
In the *Donum Vitae,* the antiabortion commitment to issues surrounding pre-embryo implantation and discarding are then applied. Research
with regard to the embryo is licit when restricted to observation, but

even observation, let alone intervention, becomes illicit when it involves risk to the embryo's physical integrity. It is judged immoral to produce human embryos for exploitation as disposable biological material. The corpses of embryos should be respected just as the remains of other deceased human beings. Cryopreservation and the discarding of unwanted embryos in the IVF process are decried as violence perpetrated against innocent persons and as a form of eugenics.

Cahill, who is sympathetic on many fronts to the Vatican position, is far less confident than *Donum Vitae* or *Evangelium Vitae* that human personhood can be secured at conception. She places the question of the moral status of the fertilized egg into the "area of uncertainty." On the one hand, she argues, the conceptus genetically has all that is necessary to develop personal identity. It is an irreplaceable human life. On the other hand, the embryo in its earliest stages simply does not look like the equivalent of a baby. It is counterintuitive to dub it as a person with equal rights. We observe that the death of an embryo is not mourned by the parents, nor have liturgies been developed to surround and sanctify its death. So, Cahill concludes, "To say that an embryo is a moral person in the usual sense simply flies in the face of common sense and common practice."[47]

In light of this employment of intuition, observation, and common sense, Cahill submits that a clear-cut, universally persuasive solution to the problem is not available at this time. Within the context of this uncertainty, however, she offers her most reasonable assessment: The fertilized ovum is a human life, to be sure, but differing moral obligations come into play at differing stages of embryo development.

> The view which I find most reasonable, and toward which I think some public consensus conceivably might be built, is that the embryo is *from fertilization* a human individual, a human life, without being a human person in the full moral sense. Its unique genotype is philosophically important both because it distinguishes this individual from other species and because it actually gives this individual the essential conditions of the possibility of its development into a full-fledged and maturely functioning adult. Thus, the conceptus has value and moral weight in the human community.[48]

Cahill here combines the weak genetic school with the developmental school and grants at best only a conditional acceptance of abortion.

Having taken a tentative stand on behalf of the moral integrity of the embryo at the point of conception, Cahill then declares that this is not a black and white matter. It should not be considered in "all" or "none" terms but rather as "more" or "less." She sees the wisdom in the developmentalist view that, though beginning with a high but still incomplete value attributed to the embryo-fetus, recognizes the differing stages of physical development that warrant differing stages of moral assessment. Picking up on the work of philosopher Carol Tauer, Cahill distinguishes the "potential person" in the embryo from its next stage, the "psychic person," and this in turn from the final stage, the "strict person" or "proper person." A *strict* or *proper* person is one who is a rational and self-conscious moral agent, something the embryo obviously is not. Cahill adds a level of respect to the psychic person, which is thought to emerge in the mother's womb when the neurological system is developed sufficiently to provide experience in the sense of response-to-sensory stimuli that is accompanied by the ability to initiate its own movements. This psychic stage of personhood garners relatively more moral weight than its merely potential previous stage but less than its later strict or proper stage. She describes her position as a "relatively conservative but not absolutist view of the value of embryonic life."[49]

I think the Cahill argument draws some distinctions and adds nuance in a most helpful way. By declaring that both conceptus and person have moral status while distinguishing them helps, because this distinction rightly fits what seems intuitively obvious. Her belief that different stages require different moral assessments also seems appropriate. Undifferentiated cells in a petri dish or preimplanted zygotes seem on the face of it to be quite different from a cooing or crying baby. The early embryo is a pre-person that is yet to become a psychic person, the latter evidently having some degree of brain action and independent nervous system.

This kind of thinking in the developmentalist mode led to the introduction of the criterion of viability in the *Roe v. Wade* decision. A viable human life—that is, one that in principle could live on its own outside the mother's womb—deserves protection. At the stage of viability, the state takes an interest in the fetus and provides some degree of legal protection. The fetus may not at this stage be able to suffer consciously or fear death, yet there is some ground for granting it protective rights.[50] We need also to be reminded that the Supreme Court refrained from defining the point at which life begins; it only defined the point at which the state would take an interest in fetal development. The Cahill line of thought squares somewhat with the court's thinking regarding development, although at no point would she want the taking of the fetus' life to be merely a matter of someone's choice. The decision to abort or not to abort requires ethical deliberation, discernment of what good might come from making a choice.

Yet I would like to explore for a moment the implications of Cahill's suggestion that the fetus is a potential person but not yet a full or proper person, and that her definition of personhood mimics the classic understanding of human rationality: A person is a rational and self-conscious moral agent. In addition to reaffirming the classic notion of the human soul as a rational and moral entity, this definition of personhood connotes individuality, independence, self-initiation, and some power of self-control. It is viability plus. That plus is a high degree of self-actualization.

Some problems arise here that need working through. First, as a developmental category this implies that there is no proper or absolute personhood, that we are all more or less on the way to becoming persons. Once committed to a developmentalist scale, consistency requires "more" or "less" judgments at every phase. Cahill has eschewed speaking in terms of "all" or "none." One might ask: How then does the category of personhood help at all in moral discernment? How can it support even what is intuitively obvious, namely, the difference between a fetus and a baby? Has Cahill effectively disqualified the category of personhood from ethical relevancy?

Second, Cahill's view of personhood parallels the Supreme Court's view of viability. Recall that the viability criterion simply defines the point at which the state takes interest, not the point at which human life begins. It tells us more about the state and about the rights of the mother than it does about the biological or moral status of the unborn child. What on the face of it looks like a criterion based on a stage of independence in the development of fetal life is in fact a relational criterion—that is, determined by the unborn's relationship to first the mother's responsibility followed by the state's responsibility. Furthermore, establishing the point of viability is situational and relational. With the advance of hospital technology, the chances of survival for fetuses removed from the womb have increased. Viability increasingly applies to earlier stages of fetal development, now generally thought to be as early as twenty-four weeks. To declare a fetus viable is by no means to declare it independent because the child is totally dependent on incubation machines. The child is in principle independent only from the mother. There is no "all" or "none" applicable to either viability or personhood.

Third, I believe that this relational dimension to personhood is undervalued in Cahill's definition. Since the demise of existentialist philosophy in the 1960s, we have come to assume that to be a person means to be a person-in-relationship. Ordinarily, relationality plays an important role in Cahill's ethical deliberations. But in this case, her choice of definition of personhood appears to distinguish it by virtue of its independence from relationship. A rational and self-conscious moral agent is a very independent entity.

However, we know psychologically that growth in what Cahill calls personhood is a delicate process determined in large part by a young child's relationship with significant others such as parents, siblings, teachers, and all those who wield influence. The image a mother and father have of a young child is quickly introjected and becomes the image the child has of himself or herself. A loving family can actually cultivate and encourage a child's growth in independence and self-confidence. Becoming a rational and self-conscious moral agent is at once a declaration of individual independence as well as a product of someone else's careful grooming and coaching. It is no accident that the growing up process for teenagers is frequently compared to what happens with birds: The fledglings are thrown out of the nest to fly on their own only after a long period of devoted nurturing.

What is morally significant about the view of personhood within the abortion debate is its contribution or noncontribution to the concept of human dignity. As I suggested earlier, dignity is phenomenally and inescapably relational. First dignity is conferred, then it is claimed. Personhood overlaps almost totally with dignity. It too is the product of an interpersonal process whereby we are first treated as persons and then we become persons. The imputing of personhood by others proleptically anticipates actually becoming a person at a later time. The ethical mandate of families or society as a whole is to treat nonpersons or pre-persons as persons so that they may become persons—that they may become healthy, rational, and self-conscious moral agents. To turn the matter around and demand that the pre-person become a person before we grant him or her dignity or a moral status equal to actualized persons is to let the tail wag the dog.

Now in this exposition and commentary I have been pressing Cahill toward the individualist camp for the sake of clarifying the terms of discussion. Despite her position that overidentifies personhood with independence, however, she can move happily in the direction of relationality and proleptic anticipation.

The distinctive characteristics of fully realized persons (rationality, free will, and derivative abilities) are not manifest prenatally at any point, and for some members of the species are never realized throughout a lifetime. Therefore, it is necessary to regard the embryo and fetus as acquiring moral status or value from their relation to qualities which they share in anticipation or by association with the functioning persons they as a rule will become.[51]

For Cahill the independent, rational, and free person is finally an ideal. When she recognizes personhood in an actual person for moral purposes, she has to borrow anticipated, yet unrealized, qualities drawn from this ideal. Less important to Cahill than to me is the relational dynamic wherein the community imputes personhood even before the person in question can claim it. That is, from my point of view, the experience of personhood and the moral claim to personhood are relational and interdependent.

Bruce Reichenbach and Elving Anderson, like Cahill, combine the genetic and developmental schools, but they take the argument a step further by focusing on the fetus as a moral end rather than a mere means. Reichenbach and Anderson grant that the fixing of the DNA at fertilization establishes uniqueness, but they are hard pressed to say that this being with human parentage is already a human person. The pre-embryo is a long way from becoming a person, because it still lacks the features we associate with personality. But it has that potential, and it will gradually actualize that potential. So, they "adopt a developmental or gradualist view, according to which the respect due to the pre-embryo, embryo, or fetus is appropriate to its stage of development. Its stage of development will correlate with our relevant obligations toward it. This means we will have differing obligations to pre-embryos than to ten-week old fetuses or to viable ones."[52]

Yet the fertilized zygote or early fetus does have moral status. Even at its earliest stages, the fetus is a potential person, a being who in time will manifest the image of God. Therefore, as a potential person, it commands respect. This does not imply that its life cannot be justifiably taken. What it does mean is that a decision to abort requires moral justification. That justification must take into consideration the interests of the potential child.

> No matter what status one gives to the fetus—actually human, potentially human, developing toward full personhood—it is a living organism with interests and an inherent potential to become a human person with a meaningful life of its own; its creation and

subsequent termination solely for the good of a third party, without any consideration of its own potential good, is treating it merely as a means and hence is immoral.[53]

In short, the potentiality of personhood is sufficient to grant enough dignity that the zygote or early fetus should be thought of as an end and not merely a means. This fetal dignity becomes one factor among others in moral deliberation; however, it is not a trump card. Reichenbach and Anderson do not take an absolutist pro-life position.

Be that as it may, the weakness of any developmentalist thesis—whether Cahill's more independent personhood, my more relational personhood, or the Reichenbach-Anderson potential personhood—is that it lacks the moral muscle to draw lines. When it comes to public policy, law, or even ethical guidance, we need to draw lines to make decision making in difficult situations manageable. One of the reasons many of us find the pope's pro-life position and the American anti-abortion movement unsatisfying is that they draw the line so soon: at ovum fertilization resulting from the sex act. Would it help if we could employ knowledge gained from embryological science combined with ethical reasoning to draw the line later in the developmental process? We now turn to a most helpful example of this kind of argument.

The Primitive Streak and the Ontological Individual

Let us refine the basic question. Usually we ask: When does life begin? Now let's ask: When does the life of an individual human being begin? No one doubts that a new life begins when, in the fertilized egg, two haploid sets of chromosomes become a diploid set of chromosomes, creating the single DNA formula for the zygote. Yet we might query, Is this a human individual? No, it is not. What seems intuitively to be the case in Cahill's scheme can be buttressed by scientific knowledge and philosophical argument.

The zygote is not yet an individual. Oh yes, it contains the DNA blueprint that will identify the person or persons it may become. But, in itself, the zygote is still a pre-embryo, a proto-embryo. Why do I say this? Because becoming a human being is a process, and the process that distinguishes the particular individual human being in question does not occur until two weeks or so following the sex act.

The moment two lovers sit up and smoke their postcoital cigarette is not the moment of conception. The man's sperm resides in the woman's reproductive tract for about seven hours or so before it is ready to fertilize an egg. During this period, lytic enzymes in the sperm are released to make it possible for the sperm to penetrate the egg's surface. It takes ten hours for the sperm to reach a readied egg, and if the sperm does not fertilize within twenty-four hours, it dies. The penetrating process and subsequent syngamy, where the two haploid sets of twenty-three chromosomes fuse to make up the full or diploid set of forty-six chromosomes, takes another twenty-four hours. The resulting cell is a zygote, which divides once about every ten hours as it journeys down the fallopian tube in the direction of the uterus. At this point the cells are undifferentiated—that is, each cell is complete and without assignment to one or another part of what will later become the body. After the sixth or seventh day, the zygote has become a blastocyst and has entered the uterus, beginning the process of implantation. The process of implantation is completed about the second week, at which point we have an embryo.

The blastocyst is not yet an individual. It is capable of dividing into two or more individuals—that is, it is capable of producing twins. Each cell contains the DNA blueprint, and if division occurs, then two, three, or more individuals with the same DNA blueprint are possible. In some cases, the blastocyst will divide and then recombine into a single entity. In certain cases—50 percent in some estimates—where abnormal fertilization or some other chromosomal defect occurs, the blastocyst is simply flushed out. Because a woman seldom discovers that she is pregnant until she misses a menstrual period, and because menstruation does not cease until after implantation, she may be totally unaware that the blastocyst process has taken place.

Gastrulation occurs approximately during the third week. Here the embryonic cells begin to differentiate, switching off certain genes and switching on others, so as to form different parts of what will become the human body. This is followed by the process of embryogenesis or organogenesis, leading up to the eighth week, wherein internal and external structures and organs develop. The nervous system responsible for coordinating bodily functions also develops at this stage. At seven-and-a-half or eight weeks the first-reflex response appears, which is what we might call activity.

The third week—the week of gastrulation—becomes philosophically important. During implantation and gastrulation, the organism is taking nutrients from the mother and the embryo is growing in an identifiably integrated fashion. At this stage, twinning is no longer possible.

Differentiation begins when the inner embryonic mass becomes surrounded by an outer or epiblastic form, and it is this process which physically distinguishes one individual from another. This process, also referred to as the *primitive streak*, is followed closely by the development of the primitive cardiovascular system, which enables nutrition to be received and growth to take place. It is here, between the second and third weeks, that an ontological human individual first makes his or her appearance.

This observation leads Norman M. Ford, a Roman Catholic moral theologian in Australia, to combine scientific knowledge with philosophical reflection in making the morally relevant assertion that we first have what we can call a person at the point where the primitive streak occurs. He argues that "after gastrulation, by the end of the third week when the neural folds have been formed and the primitive cardiovascular system is functioning to enable nutrition and growth as a whole to take place, there are sufficient reasons to justify asserting that a living individual with a human nature has been formed. Consequently, a human being or person is present."[54] What he dubs as an ontological individual person is contingent on two items. First, the embryo is no longer subject to twinning, so only one individual is possible and not more. Second, he appeals to a holistic principle: The embryo functions as an integrated whole with internal differentiation and external relationship. Prior to this stage of holistic integration, we do not have a living human body; rather, we have only a mass of pre-programmed, loosely organized developing cells until their clock mechanisms become synchronized and triggered to harmoniously organize, differentiate, and grow as heterogeneous parts of a single whole human organism.

Ford goes on to stress that prior to this stage it would be pointless to speak about the presence of a true human being in an ontological sense. A human individual could scarcely exist prior to a definitive human body being formed. The concept of form is multivalent here. It refers to the physical integration of the embryo. But it also recalls the concerns of Aristotle, Thomas Aquinas, and the contemporary Roman Catholics regarding creationist ensoulment. In this tradition the soul is understood as the immaterial rational component to human nature associated with the form of the body. A human being is a unity of body and soul, so there must be a bodily form if such a unity is to be perceived. This leads Ford to hypothesize that here, at the onset of the primitive streak, the human soul is created. "The formation of an ontological individual with a truly human nature and rational ensoulment must coincide."[55]

Thomas A. Shannon and Allan B. Wolter, O.F.M., want to apply such scientific and philosophical observations to Roman Catholic thinking about abortion. They affirm with Catholic tradition and with today's Vatican that from the moment of conception the life of every human being needs to be respected, and they affirm that the human soul is immediately created by God. Yet they want contemporary science to inform the tradition. This leads them to suggest that the concept of conception be revised. Instead of being identified with the sex act, conception refers to the process that is completed about the time of the primitive streak. "Biologically understood, conception occurs only after a lengthy process has been completed and is more closely identified with implantation than fertilization."[56] In keeping the Vatican terminology but changing the definition, Shannon and Wolter open the door to pregnancy intervention within the first two weeks, while still maintaining a closed door to abortion on demand after the embryo has attached itself to the mother's body.

Shannon and Wolter along with Ford have in effect provided support for the creationist position and have even identified the moment of ensoulment. They have also drawn a line after which personhood can be said to have begun.

> We find it impossible to speak of a true individual, an ontological individual, as present from fertilization. . . . This means that the reality of a person, however one might define that term, is not present at least until individualization has occurred. Individuality is an absolute necessary condition for personhood.
>
> We conclude that there is no individual and therefore no person present until either restriction or gastrulation is completed, about three weeks after fertilization. To abort at this time would end life and terminate genetic uniqueness, to be sure. But in a moral sense one is certainly not murdering, because there is no individual to be the personal referent of such an action.[57]

The implications for the abortion controversy are clear. If we accept the thesis that something like implantation or the appearance of the primitive streak is ethically decisive, then pre-implantation abortion would not be morally illicit. The use of an abortificient such as RU-486, or some other morning after pill, would not be considered murder. To abort following implantation, however, would place that action in a different moral category. The implications for embryo research and the discarding of defective zygotes is also clear. Fertilized eggs in petri dishes are manipulatable and discardable.

Does this automatically require that pre-embryos have no moral status? Even if preimplanted zygotes do not yet have intelligence or the capacity for human relationships, they still carry a genome that will develop within certain parameters into a specific person or persons. How does this count? Could we say that some claims for moral or legal protection can still be made, even if such claims might not be absolute?

A Noticeable Lack
of Protestant Connections

In sorting our way through the abortion controversy to find relevance for genetic screening and selective birthing, I have attended primarily to the thinking of Roman Catholics since mainline Protestants (and even evangelical pro-life Protestants) have had comparatively little to say about the implications of abortion ethics to genetics or vice versa. For example, the 1991 "Social Statement on Abortion" by the Evangelical Lutheran Church in America rehearses many of the issues already argued in the 1970s without taking a stand regarding the morality of abortion on demand. Its most forceful statement—"The position of this church is that government has a legitimate role in regulating abortion"—constitutes a bald acceptance of the ethical mess we are in. No mention is made of the issues arising over genetic screening.[58] The Methodist task force on genetics recognizes the value of screening for genetic defects in prenatal diagnosis, but no connection is drawn to the abortion controversy.[59] The World Council of Churches (WCC) draws the connection and asks, "When does individual life begin?" Their answer: not at fertilization. At this early stage, the WCC document says, "the specific interrelationships among cells that later characterize the whole organism . . . are not yet permanently established."[60] The WCC position could logically endorse the discard of genetically unacceptable pre-embryos, but this is not directly asserted. The United Church of Canada grants moral approval to abortion when it is the "lesser of two evils," but it offers no precise application to genetic screening.[61] The United Church of Christ (UCC) in the U.S. statement on genetic engineering supports "genetic screening of pregnancies at risk," but this is as close as it gets to making the connection between abortion and genetics.[62] Theologian and ethicist Ronald Cole-Turner comments on the UCC statement and applies it to Protestants in general: "When it comes to the central moral issue—whether or not to terminate a pregnancy if a defect is identified—these professionals tend to be nondirective. . . . Does the prediction of a genetic disease call for an abortion?"[63] As yet there is no answer.

All of this leads to a somewhat sad conclusion. As we approach the era of selective abortion for purposes of sorting out desirable genes from undesirable genes, most Christians are not ethically ready. Despite the fact that massive intellectual resources of a theological and ethical type have been invested in thinking through the abortion controversy, we are unprepared for the kind of decisions large numbers of prospective parents will be confronting. Much thought has been given to the issue of abortion on request and to the question of when human dignity begins, but what we need now are middle axioms to guide the choices that will inevitably confront the next generation of parents-to-be. At this point certain minimalist middle axioms present themselves. Let me make some recommendations.

First, it is better to weed out defective or undesirable genes prior to conception rather than afterward. Whether or not the conceptus has full personhood and full dignity comparable to living adults, ethicists certainly agree that the fertilized zygote has already achieved a moral status deserving a certain level of respect and honor that resists brute manipulation or irreverent discarding. Genetic selection or even manipulation in the sperm or ovum prior to fertilization, prior to the DNA blueprint of a potential person, seems obviously more defensible.

Second, whether prior to or subsequent to the appearance of the primitive streak, the choice for selective abortion should be the last resort. Prefertilization selection, when possible, should be given priority. Prenatal fetal gene therapy should also be given priority.

Even though abortion on request is legal, not all grounds for requesting it are ethical. In the case of selective abortion, a decision based solely on the desires of the parents without regard for the well-being of the child is unethical. Recall Martin Luther's words with which we opened this chapter, "Even if a child is unattractive when it is born, we nevertheless love it."

Third, the motive of compassion that seeks to minimize suffering on the part of children coming into the world should hold relative sway when choosing for or against selective abortion. Compassion, taken up as the principle of nonmaleficence in bioethics, constitutes the way that parents show love toward children-to-be. In those rare cases—3 percent to 5 percent of prenatal diagnoses—in which the genetic disorder is so severe that no approximation to a fulfilling life is possible, the decision to abort can be understood as a form of caring for the baby as well as self-care for the parents. Yet we must acknowledge that this is a judgment call. No clear rule tells us exactly when the imputed dignity of the unborn child may be trumped by a compassionate decision to abort.

Fourth, we should distinguish between eugenic purposes and compassion purposes when engaged in genetic selection, genetic selection at either the prefertilization or abortion stage. The goal of eugenics is to reduce the incidence of a certain genetic trait—usually an undesirable trait—in the population. Eugenics is social in scope and derives from some social philosophy. At this point, bioethicists tend to oppose eugenic policies because, if practiced on a large scale, it could reduce biodiversity and, more important, connote the political totalitarianism of the Third Reich. The compassion or nonmaleficence principle, when limited to the concrete situation of a family making a decision regarding a particular child, is much more acceptable. The line between eugenics and compassion, however, is not a clear one because we may eventually argue, based on the principle of compassion, that the attempt to rid future branches on a family tree of an autosomal recessive gene, such as cystic fibrosis, makes good eugenic sense.

Fifth, we should distinguish between preventing suffering and enhancing genetic potential. Genetic selection based on the compassion principle to help reduce suffering is understandably an act that, in at least a minimal sense, is directed toward the well-being of the child. In the future, when genetic selection and perhaps even genetic engineering make it possible for designer babies to have higher-than-average intelligence or good looks or athletic prowess, then we will move closer to the perfect child syndrome. The risk of commodifying children and evaluating them according to standards of quality control increases, especially when they are sold to paying parents. That there is risk of commodification does not in itself provide sufficient warrant for prohibiting enhancement. Yet it will call forth more intensified attention to our fundamental principle: God loves us regardless of our genetic makeup, and we should do likewise.

5

Sex and Baby Making
in Christian Thought

*It is above all in raising children that the family fulfills
its mission to proclaim the Gospel of Life.*
—Pope John Paul II, *Evangelium Vitae*

W hat is the relationship between sex and baby making? Or, more
specifically, what is the connection between the pleasure of sexual intercourse and the procreation of children? This has been a theological issue almost from the beginning of the Christian era right down
to the present day. To see where we are, we need to see where we have
been.

As we look for theological resources within the Christian tradition
that bear on the issues surrounding baby making and the love of children yet to be born, such resources seem obscured. They seem se-
questered backstage, because the big show on the front stage is sex. The
drama of sexual morality seems to have drawn the biggest audience in
the history of the church, drawing so much attention that we need an
occasional intermission just to view the needs of children.

Our task in this chapter will be to review the main drama—sex, but
to stay in our seats for the intermission to watch the extras—the children, lingering around the stage edge. The two lead actors, sex-for-
pleasure and sex-for-babies, will appear again and again as the scenes
shift from the ancient writings of Augustine, Thomas Aquinas, Martin
Luther, and John Calvin, as well as the views of the Vatican in the twentieth century. The curtain will close just after theologian Vladimir
Solovyev's oration on the meaning of love, a love that transmutes human sexuality into a divine blessing.

As a modern liberal audience watching from a pluralist context, we
might find it difficult to understand just what our Christian forebearers believed and practiced. Because they could not make up their
minds on whether marriage was a duty to God or merely an approved
means for channeling lustful desire, they affirmed both views. On the
one hand, marriage and childraising were viewed as a duty because

God had commanded the man and woman in Genesis 1:28 to "be fruitful and multiply." On the other hand, lust was considered a sinful disease; perpetual virginity was the preferred cure. Celibate priests, brothers, and nuns took vows of chastity, and, if some of these persons were blessed with a lack of lust—that is, with no desire for sex—then they were considered especially virtuous. For the average person with an average sexual desire, however, continence was the preferred option—that is, lust but no sex. If the single life either as celibate or continent seemed too difficult to maintain, then marriage was offered as a third-rate alternative. Get married! Channel your lust! Avoid fornication and adultery and, if possible, even avoid enjoying sex with your spouse! Continence within marriage is better than sex within marriage. And sex without passion is better than sex with passion. If you let your passions get the best of you while in bed, then you would be condemned for being an "ardent lover." To have sex without the passion of ardent love was considered a moral achievement.

Hence, our ancient ancestors worked with a hierarchy of virtue: chastity was best, continence second best, and ardent love within marriage, as third best, was morally above fornication and adultery, though not by much. Slipping into ardent love could be redeemed, however, if the husband and wife engaged in sexual intercourse with only one objective in mind, namely, making babies. Baby making became the way to rescue one's immortal soul from the threat of mortal sin.

What can account for such moral constipation? Such rigidity? Such a failure to appreciate human nature and the God-given joys of intimacy and mutuality? Our theological and ethical forebearers lived in a different time with different challenges. They revered the same Jesus Christ and the same announcement of God's grace that faithful Christians do today, but they saw the challenges somewhat differently. Despite the initial strangeness of their conclusions and the dogmatism of their pronouncements, they proffered enduring insights that remain instructive, even if not binding, to our present generation.

In this chapter I will take up three tasks. First, I will point out what I believe to be the very unsatisfactory connection between sexuality and procreation made by the long Christian tradition. From Augustine through Thomas Aquinas and the Reformers, Martin Luther and John Calvin, right down to today's Vatican and the beliefs of Pope John Paul II, the misinformed assumption has been that we ought not to have sex without babies or babies without sex. Second, buried within this very same tradition is a hidden treasure, namely, the love of children. I recommend that we dig up this treasure, brush the dirt off, and shine it up for decorating contemporary ethics. Third, I recommend that theologians in the next generation sever the tie between sexuality and procreation, and that we look for an independent ethical justification for healthy sexual relations. I suggest that Vladimir Solovyev's treatment of sexual love in the service of self-transcending divine love provides a model for directions that theological ethicists might take.

Augustine and the Love of Children

The church's official position that began to take shape during the formative centuries immediately subsequent to the New Testament and culminating in the magisterial formulations of Augustine is this: Sexual intercourse should be avoided if possible; but if unavoidable, it should then take place only within marriage and only for the purpose of begetting children. Augustine worked with a relative scale of values: Unmarried virginity is best; next best is continence—that is, sexual abstinence within marriage; and next in line is marriage with intercourse. Marital intercourse, however, should be engaged in solely for the purpose of procreation and not for satisfying lustful desires. The problem with lust, whether outside of marriage or even within marriage, is that it expresses a this-worldly bodily passion rather than a spiritual virtue. To pursue spiritual virtues one should be continent. Continence is a spiritual virtue that befits life in God's holy city. If one is too weak in spirit to be continent, then the next best thing is to place one's lustful passions—one's concupiscence—under the direction of a spiritually conceived purpose, namely, procreation.

It is important to note that Augustine's position does not rely on the assumption that it is divinely ordained or intrinsically good that we produce children. Those faithful to Jesus Christ are no longer obligated by the Genesis mandate to "be fruitful and multiply," nor are we obligated to provide heirs for the land as were the patriarchal families of ancient Israel. Our task, says Augustine, is to concern ourselves not with birth but with rebirth, not with generation but rather regeneration—that is, with bringing new persons to faith and to baptism. Augustine is not motivated by an intrinsic good attached to population growth; but rather, his argument supporting the tie between sex and childbearing is primarily a concession to sin, primarily a practical strategy for winning the battle raging within the human soul between the flesh and the spirit.

Yet if we pause to read between the lines, I believe we can find an additional argument: the protection of children. This bishop of Hippo wanted to ensure that when a child was born into this world, it would be loved by the parents. Sex-for-pleasure only, feared Augustine, might produce the deadly combination of a child with unloving parents. Now let me track these arguments.

Let's start with Augustine's three watchwords for marriage: "children, fidelity, and sacrament" (*proles, fides, sacramentum*).[1] Beginning with the assumption that "freedom from all sexual intercourse is both angelic exercise here and continues forever," he concedes that sex for begetting children is still good, though a lesser good.[2] Within the marital bond, a husband and wife should be faithful, and faithfulness consists in avoiding intercourse with anyone outside the marital bond.

> Intercourse within marriage for the sake of begetting children has no fault. The satisfying of lust on the part of either the husband or the wife within a covenant of faithfulness to the marriage bed, however, is a venial fault. Adultery or fornication is a deadly fault. Continence from all intercourse is better even than intercourse within marriage done for the sake of begetting children. . . . Marriage and continence are two goods, whereof the second is better.[3]

In short, marriage is good, lust is evil, and marital sex is a mixture of good and evil.

What about Adam and Eve in Paradise before the Fall? Was their marriage a mixture of good and evil? No. It was simply good, because they could have procreated without lusting. The reason God made humanity in two sexes was for the purpose of making babies. "They were created male and female, with bodies of different sexes, for the very purpose of begetting offspring, and so increasing, multiplying, and replenishing the earth; and it is great folly to oppose so plain a fact."[4] In affirming the procreative purpose of sexual differentiation and marital union, however, Augustine scratches his head and asks: But how could Adam sow his seed in Eve without sinning? How can we have sex without sin? His answer: through the power of the will. After all, he argues, the spiritual struggle in which we all engage takes the form of mastering our physical desires through the will power of the soul. Adam and Eve prior to the Fall had not been introduced to this struggle, so in their innocence they did not have to subdue their lust through the power of the will. Their wills were completely subservient to God's will.[5] Therefore, concludes Augustine, the first man and first woman engaged in sexual relations for the purpose of procreating new members of the Kingdom of God, and they did so willfully and without passionate desire. Employing the extended metaphor that was common to the ancient world—comparing sexual intercourse with sowing seed in fertile ground—Augustine writes, "the man, then, would have sown the seed, and the woman received it, the generative organs being moved by the will, not by lust."[6] In this way the Eden union of Adam and Eve becomes the model for our ideal marital union—that is, procreative but without lust.

Furthermore, the marital bond is permanent. Why? Because it is a sacrament. For Augustine, the sacramental quality of marriage is the warrant for prohibiting divorce under all conditions. Because marriage is sacramental, all divorce constitutes unfaithfulness, adultery. "The marriage compact is not done away with by divorce," writes Augustine, so that a man and a woman continue as wedded persons "one to another, even after separation, and commit adultery with those with whom they shall be joined."[7] What is the theological justification for this position? Is it a law of nature? Is it built into creation? No. The indissoluble character of the sacramental bond of marriage is modeled after—or better, participates in—the indissoluble character of Christ's bond with the church. The church is one. Christ is one. The bond of Christ with the church is everlasting. Marriages between faithful members of Christ's church are supposed to emulate Christ's unbreaking faithfulness to us. Such thinking can be buttressed with scripture: "This is a great mystery, and I am applying it to Christ and the church. Each of you, however, should love his wife as himself, and a wife should respect her husband" (Eph. 5:32–33). It is this sacramental tie to God's redeeming work in Christ and to the everlasting character of salvation that undergirds Augustine's notion of an unbreakable marriage bond.[8]

Although Augustine says that "childbearing is the end and aim of marriage,"[9] the proscription against divorce remains even if the parents are biologically unable to have children. "Although women marry and men take wives for the purpose of procreating children, it is never permitted to put away an unfruitful wife for the sake of having another to bear children."[10] The doctor of the church here interprets Jesus' repudiation of divorce to be so complete as to make null and void the Mosaic permission to divorce, permission previously granted on account of human hardness of heart. The regenerate Christian operates out of the sacramental tie of Christ to the church, not out of concessions to human sin. The net effect on the ethics of marriage, then, is that apart from childbearing and even apart from sexual intercourse, the marital bond retains its abiding integrity.

Earlier I suggested that between the lines we can read that Augustine is taking a stand in behalf of the love of children. He is opposed to cruelty to children, especially in the form of infanticide. The surrounding pagan culture of the Roman empire emphasized sex-for-pleasure, and this attitude appeared to be tied to the deliberate elimination of children in order to eliminate impediments to that pleasure. Infanticide was the means, which outraged both Jews and Christians. Centuries prior to Augustine, Philo of Alexandria had reported his outrage at the practices of parents who strangle their infants, drown their children by attaching weights and then dropping them into water, or exposing their children in the wilderness to the elements and wild beasts or carnivorous birds. Such parents are guilty of murder, charged Philo. Why would parents indulge in such cruelty? Because of their exclusive focus on the pleasure of sex and their unwillingness to take responsibility for the children that result. As lovers of pleasure who mate without any intention of caring for their progeny, such parents are like pigs and goats yielding to their undiscriminating animal drive for the satisfaction that sexual intercourse gives.[11]

In his apologetic defense of the Christian faith from the constraints and even persecutions of the Roman authorities, Tertullian alluded to the surrounding practices of child sacrifice in religious rites, infanticide, and abortion. Tertullian had to defend the church against false accusations that the Eucharist included the slaying of infants and the devouring of human flesh and blood. He rhetorically invoked the "look who is talking" argument by pointing to the Roman practice of human sacrifice on behalf of the god Saturn. Then he moved on to discuss parents murdering their children. "In regard to child murder," Tertullian wrote, "it does not matter whether it is committed for a sacred object, or merely at one's own self-impulse. . . . It is certainly the more cruel way to kill by drowning, or by exposure to cold and hunger and dogs."[12] He proceeded to add that all forms of murder are forbidden to the Christian, and this includes the aborting of an unborn fetus. "To hinder birth is merely a speedier form of killing. It does not matter whether you take away a life that is born, or destroy one that is coming to birth. That is a person who is going to be one. You already have the fruit in the seed."[13]

With these factors determining Augustine's context, the African bishop in his own way sought to cut off the growth of child abuse by attacking its apparent roots, namely, sex-for-pleasure.[14]

It is one thing for married persons to have intercourse only for the wish to beget children; it is another thing for them to desire carnal pleasure in cohabitation. . . . Those who do this, although they are called husband and wife, are not such; they retain no vestige of true matrimony, but pretend the honorable designation as a cloak for criminal conduct. Having proceeded thus far they are betrayed into exposing their children who are born against their will. They hate to nourish and retain those whom they were afraid they would beget. This infliction of cruelty on their offspring so reluctantly be-gotten unmasks the sin which they had previously practiced in darkness, and drags it clearly into the light of day. Sometimes [Ali-quando], indeed, this lustful cruelty, or, if you please, cruel lust, resorts to such extravagant methods as to use poisonous drugs to secure sterility [poisons of sterility, *sterilitatis venena*]; or else, if unsuccessful in this, to destroy the conceived seed by some means previous to birth, preferring that its offspring should rather perish than receive vitality; or if advancing to life within the womb, should be slain before it was born.[15]

In commenting on this text, John T. Noonan points out that this is the only passage in which Augustine deals with artificial contracep-tives, "poisonous drugs to secure sterility," a notion which eventually had an impact on Roman Catholic canon law. There is no question here that Augustine categorically opposes contraception, abortion, and infanticide.

There is a close association in Augustine's mind, and in contem-porary practice, of infanticide, abortion, and contraception. The association gives a sting to his critique. But the acts are distin-guished. The fetus in the womb, not yet alive, is the fetus in the forty days before ensoulment. The "poisons of sterility" are in-tended to achieve their deadly affect before conception; the other means are used if they fail, and a fetus has been conceived.[16]

My point in retrieving this history is to refocus our eyes. What we normally look at today, when reviewing our ancient forebearers, is their apparent restrictive association of sex with procreation and their pro-scriptions against contraception and abortion. Yet if we blink and refo-cus, we can see something else going on here as well, namely, a concern for the welfare of children yet unborn. No doubt that from the per-spective of modern eyes, the ancient Augustine looks like a killjoy, re-stricting sexual pleasure by invoking a higher purpose. And no doubt that to advocates of abortion-on-demand, he looks like an atavistic impediment to progress in women's rights. Our contemporary perspective is that of the grown-ups, the adults who wish to defend sex-for-pleasure or defend the right to reproductive privacy. With a slight shift in the angle of vision, however, the children of the future come into view.

Thomas Aquinas and Crimes without Victims

We can find something similar in the thinking of Thomas Aquinas. The tradition that surrounds Aquinas includes vital concepts such as "natural law" and "sins against nature."[17] A sin against nature is one that violates the order of nature in such a way as to injure God, the ordainer of nature. Marriage and sexual intercourse have been ordained by God and, when we humans frustrate that order, God is injured. Within marriage every extravaginal ejaculation is a sin against nature. Outside of marriage, a list of sins against nature includes masturbation, sodomy, and bestiality. What all these sins have in common is that procreative insemination is rendered impossible. Because conception is prevented, nature is frustrated.[18]

Nature is not frustrated, of course, when sexual intercourse within marriage results in children. "The marriage act is not a sin," Aquinas says. In fact, "it is meritorious." His argument includes a positive affirmation of our physical bodies in the material world. "If we suppose the corporeal nature to be created by the good God, we cannot hold that those things which pertain to the preservation of the corporeal nature and to which nature inclines are altogether evil." And, because we are directed by nature toward coitus as a means for begetting children, "it is impossible to maintain that the act of begetting children is altogether unlawful." One thing is forbidden, however: enjoyment. For Aquinas, the arguments regarding natural law do not apply to the enjoyment of ardent loving that accompanies the marital union because such enjoyment implies a passion that escapes the control of reason. Sexual passion can be tolerated; however, if prior to the act the lovers, in full control of their reason, direct their passions toward baby making.[19]

In this life it is baby making that justifies sexual desire and passion. But what about the next life? Will there be sexual distinctions in heaven? Yes, says Aquinas. Our sexual identities will perdure in heavenly felicity because they belong to the perfection of our human nature. However, sexual union for procreation will no longer be necessary.[20]

Aquinas addressed, in the twelfth century, an issue that western society took up again in the late 1960s, namely, crimes without victims. It seems clear, noted Aquinas, that adultery, seduction, and rape are injurious to our neighbor—that is, they create victims.[21] Therefore, these activities violate our mandate to love our neighbor, and the mandate to love God and love neighbor is the natural law ordained by God. Surely it is a sin to hurt another person whether by sexual abuse or by any other means. But, asks the great scholastic theologian, what about unnatural activities in which no other person is injured, in which no victim is created? Such things as masturbation, sodomy, and intercourse with animals injure no one. Could we remove such benign sexual acts from the list of sins? No. Why? Because they are sins that are committed against our human right reason and against God's natural order. Even if there is no human victim, God is victimized.[22]

If the fundamental precepts of the natural law are to love God and love our neighbor, then it would appear that a sexual sin without a human victim merely fails to love God. Yet this is not at all the case. Aquinas assumes that the result of intercourse, as programmed by nature, is offspring. Intercourse without regard to offspring betrays a lack of love for the offspring—that is, a lack of love for the neighbor unborn. Who is hurt? An injury is done to the unborn children when parents fail to bring them into the world, provide them with education, and cultivate their life of faith. In short, the neighbor offended by extravaginal ejaculation is the child who now will not see the light of day.[23]

What Aquinas wants is for children to be raised and educated in the knowledge of God and to live the life of faith. Christian education is the responsibility of the family and the church, and providing the world with new children for baptism and living the godly life is the end of marriage. The end is not merely to fulfill a natural drive or merely to produce more children to perpetuate the race or enlarge the world's population. If a child could not have access to the sacraments and to nourishment of the soul, then it would be better that it had not been born. This is not a numbers game; rather, it has to do with the quality of life, the spiritual quality of life. Noonan comments, "The universal acceptance of religious education as an element in the good of offspring is an emphatic rejection of the criterion of quantity. What is valued, in the very definition of the procreative requirement, is children of a certain quality."[24]

The Protestant Reformation
and the Raising of Children

The Protestant Reformers inherited the Augustinian and medieval mind-set, which includes this emphasis on children. On the one hand, they presumed early on that celibacy constituted the purest expression of faith and that sexual desire could be rendered virtuous only when expressed within marriage and for the sake of baby making. On the other hand, as the Reformation took shape, they sought to liberate the joys of marital love and the raising of children from the oppressive monastic mind-set. They experimented with the theological thought that sexual union was God's gift prior to the Fall, and that God takes delight, as we do, in passionate love and in devotion to children. These two views—reverence for celibate faithfulness and celebration of family life—seem to be in mortal conflict. Yet in the transitional period of the sixteenth century, the Reformers found themselves affirming both.

Like Augustine, Martin Luther began by presuming that sexual lust is a sign of the fall into sin and that one value of marriage is that it helps stem the damage that lust can do. And like the monastic tradition that preceded him—Luther was an Augustinian monk—he spoke with high regard of the celibate life as the ideal life. Chastity, understood as sexual fidelity within marriage, turned out to be Luther's moral norm. Yet there is a higher form of chastity, namely, virginity. The fulfillment of this ideal is limited to very few, however. "Yet there are some (although few) exceptions whom God has especially exempted—some who are unsuited for married life and others whom he has released by a high supernatural gift so that they can maintain chastity outside of marriage."[25] Luther's logic is this: If you are born without sexual desire, then consider it a divine gift and pursue celibacy outside marriage; however, if you like most people are born with sexual desire, then your divine call is to pursue marriage and marital fidelity.[26]

John Calvin agreed with this view. "Continence is a special gift of God," wrote the Geneva Reformer, a gift that distinguishes a class of men who on account of celibacy can devote their lives more fully to the affairs of the Kingdom of Heaven. For most of us who do not belong to this elite class of spiritual athletes, marriage is the norm.

> Now, through the condition of our nature, and by the lust aroused after the Fall, we except for those whom God has released through special grace, are doubly subject to women's society. . . . Hence, those who are troubled with incontinence and cannot prevail in

the struggle should turn to matrimony to help them preserve
chastity.[27]

We can see here in his *Institutes* that Calvin, like most other theologians of the era, did not consider the woman's point of view. The pre-
sumption all along has been that the problem of lust is a male problem
and that the solution is taking a bride. Even the Reformation failed to
ask openly just what the problem might look like from the woman's
perspective and whether or not marriage constituted a solution. And,
despite Calvin's belief that marriage was instituted by God—Calvin says
our lust drives us to choose a mate and thereby live in community—the
assumption continues that lust is a product of the Fall, hinting that human existence before the Fall would be celibate. Sex must be thought
of as unclean, therefore, and restricting sex to marriage only partially
cleans it up.

Because the vast majority of mortals do daily battle with lustful desires, marriage becomes the prescribed norm. Does this make marriage
a mere concession to sin then? Not according to Luther. Like a chick
struggling to hatch from its egg, Luther struggled to extirpate himself
from his medieval shell by excoriating the monastic suppression of the
sexual drive, and to liberate tender human emotions, by placing our intimate human joys within God's providence.

So to understand Luther here, we need to note some of the nuances
that occurred during the Reformation. Luther began to think of marriage as ordained by God in the Garden of Eden before the Fall. Sexual
pleasure is God's gift to the human race and so should be revered and
treasured, not denigrated. But Christendom on the eve of the Reformation had not looked at it this way. As we have noted, celibacy had become the spiritual norm, making marriage a lower form of faithful living. By pressing Augustinianism to an extreme, far beyond its intended
limit, medieval monasticism held celibacy as such a high ideal that family life appeared lowly in comparison. This practice disturbed and an-
gered the rebellious monk who wanted to celebrate both chastity and
marital fidelity. He reports an experience of consciousness raising.

> When I was a boy, the wicked and impure practice of celibacy had
> made marriage so disreputable that I believed I could not even
> think about the life of married people without sinning. Everybody
> was fully persuaded that anyone who intended to lead a holy life
> acceptable to God could not get married but had to live as a celi-
> bate and take the vow of celibacy. . . . Therefore it was a work

necessary and useful for the church when men saw to it that through the Word of God marriage again came to be respected and that it received the praises it deserved. As a result, by the grace of God now everyone declares that it is something good and holy to live with one's wife in harmony and peace even if one should have a wife who is barren or is troubled by other ills.[28]

Note here how Luther presumes he is addressing a male audience; only men wrestle between celibacy and taking a wife. However, there are times when he becomes aware of the woman's unexpressed point of view. After excoriating heathen literature and complaining about men who see women as only a necessary evil, Luther defends women on two counts. First, women have their complaints to raise against men too. "I imagine that if women were to write books they would say exactly the same thing about men."[29] Second, women's bodies are to be positively appreciated. So are men's bodies. Marriage is the place where mutual appreciation of the physical bodies that God has given us is to take place. God "wills to have his excellent handiwork honored as his divine creation, and not despised. The man is not to despise or scoff at the woman or her body, nor the woman the man. But each should honor the other's image and body as a divine and good creation that is well-pleasing unto God himself."[30]

Harvard Reformation historian Steven Ozment describes the transition from the Middle Ages to the Reformation this way:

> Women and marriage were widely ridiculed in proverbs and jokes, the biblical stories of the downfall of Adam, Samson, and David at the hands of women had gained popularity, and the advocates of virginity and celibacy never missed an opportunity to remind the lovestricken of the sacrifices and suffering that marriage and parenthood entailed.
>
>   It may seem surprising to learn that Martin Luther was a leading defender of the dignity of women and the goodness of marriage.[31]

In short, the traditional elevation of celibacy with its body-denying value system was gradually turned upside down by the Wittenberg reformer, making the choice of marriage attractive and the begetting of children a noble vocation.

Like his predecessors, Luther thought of marriage in terms of sacrament. Luther certainly believed the marital bond to be indissoluble, to be sure, but this view did not govern Luther's sacramental reasoning.

Rather, he reasoned that the unity of husband and wife emulates the unity of Christ's two natures. Luther defined a sacrament as "a sacred sign of something spiritual, holy, heavenly, and eternal."[32] Human marriage is a sign of the holy marriage of the two natures in Christ and of Christ to the church, which makes the marriage sacramental. His emphasis was more on sign of the divine reality than on indissolubility.

> The estate of marriage is a sacrament. It is an outward and spiritual sign of the greatest, holiest, worthiest, and noblest thing that has ever existed or ever will exist: the union of the divine and human natures in Christ. The holy Apostle Paul says that as man and wife united in the state of matrimony are two in one flesh, so God and man are united in one person Christ, and so Christ and Christendom are one body. It is indeed a wonderful sacrament.[33]

Despite Luther's belief that matrimony is sacramental, the tradition that bears Luther's name has declined to view the marriage rite as a sacrament on a par with baptism and the Lord's Supper. Why? Marriage, though an estate instituted by God prior to the Fall, is universal. It belongs to the order of nature, while Christian Sacraments belong to the order of redemption.[34] Luther's notion of the two kingdoms stipulated that laws governing marriage should be proffered by the state, not the church, and that they should apply to Christian believers and nonbelievers alike.[35] Marital disputes are to be brought before civil courts, not ecclesiastical courts. This does not mean that the relations of husband and wife escape God's authority, however. The civil authority rules only by divine authority, and civil law should reflect divine law. The point we want to make here is that for Luther and his followers marriage is an order of creation, not redemption, and church sacraments belong in the latter category.

Calvin similarly held that "marriage is a good and holy ordinance of God," but this in itself is insufficient grounds for calling it a "sacrament." Calvin employed *argumentum ad absurdum* to refute church tradition on this matter. Farming, building, cobbling, and barbering are similarly lawful ordinances of God, but these are not deemed sacraments. Marriage is no different.

Exegetically, Calvin objected to the Bibles of his day that translated the word "mystery" as "sacrament" in Eph. 5:33, a mistranslation that leads to a misinterpretation. Paul here exhorts a man to love his wife just as Christ loves the church. He is not sacramentalizing marriage; in fact, Paul makes it clear that "mystery" applies to "Christ and the

Church," not to marriage. And to add confusion on top of confusion, Calvin complained, the medieval church of Rome, after voicing disdain over sexual intercourse as an impurity, even went so far as to include the sex act in the sacramental act. Why after disdaining sex should the church then turn around and speak of it as sacramental? Calvin felt that this was contradictory. "There is another absurdity in their dogmas," he wrote, "they affirm that in the sacrament the grace of the Holy Spirit is conferred; they teach copulation to be a sacrament; and they deny that the Holy Spirit is ever present in copulation."[36] Almost because of his assumption that sexual activity constitutes an impurity, Calvin could argue against deeming marriage a sacrament. In sum, we note that as the sacramental practice of the Reformation took on its distinctive shape, the Protestants continued to celebrate the wedding rite but reserved the term *sacrament* for baptism and Eucharist.

Yet the sacramental feel of marriage was not lost on Luther. Nor did he ignore the intrinsic beauty of a loving relationship between a woman and a man. He tacitly assumed that procreation is the purpose of sexual intercourse, of course; yet he also appreciated marital love as a good in itself. "The love of a man and a woman is (or should be) the greatest and purest of all loves," he wrote.[37] Luther treasured the wanting of the beloved by the lover. He thought that even if the human race had not fallen, "the love of bride and groom would have been the loveliest thing."[38]

The loveliness of a woman and man sharing mutual intimacy could not be subordinated completely to the rule that sex is only for baby making. Luther seemed to make room for the pleasure of sex, an attitude which the church earlier had disdained. This is reflected in his thoughts on divorce. What if one of the marriage partners decides to abstain from sexual relations and, despite the protestations of the spouse, remains abstinent? Divorce on grounds of desertion was already being practiced in the sixteenth century. Does this apply here? Luther thought so. Unilateral abstinence is a form of desertion. The Apostle Paul had suggested that couples might abstain from sexual relations by mutual consent, but by mutual consent only. Forced abstinence is something else. If after counsel and discussion one partner still insisted on abstinence, then the other would be free to divorce and remarry.[39] There seems to be some appreciation here for sex apart from procreation.

Turning to procreation, as with so many aspects of ordinary human existence, Luther marveled at the wonders of nature and viewed birth as a miracle. In fact, the whole process of insemination, pregnancy, and delivery seemed to him to be miraculous. His understanding of the relationship of sperm to fetus certainly could be refined by advances in biology, but no science could improve on his ear for the music of nature.

> Surely it is most worthy of wonder that a woman receives semen, that this semen becomes thick and, as Job elegantly said (Job 10:10), is congealed and then is given shape and nourished until the fetus is ready for breathing air. When the fetus has been brought into the world by birth, no nourishment appears, but a new way and method: from the two breasts, as from a fountain, there flows milk by which the baby is nourished. All these developments afford the fullest occasion for wonderment and are wholly beyond our understanding, but because of their continued recurrence they have come to be regarded as commonplace, and we have verily become deaf to this lovely music of nature.[40]

More than legitimating marital love, marriage should lead us to bring new children into the world and, even more important, to raise those children in the knowledge of God's grace. It is not enough for Luther to seek children as inheritors of the family property. He excoriated the royalty of his day for limiting the number of children in order to engineer inheritance patterns. Children should be borne for their own sake, and parents have a divinely ordained mandate to care for their children while educating them into the godly life. Luther's own love for children sounded the deepest chords within his soul. He praised infants who seem to have no temporal cares and only happy speculations and treasured children at play, believing that such play pleases God.

As a father of six who watched two daughters die, Luther felt the unmerciful pain of grief so profoundly that the theodicy question challenged his faith. The death of thirteen-year-old Magdalene, in 1542, overwhelmed him. Griefstricken, he and wife Katherine could not expunge from their minds' eye the features, words, and movements of their deceased daughter. Though he wanted to thank God that his beloved Magdalene had escaped the sufferings of the physical world and entered a heavenly realm beyond earthly limits, he admitted that he wished he could have kept her longer. Even meditation on the death of Christ could not provide the comfort that he knew—theologically knew—it should. Luther was angry with God. Ozment writes,

> I know of no other occasion in Martin Luther's life on which his theology and faith were not a match for the enemies who threatened him. He defied the emperor, German princes, and several

popes; he cursed and taunted the devil; and in the last years of his
life he shouted down in the most unforgiving way what he perceived to be an international conspiracy of Jews, Turks, papists,
and bad Christians, who plotted to undo his Reformation. His theology and faith truly failed him only at the death of a child. Some
might find it disappointing that the great reformer could love a
child more than he trusted God.[41]

Yet, as seemed to be the case all through his life, Luther's faith could be
fueled by despair. Faith seemed curiously strengthened when challenged by doubt. In his grief, Luther wrote a song for Magdalene, whom
he had nicknamed Lena.

> I, Lena, Luther's beloved child
> Sleep gently here with all the saints
> And lie at peace and rest
> Now I am our God's own guest
> I was a child of death, it is true,
> My mother bore me out of mortal seed,
> Now I live and am rich in God.
> For this I thank Christ's death and blood.[42]

When not grieving the loss of a child, Luther could say that our children belong first to God and only secondarily to their parents. This
makes education in the godly life a godly activity. "Most certainly father
and mother are apostles, bishops and priests to their children, for it is
they who make them acquainted with the gospel."[43] With both carrot
and whip, Luther argued that Christian families should raise children
with utmost devotion, discipline, and dedication.

> But this at least all married people should know. They can do no
> better work and do nothing more valuable either for God, for
> Christendom, for all the world, for themselves, and for their chil-
> dren than to bring up their children well. . . . For bringing up
> their children properly is their shortest road to heaven. In fact,
> heaven itself could not be made nearer or achieved more easily
> than by doing this work. . . . Hell is no more easily earned than
> with respect to one's own children. You could do no more disas-
> trous work than to spoil the children, let them curse and swear,
> let them learn profane words and vulgar songs, and just let them
> do as they please.[44]

Though perhaps surprising to a reader who assumes Luther never spoke
of works earning entry into either heaven or hell, the Reformer uses here

the reward of heaven and the fear of hell to drive home his point: Raising children well is of inestimable importance.

Procreative and Unitive Sex

We have just taken a brief look at the Augustinian tradition in its formative role for both Roman Catholic and Reformation Protestant teaching. Now let us jump to the twentieth century. Whereas our formative Christian forebearers largely assumed that sex and procreation belonged inevitably together, the momentum in contemporary culture is to divide them. This is a momentum that Roman Catholic leadership for the most part is trying to thwart; yet, even here, subtle movement can be discerned.

In his encyclical letter of 1930, *Casti Connubii,* Pope Pius XI draws on Augustine's three watchwords for marriage in order to emphasize that procreation is central.

> The saintly Doctor [Augustine] shows that the whole doctrine of the Christian church is excellently summarized under these three heads: *Fidelity* signifies that outside the matrimonial bond there shall be no sexual intercourse; *Offspring* signifies that children shall be lovingly welcomed, tenderly reared, and religiously educated; *Sacrament* signifies that the bond of wedlock shall never be broken. . . . Among the blessings of marriage offspring holds the first place.[45]

The pope here clearly believes that producing offspring is built right into the very nature of the conjugal act and that sex without baby making is inconceivable. The point the pope wants to make is that contraceptive measures should be forbidden. He says that deliberately depriving sex of its natural power or efficacy through birth control is an act that is shameful and intrinsically immoral.

Yet there is more in *Casti Connubii* worth noting. First, personalist themes can be discerned. What some call the *unitive dimension of love and marriage* is clearly affirmed. "The love of husband and wife . . . holds pride of place in Christian marriage," says Pius XI, "this mutual inward moulding of husband and wife . . . can in a very real sense . . . be said to be the chief reason and purpose of matrimony."[46] Lisa Sowle Cahill sees this personalist emphasis on reciprocity between spouses as destabilizing the previous procreation-centered description of the marital act.[47] We have here a 1930 foundation on which future Roman Catholic affirmation of sexual love could be built.

I also note how the pope waxes with more than minimum eloquence regarding the value of children. Children shall be "lovingly welcomed, tenderly reared and religiously educated," he says. What kind of construction should we put on this? A cynical construction might lead us to say that the Roman Pontiff only wants us to make more babies so we can have more Catholics. It is the brute production of offspring that the pope wants, not children with whom we live and share our lives. The more positive construction, which I offer here, is that the Holy Father is giving voice to a significant strain within the long Christian tradition that imputes dignity to children. Just as Jesus gathered children around himself and spoke of their special relation to the Kingdom of God, so also does the Christian church guide our obedience to Jesus' commandment to love our neighbor with special attention given to children.

What was a mere crack in the door for *Casti Connubii* becomes, three decades later, an opening toward personalized loving. "Marriage to be sure is not instituted solely for procreation," say the drafters of *Gaudium et Spes* during the Second Vatican Council. The unitive dimension of marriage clearly dominates as Vatican II roots the marital union "in the conjugal covenant of irrevocable personal consent." Celebrated here are the twin qualities of love and human dignity.

> This love is an eminently human one since it is directed from one person to another through an affection of the will. It involves the good of the whole person. Therefore it can enrich the expressions of body and mind with a unique dignity, ennobling these expressions as special ingredients and signs of the friendship distinctive of marriage. . . . Such love, merging the human with the divine, leads the spouses to a free and mutual gift of themselves, a gift proving itself by gentle affection and by deed.[48]

Mutual loving acts of gentle affection are, *Gaudium et Spes* continues, "by their nature ordained toward the begetting and educating of children." Although the value of marriage extends well beyond mere procreation, to be sure, it necessarily includes procreation. I simply note that although marriage here is at first rooted in the covenant of a man and woman who freely will to enter into a lifelong relationship, at this point it is natural law that is invoked to nail down the unbreakable connection between marital unity and procreation.

The principle that marriage has been ordained by God through nature to issue in offspring has corollaries that occupied the church during the 1960s, namely, the forbidding of birth control and abortion. Conceiving children is proper to marital love, and protecting what they conceive is proper to human dignity. Methods of regulating human procreation ought not to be undertaken; rather, we should trust the designs of nature more than we trust our own judgment in matters of family planning. And, most assuredly, in reverence for the dignity of each life begun at conception, each child in the womb should be protected. "Therefore from the moment of its conception life must be guarded with the greatest care, while abortion and infanticide are unspeakable crimes."[49]

The attitude toward children here is striking in its lack of attention given to children as persons. Certainly the proscriptions against abortion on the grounds that the conceptus has dignity is a positive affirmation of each child's personhood. But it ends here. The concern of *Gaudium et Spes* is with the morality of the parents and the fulfilling of their conjugal and procreative duties. Children are subordinated to these ends. Although the Vatican document reiterates the now familiar vocation of bringing children into the world and providing them with religious education, the goal of this task seems to have more to do with the fulfillment of marriage than it does with the welfare of the children themselves. "Children contribute in their own way to making their parents holy."[50]

Now let us turn to a related question: Must each act of sexual intercourse be individually considered open to the possibility of baby making? Or might we take a married couple's sex life as a whole into consideration and celebrate its unitive value along with its procreative value? If the latter, then contraceptive measures might be taken for a season and then removed when the parents-to-be decide they are ready to beget progeny. Thinking in terms of the marital relationship as a whole rather than in terms of individual sexual acts, one could affirm both the procreative purpose of marriage in concert with the use of contraceptive technology as a means for guiding the times at which children would be born.

In the Pontifical Commission for the Study of Population, Family, and Birth, which was instituted by Pope John XXIII and reconstituted by Pope Paul VI, the majority of commission theologians agreed that the desire to beget children, expressed over the whole of a given marriage, plus the whole of the couple's sexual life together would be adequate to fulfill the unitive and procreative ideals. Love and procreation are not so linked that a couple who deliberately renders coitus sterile attacks its meaning as an expression of mutual self-giving. The meaning of marriage is found in the communal relationship of the persons involved, not in their acts, sexual or otherwise. Pope Paul VI, however, rejected this line of thinking. Instead he sided with the commission minority and argued that each sexual act must be individually considered open to the possibility of procreation. This means no artificial measures to prevent conception could be employed in any instance. This position is made clear in the pontiff's *Humanae Vitae:* "Each and every marriage act must remain open to the transmission of life."[51]

This delimitation of sexuality to procreation should not obscure the significant progress in the Catholic understanding of marriage, according to scholars such as Richard McCormick and Lisa Sowle Cahill. In reviewing the long history of theology in light of twentieth-century reinterpretations, McCormick identifies three stages of development: (1) the couple must positively pursue procreation; (2) the sex act is licit if it does not positively exclude procreation; and (3) sexual intercourse becomes licit even though there is the intent to avoid procreation. McCormick sees the *Humanae Vitae* as a setback in this otherwise identifiable trend.[52]

Cahill interprets *Humanae Vitae* more appreciatively as moving procreation alone out of the center by affirming "two great realities of married life," namely, "conjugal love" and "responsible parenthood." In the tradition of *Gaudium et Spes, Humanae Vitae* speaks of a man and woman's love in terms of "communion" and "reciprocal personal gift of self" as well as "a very special form of personal friendship."[53] In the race between the procreative and unitive values of marriage, the unitive value, though behind, seems to be gaining. "Catholic thinking about sexuality is on a trajectory toward appreciation of the interpersonal dimension as primary, with procreation in secondary place."[54]

More on Procreative
and Unitive Sex

It was well into the pontificate of Pope John Paul II that the Congregation for the Doctrine of the Faith published *Donum Vitae,* its treatise of *Instruction on Respect for Human Life in Its Origin and on the Dignity of Procreation.* This document, reiterating what Paul VI said in the *Humanae Vitae,* states that there is an inseparable connection between the two meanings of the conjugal act, namely, the unitive and the procreative. The justification for this position, as well as the justification for the wholesale rejection of reproductive technologies in general, is based on a natural law theory regarding the nature of marital acts and their ties to baby making. The foundational appeal to nature here follows two steps: first the nature of the individual human being and, then second, the nature of the marital act.

The first step toward establishing an ethical foundation is the iteration of an anthropological assumption: Each individual human being is a composite unity of two things, a physical body and a spiritual soul. We have a double nature present in a unified totality. Human striving can lead to true self-realization only when both the corporeal and spiritual dimensions contribute to the unified totality. This is a pro-body stance. Each individual person is uniquely constituted not only by his or her spirit, but by his or her body as well. The words of John Paul II are cited: "Thus, in the body and through the body, one touches the person himself" or herself in "concrete reality." This means, among other things, that the human body ought not be reduced to a mere complex of tissues, organs, or functions that are evaluated in the same way as the body of animals. Rather, the human body is constitutive of the person who manifests and expresses himself or herself through it.

This anthropological assumption provides the basis for attacking modern reproductive medicine on the grounds that it is depersonalizing, dehumanizing, and denies us human dignity. It treats a human being as if he or she were merely material, subject to external design and manipulation. Our bodies become mere instruments of our technological wills. We become divided against ourselves when a disembodied will manipulates our corporeal reality. To the extent that reproductive technology disembodies baby making, it is morally illicit. Siding with the Vatican on this point, Paul Lauritzen argues that the disembodiment of the human self through technology "sets the stage for the objectification and commodification of reproduction."[55]

What Roman Catholics know as the moral law issues from this body-soul composite unity. "The natural moral law expresses and lays down the purposes, rights and duties which are based upon the bodily and spiritual nature of the human person." Therefore," the framers of *Donum Vitae* say, "this law cannot be thought of as simply a set of norms on the biological level." Going beyond mere biology, they rise to the level of human reason, to the rational order, wherein the human "is called by the Creator God" to "direct and regulate our lives and actions." Such actions include how we are "to make use" of our "own body."[56]

I note a double problem of coherence here. On the one hand, the appeal for a moral norm seems at first to be an appeal to nature but, on the other hand, this is immediately obviated by an additional appeal to our rational apprehension of God's will. If the Creator God regulates our life and actions, then the ground of moral law must be found ultimately in the Creator's will that we employ our rational capacities and not simply in the nature of the creatures. If the divine will can be discerned independently of created nature—say, through special revelation—then the appeal to natural law would be superfluous. No necessary connection is made here between the transcendent Creator's will and our creaturely nature. No necessary connection to our biological or physical nature, that is.

It is according to our rational nature, not our physical nature, that the Creator calls us to discern our moral responsibility. This action alerts us to a second problem of coherence. On the one hand, our bodily nature is said to be essential to our human nature yet, on the other hand, this nature is disregarded when establishing a foundation for morals by appealing strictly to our rational souls. The use of "use" language here—wherein the soul uses the body—could betray a return to the classic soul-body dualism in which the soul is considered the higher nature and the body the lower nature. This dualism, which *Donum Vitae* seems to fear will allow technological impersonalism to dehumanize us, is implicitly reaffirmed by this natural law theory.

Creationism and Baby Making

That the dualism is meant to be ontological becomes clear at the point where the Vatican document subtly interjects creationism. *Creationism,* as we discussed in an earlier chapter, means something quite specific, namely, that at the moment of conception "the spiritual soul of each" of us is created by God as part of God's plan for each of us to live eternally in the divine presence.[57] Sperm and ovum provide the physical zygote that will eventually produce our body; God provides the soul. Each of us is heir to both earth and heaven, to both the biology of our parents and the intervention of God. How might one arrive at this conviction? By observing biology? Not likely. By discovery in our rational thought processes? Not likely. The doctrine of the special creation of each individual soul arose during the patristic period in controversy with opposing points of view. It derives from dogma, tradition, and church authority.

The concept of creationism in the church's tradition was raised as an alternative to Origen's view of pre-existence and Tertullian's view of traducianism. Augustine rejected Origen's idea—the immortal soul pre-exists and is imparted to a mortal body during the birth process—on the grounds that Origen presumed a clean soul and a dirty world, failing to appreciate the goodness of God's physical creation.[58] Traducianism, the idea that we inherit our souls from our parents during the procreative act, is the more fascinating idea. In Tertullian's version, we find the extended metaphor of the seed being planted. Tertullian contended, over against pre-existence of the soul, that the body and soul come into existence together at the same time—the time of conception. Employing the ancient analogy comparing sex to agriculture, he says that we humans produce two kinds of seed—one for the body and one for the soul, and both get sown in sex. The point to be observed here is this: The soul seems to be a substance that can be passed on from the parent—actually a seed from the father planted in the body of the mother—right along with the bodily seed. Tertullian arrives at this idea via a sort of phenomenology of sexual passion. When finding himself exhausted after making love, he feels that some of the power of his soul has been expended and deposited in his lover.

> In that very heat of extreme gratification when the generative fluid is ejected, [don't we] feel that somewhat of our soul has gone from us? And do we not experience a faintness and prostration along with a dimness of sight? This, then, must be the soul-producing seed, which arises at once from the out drop of the soul, just as that fluid is the body-producing seed which proceeds from the drainage of the flesh. . . . And finding their way together into their appointed seed-plot, they fertilize with their combined vigour the human fruit out of their respective natures.[59]

One of the theological reasons for following such a line of thought was to make the connection between Adam's soul and each individual soul, just as each of us is heir to the bodies of Adam and Eve. Both body and soul have been passed down through Adam and Eve's progeny, and together they carry both the original nature—the *imago dei*—plus original sin. Augustine did not find this argument convincing, although it looked better to him than did the pre-existence argument. Augustine wavered between traducianism and creationism, and was satisfied that he could not make up his mind. He was confident that, regardless of which anthropological theory might be correct, no saving doctrine was at stake in the debate.[60] In comparison to Augustine, today's Vatican believes there is a great deal at stake.

Returning to the path of the Vatican argument, natural law theory intends to direct our gaze on the nature of the individual body-soul union and to the nature of the marital union. The divine will is said to be written into human nature; therefore, if we read human nature carefully, we can discern its divinely appointed telos or purpose. Nature tells us that marital love and baby making go together. Any reproductive technology that, given sexual intercourse, helps facilitate the natural process of procreation is morally licit; whereas any disconnecting of procreation from the sex act constitutes a departure from natural law and is morally illicit.

It follows that assisted reproduction, which bypasses sexual intercourse, will be deemed illicit. Contraception that gives us sex without babies is illicit. Now babies without sex becomes illicit for the same reason. Artificial insemination with husband's sperm (AIH) and in vitro fertilization (IVF) make procreation possible without sexual union. The problem with contraception is that, even though it supports the unitive dimension of love, it sheds the procreative dimension. The problem with homologous fertilization methods such as AIH or IVF is that, even though they support procreation, they do so without necessarily supporting the unitive dimension.

Key here is that the unitive dimension of marriage is understood in terms of one specific sexual act tied directly to the procreation of a child. It does not refer to the ongoing loving relationship of a man and a woman in marriage. "Homologous artificial fertilization, in seeking a procreation which is not the fruit of *a specific act of conjugal union,* objectively effects an analogous separation between the goods and the meanings of marriage."[61]

The Congregation for the Doctrine of the Faith's *Instruction* raised the sensitive question regarding the texture of the mother-father relationship that, when taken as a whole inclusive of sexual activity, would at times yield children and other times would not. In light of this it would seem logical to ask: Might the unitive dimension of marriage include the ongoing sexual sharing of two people in a bond of love, and might we view these two people as dedicated to the procreating and nurturing of children as their vocation? Might this holistic rendering of marital unity count in moral discourse? No. This line of thinking is rejected outright. "The question is asked whether the totality of conjugal life in such situations is not sufficient to ensure the dignity proper to human procreation." Considered here are those infertile or planning parents who find it necessary to resort to assisted reproduction if they are to make babies at all. Their desire to procreate counts no more than their ongoing marital love. "This good intention is not sufficient for making a positive moral evaluation of *in vitro* fertilization between spouses. The process of IVF and ET [embryo transfer] must be judged in itself and cannot borrow its definitive moral quality from the totality of conjugal life of which it becomes part nor from the conjugal acts which may precede it."[62]

What follows is the inheritance myth in full operation. Having proscribed homologous fertilization methods, the heterologous methods then receive no sympathy. The document asserts that heterologous artificial fertilization such as artificial insemination with donor sperm (AID) or surrogacy, wherein one of the gametes comes from someone other than the mother and father engaged in the sex act, is morally illicit. A man and a woman should "collaborate with the power of the Creator" in the sex act, and they should "become a father and a mother only through each other." This concept of divine-human collaboration is said to cede rights to the child, the right to be conceived, carried in the womb, and brought into the world by the same parents who will raise him or her within an intact marriage. "It is through the secure and recognized relationship to his own parents that the child can discover his own identity and achieve his own proper human development."[63] In short, the full realization of a child's identity and development require a direct connection between genetic and social parentage.

Although the foundation for Vatican ethics is touted to rest on natural law, nothing could be further from the case. It rests primarily on the distinctively theological commitment to creationism—that is, to the belief that God creates a soul *de novo* for each individual person at the moment of conception. Then, somehow the dignity or inviolability of this divine action for the individual person becomes transferred to the sex act on the part of the parents. From these two closely related theological commitments, the proscriptions against all technologically assisted reproductive methods follow. But it must be noted clearly that this commitment to creationism is a distinctively dogmatic import to both biology and rationality. It is not discernible by any method of observing the natural world. To say that procreation is mandated by the sex act is a claim that bypasses any kind of testimony by natural law; it is an appeal to a dogmatically determined concept of nature and not to something observed in or about nature.

My analysis here differs in part from that of Paul Lauritzen. Lauritzen believes he has gotten to the bottom of the Vatican argument by identifying the appeal of *Donum Vitae* to embodiment. He believes that the emphasis on body-soul unity is a separate and more fundamental commitment than the natural law commitment. I disagree, noting how the text flatly states that "the natural moral law expresses and lays down the purposes, rights, and duties which are based upon the bodily and spiritual nature of the human person."[64] But here I wish to stress a different point, namely, the Vatican is less than fully serious when it identifies the integrity of human embodiment discerned through natural law as foundational. Lauritzen writes,

> The appeal to keep procreation and intercourse together, therefore, is not simply rooted in a natural law reasoning but reflects a more general recognition that personal love is expressed in the language of the body and that an act of sexual intercourse that both expresses love and is aimed at procreation unites body and spirit in the bringing into existence of new life. To create new life without sexual intercourse is thus to fail to accord human reproduction its full dignity.[65]

What Lauritzen fails to see, I think, is that the alleged unity of body and spirit in either sexual intercourse or procreative conception gains its moral status from the dogmatic assumption that this is the moment when the human soul is created. The unity of body and spirit that is supposed to characterize the love between mother and father gains its moral status by borrowing it from the unity of the zygote's body and spirit created by God at the moment of conception. All that counts here for *Donum Vitae* is the connection in time and space between fertilization in the sex act and the act of divine intervention in soul making.

Lauritzen rightly interprets a subordinate argument in *Donum Vitae* regarding the risk that the technologization of reproduction might lead to the commodification of children. The Vatican document stresses that each child should be the fruit of his or her parents' love. The child ought not "be desired or conceived as the product of an intervention of medical or biological techniques; that would be equivalent to reducing him to an object of scientific technology. No one may subject the child that is coming into the world to the conditions of technical efficiency, which are to be evaluated according to standards of control and dominion."[66] Lauritzen interprets this caution against dehumanizing as a caution against disembodying, trying to dominate one's body by the spirit through technology. Reproductive technology "turns our bodies into mere instruments of our wills . . . insofar as assisted reproduction disembodies procreation, it is deeply flawed." This disembodiment through technology may lead to the objectifying and commodifying of the children who result. "Persons will be treated as less than fully human; children will be thought of largely as commodities; and interventions into the reproductive process will be judged solely by criteria of technical efficiency in producing the desired product."[67] The Vatican caution here is well taken. So is that of Paul Lauritzen.

Still, more needs to be said. Reproductive technology does not *necessarily* objectify and commodify. Technology can be a tool used to express love in baby making. We found this to be the case with Martha and Phil who were discussed in chapter 2. AID was the tool whereby their marital relationship created a family relationship. The quality of their parental love for their two children is in no way diminished by a technologically assisted birth process. Theologian Richard McCormick notes that the attitude of parents and technicians can be every bit as reverential and respectful as they would be when a child is naturally conceived.[68] Reproductive technology can be a means to a loving end.

For the papacy, this analysis of means and ends and the proffering of a doctrine of human dignity is much more than merely an item of philosophical or ethical speculation. We see here a passionate commitment to protect the lives of the innocent, and it is this passion that drives Pope John Paul II in the *Evangelium Vitae* to rally the world to protect children and the elderly from what he perceives to be the rampant "culture of death." The practice of euthanasia and physician-assisted suicide, along with the practice of abortion and its associated reproductive technologies, are the weapons the strong wield in their war against the weak and defenseless. We are facing a *"war of the powerful against the weak,"* warns the pope, a *"conspiracy against life."*[69] He calls for a renewal of culture through the strengthening of families, the task of which is to raise children. "It is above all in *raising children* that the family fulfills its mission to proclaim the *Gospel of Life*."[70] And, to get beyond the limits of the inheritance myth, the Holy Father advocates adoption for unwanted children who need homes.

> A particularly significant expression of solidarity between families is a willingness to *adopt* or *take in* children abandoned by their parents or in situations of serious hardship. True parental love is ready to go beyond the bonds of flesh and blood in order to accept children from other families, offering them whatever is necessary for their well-being and full development.[71]

When it comes to summarizing the concerns of Pope John Paul II, Lisa Cahill and Thomas Shannon note three distinctive emphases to his pontificate. First, John Paul II makes a concentrated effort to ground his reflections in appropriate scriptural accounts of the meaning and destiny of human life. This effort is amply illustrated in his *Evangelium Vitae* where he appeals to the Genesis account of Cain and Abel, the Ten Commandments, and the New Testament gospels. Second, he employs personalist language to understand human experience. Along with dignity, the concepts of personhood and relationality become courts of final appeal in the *Evangelium Vitae.* Third, he portrays women and men as equal partners in marriage and family life. In the *Evangelium Vitae,* he trumpets the cause for a "new feminism," according to which women should be equal to men while avoiding a repeat of the misdeeds of patriarchy.[72] In his book, *Crossing the Threshold of Hope,* the pope takes a strong stand against pro-choice, while declaring himself "pro-woman, promoting a choice that is truly in favor of women; and this includes the church standing by and supporting women who have had abortions."[73]

Along with his predecessor, Paul VI, John Paul II identifies openness to procreation as morally necessary with each sexual act. The unitive and procreative meanings of the conjugal act are inseparable. To employ contraceptive technology, according to the Holy Father, is to manipulate and degrade human sexuality, especially the dimension of self-giving. Cahill offers the most optimistic of possible interpretations of the pontiff here: Mutual self-giving love is not only equal but primary as the meaning of marriage. Cahill and Shannon want to take us beyond seeing procreation as a mere Augustinian justification of sexual desire and acts of lust; they want us to advance toward a wholesome view of loving commitment between a man and a woman in a marriage bond. Yet there is still work to be done. "What is needed is a sexual ethics that recognizes both the physical and interpersonal aspects of sexuality, marriage, and parenthood. . . . The centrality of love as a norm in sexual morality is consistent with the personal character of the 'one-flesh' union of Adam and Eve, with Jesus' emphasis on the involvement of one's deepest attitudes and commitments in one's moral activity, and with the Thomistic tradition's stress on distinctively human characteristics as most important to human nature and as essential to friendship, with the post-Vatican II teaching on marriage as a personal relationship of commitment, and with John Paul II's view of sex as the language of mutual self-gift."[74]

Sex without Babies,
Babies without Sex

In arguing against the Augustinian legacy that ties sex to reproduction, bioethicist Joseph Fletcher announces with considerable fanfare that things are changing. The new reproductive technologies permit us to separate sexual intercourse from making babies. During the sexual revolution of the 1960s, we sought sex without babies; now with the genetic revolution, we find we can have babies without sex. What then is the value or purpose to human sexuality? That remains to be seen. Fletcher writes, "Love making and baby making have been divorced. Sex is free from the contingencies and complications of reproduction, and sexual practice can now proceed on its own merits as an independent value in life."[75] Freedom has been thrust on us and we will have to decide, both culturally and individually, just what sexual intimacy means and what ethical principles will guide our bringing children into the world.

As we have just seen, the era of contraception and abortion—which gives us sex without babies—and the era of reproductive technology—which gives us babies without sex—are provoking a conservative backlash. It is not only the Vatican that wants to return to the premodern era in which nature rather than choice determined the relation of sex to baby making but also essentialist or pro-life feminists, some who, like Sidney Callahan, draw on Roman Catholic tradition to reroot sexuality and childbearing in nature. The "view of sexuality that I and most pro-life advocates share sees procreation as equal to the values of love, desire, and unity," writes Sidney Callahan, "the link between sex and procreation cannot and should not be broken. Sexual expression should be confined to those committed pair bondings that can serve procreation if need be."[76] Then with almost an appeal to sociobiology she adds, "Erotic pleasure is viewed as nature's ingenious way of ensuring genetic selection. Courtship, love, and sexual preference are means of selecting the best genes for the next generation and ensuring reproductive success."[77]

Sidney's husband, Daniel Callahan, disagrees, saying, "Sidney says that 'to totally separate sexual activity from reproduction becomes an exceptional case.' Exactly the opposite is true: It is reproductive sexuality that is the exceptional case. . . . Biology does not necessarily provide a better guide to developing moral standards than reason and sober human reflection on experience."[78] Then he goes on to add, "I take it to be a mark of human progress that many, including myself, have come to reject the view that sexuality and procreation are 'a process that is intrinsically whole.' On the contrary, the process is divisible, and our common moral problem is to decide how to make the proper distinctions and divisions."[79]

Cahill and Shannon, as we have seen, also have an investment in distinguishing—but not completely separating—sex and baby making. These two celebrate what they perceive to be a positive transition currently underway. "The major modern shift in the Catholic understanding of sex is to link it in an equally fundamental way with the interpersonal communion (love) of the partners, and so to give it an intrinsically positive meaning."[80] Cahill applauds this addition of the unitive to the procreative value of sexual intercourse, yet she is critical of the Vatican for not going far enough to draw out further implications. The history of *Humanae Vitae* and *Donum Vitae* demonstrates that church leadership focuses too much on sex as a physical act, while ignoring the place of sex within the ongoing relationship of love. Furthermore, a fuller appreciation of the love bond should permit some sex without baby making—that is, contraception should not be strictly prohibited. In addition, Cahill and Shannon are somewhat more open than the Vatican is to baby making through reproductive technology without sex.

> It is dubious, however, that the experience of married persons, parents or not, clearly warrants the assertion that the love which their sexual relationship expresses must be incompatible both with occasional artificial avoidance of conception and with the use of artificial means to bring about conception without the sexual act. It is the committed love relationship of the couple in its totality that gives the moral texture both to their sexuality and to their subsequent roles as parents. It is from the wholeness of the relationship that their specific physical acts of sex and conception take their moral purpose.[81]

Cahill and Shannon further contend,

> Within the trinity of love, sex, and procreation, it is love that is fundamental, most humanly distinctive, and thus most morally important. Sex and procreation are not merely dispensable goods, but their moral meaning can be defined fully only within the interpersonal relationship of the persons who cooperate in realizing these goods.[82]

Lutheran theologian Gerhard Forde, like Shannon and Cahill, keeps one foot in the sex-procreation tradition, while stretching the other foot in the direction of loving children.

> Procreation is not, indeed, the only justification for sexual intercourse, but it is a part of the reality being symbolized. . . . Society

has always had and must take a vital interest in its children and must pay attention to them today. Children all too often are the victims sacrificed on the altar of sexual gratification. This too is the concern of the civil use of the law.[83]

Although Forde can distinguish between sex and baby making, he, like the tradition before him, seems to assume that keeping this connection protects us against abandoning our responsibility to children. I maintain, in contrast, that once we have crossed the Rubicon of choice we must lodge the sense of responsibility for children in choice—that is, we must persuade by ethical argument that people should devote a significant portion of their lives to loving and protecting the dignity of children. This ethical mandate is valid with or without sex.

It seems to me that the time has come for ethical leaders to help find a justification for healthy sexual relations in something other than baby making. Even an appeal to what happens in nature will show that, at least for the human species, only some sex acts result in pregnancies and only some pregnancies result in babies. An appeal to culture will show that the sexual dimension of human relations is power packed with drama; "love makes the world go 'round," so to speak. Sheer observation of the phenomenon of sexuality shows that it cannot be reduced to brute biological procreation, and the slightest contact with Christian theology shows that the quality of human relations cannot be reduced to a brute biological act of copulation in the service of procreation. The spread of contraception and advance in reproductive technology has borne us beyond the Rubicon into the land of choice, wherein the connection between sex and baby making is increasingly a matter of choice. The time is ripe for Christian ethicists to reexamine our theological resources and raise the question: How can a healthy sex life be grounded in something other than brute procreation?[84]

The Transformatory Power
of Sexual Love

Fortunately, fulfilling sexual relationships have an intrinsic tie to love. Love is a rather significant theological category. Might there be something here worth teasing out? The work of Vladimir Solovyev, the early twentieth-century Russian Orthodox theologian, provides an example of the kind of theological reasoning that is called for. As we turn toward the new millennium, we may find we need to garner social-scientific resources, which were not available to Solovyev, in pursuing a theology of sexuality; nevertheless, his work shows that jewels of understanding can be found in the rich treasure box that is Christian theology.

Solovyev proffered a natural law argument in support of sex without babies. He began by observing in nature that the multiplication of living creatures may take place without conjugal sex. Many organisms multiply in a nonsexual fashion by segmentation, budding, spores, or grafting. When we rise to the level of life forms where sexual differentiation plays an important role, Solovyev discovers a fascinating formula. En route to his formula he constructs a scale. At the bottom of the scale he puts cold-blooded animals such as fish. Fish produce embryos on a colossal scale, eggs by the millions. And these eggs are fertilized by the male outside the female's body, which indicates that fish are not driven by a sexual impulse in the humanly understood sense. On the next step up on the scale we find amphibians and reptiles, where the rate of increase is less than that of fish and where sexual contact between males and females is increased. Among birds, a higher step up on the scale, the rate of multiplication is less; but we find, in these life forms, mating patterns and continuous mutual attachment. In mammals we find a still slower rate of procreation but a more intense sexual impulse, even if the sexual impulse is seldom connected to continuous mutual attachment. At the top of the scale is the human race, where the rate of procreative increase is the smallest, yet sexual love attains its "utmost significance and highest strength." This leads Solovyev to conclude that sexual love and multiplication of the species are *in inverse ratio* to each other. The stronger the one, the weaker the other.

> So, if in this way, at the two extremes of animal existence we find on the one hand increase without any sex love, and on the other hand sex love without any increase, then it is perfectly clear, that these two phenomena cannot be ordered in indissoluble connection with one another—it is clear, that each of them possesses its own independent significance, and that the meaning of the one cannot consist in its being a means to the other.[85]

Solovyev has disengaged the unitive dimension from the procreative dimension in order to treat human loving in an independent fashion. What has been missing in much of the classic and contemporary moral discussion in western theology is the personal dimension of love—that is, that the most meaningful sexual love is shared with a particular person, the beloved. Because it is love of a particular person, this love loses dignity if it is subordinated as a means to some further end such as baby making. If we look closely at the role of sexual love in the human world, we will see that "it is incomparably greater, than in the animal world, and assumes that individual character, in virtue of which *just this* person of the other sex possesses for the lover unconditional importance, as unique and irreplaceable, as a very end in itself."[86]

Theologically speaking, what is the justification of sexual love? Is it procreation? No. Sexual love—and we need to underscore *love* here, so what we are about to say would not apply to prostitution, rape, or objectified sex, all of which could lead to procreation—in its most beautiful form entails a profound encounter of one person with another. It entails self-transcendence and opens oneself to transformation. Authentic love that is evoked in us through sexual bonding with another person leads to imputing unconditional significance to the beloved, and this elicits the development of a self-transcending individuality in the lover.

If we understand the human predicament as at least in part caused by egoism—that is, if much human suffering is caused by a self-centeredness or even pride that makes us unempathetic to the feelings of others and permits our manipulating or using others to accomplish our own ends—then a loving relationship in which another person is encountered as other will have a salutary impact. We would hope that rational thinking, wherein our minds lift our thoughts toward universal truths, could carry us beyond our particular selves so that we can see ourselves as parts of a larger reality. But even rational thinking can easily be subverted by self-interest and become one more expression of egoism rather than its antidote. However, sexual love with a particular person, the beloved, may be able to accomplish what even universal reason fails to do. Solovyev speaks with eloquence.

> There is only one force, which can from within sap egoism at the root, and effectively undermine it, namely love, and chiefly sex-love. The falsehood and evil of egoism consists in the exclusive acknowledgement of absolute significance for oneself and in the denial of it for others. Reason shows us, that this is inconsistent and unjust, but love directly proved by facts, does away with such wrongful relations, compelling us not by abstract knowledge, but by inward feeling and the will-to-live to recognize for ourselves the absolute importance of another.[87]

Solovyev goes on to contend that authentic love is connected to immortality by virtue of its particularity, its ability through relationship to establish individuality. He believes that eternal salvation is for persons, for individuals. And love—not vague altruistic love but passionate, personal love—exerts individuating power.

> It is self-evident that art, science and politics, which give the content of the separate impulses of the human spirit and satisfy the temporary historical needs of mankind, do not by any means communicate the absolute, self-sufficient contents of human *individuality*, and therefore stand in no need of immortality. Of this, only love stands in need, and only love can attain it. True love is that which not only affirms in subjective feeling the unconditional significance of human individuality in another and in oneself, but also justifies this unconditional significance in actuality, effectively rescues us from the inevitableness of death and fills out our existence with an absolute content.[88]

What is the warrant for the audacious claim that love of a particular person gains the qualities of absoluteness and even immortality? The answer: faith. "The concern of genuine love is above all based on *faith*," says Solovyev. It must be based on faith, because empirically our beloved, and even ourself, is ephemeral—that is, subject to deterioration and death. Only God has the power to confirm our love through the gift of immortality, a gift that we share with the very life of God in Godself. He argues, "the radical meaning of love, as has already been shown, consists in the acknowledgement for another creature of unconditional significance. But this creature in its empirical being, as the subject of actual sensuous reception, is not possessed of unconditional significance: it is imperfect in its simplicity and transient to its existence. Consequently, we can assert unconditional significance for it only by faith, which is the assurance of things hoped for, the conviction of things not seen." Then he adds, "we must, by faith in the object of our love, understand the affirmation of this object as it exists in God, and as in this sense possessing everlasting significance."[89]

This faith is a faith in God who transcends the present physical state of existence. This faith will be confirmed eschatologically when not just individuals but the whole of physical reality will be consummated into the fullness of the divine life. The salvation of each of us individually is dependent on the salvation of the whole of creation, and this is the assurance of things hoped for. Solovyev's magnificent description of eschatological felicity takes on a mystical tone as he describes the oneness of all things, a oneness that balances and integrates part and whole, individual and all.

Perfect all-oneness in accordance with its own conception and equality of right between the one and the all, between the whole and the parts, between the general and the particular. The fullness of the idea demands that the greatest possible unity of the whole should be realized in the greatest possible independence and freedom of the particular and single elements—in themselves, through them, and for them. In this tendency the cosmic process attains to the creation of living individualities, for which the unity of the idea exists in the likeness of the race, and is felt in its full force in the moment of sexual impulse, when the inward unity or community with the 'other,' with the 'all,' receives its concrete embodiment in the relation to a single person of the other sex, who represents in itself this complementary 'all' in one.[90]

The sexual impulse is by no means reducible to human concupiscence or even the forces of genetic self-preservation; rather, it is an icon, a doorway that opens up a pathway between the particular and the universal, between the part and the whole, between time and eternity, and between the profane and the holy. No more grand or sublime justification for the value of sexual love could be offered than to ground the passionate embrace of two people in the divinely appointed unity that binds all things in heaven and earth into eternal blessedness.

6

Visions of the Future
and Ethical Foundations

Over and above their present-at-hand reality
human individuals are related, as persons, to a
still open destiny and thereby to God.
—Wolfhart Pannenberg[1]

What about ethical first principles? When dealing with the ethical
challenges posed by the new reproductive technologies, which
foundational principles do we appeal to for ethical guidance? There are
a number of questions we can ask here to help refine the issues. First,
must we appeal to strictly biblical-theological commitments, or might
a secular-humanist ethic suffice? Second, if we opt for a distinctively
theological approach, must we distinguish between an ethic for believers in Christ and another ethic for nonbelievers? Or, to put it another
way, are ethical principles derived from a stance of faith so different
from other religious or secular commitments that there is no overlap of
shared commitment? Is there a disjunction or conjunction between
Christian and non-Christian ethics? Third, can we distinguish within
the theological approach two modes of pursuing ethics, one that overlaps with secular-humanist approaches and one that does not? Fourth,
if so, must these two modes of pursuing theological ethics be sharply
separated or can they be thought of as complementary?

This chapter, like tree climbing, will proceed algorithmically, beginning where the ethical trunk forks into secular and theological branches
by offering a brief exposition of the works of bioethicist Joseph Fletcher
and ethicist Trutz Rendtorff. Fletcher tries to defend a strictly humanist
focus on human well-being, and the cultural power of this secular approach is manifest in the influential field of biomedical ethics. Returning
to the fork, we will then follow the Rendtorff branch of theological ethics
to the point of its next divide, the distinction between Protestant evangelical ethics and Roman Catholic natural law ethics. Here we will look
briefly at theologian Karl Barth's understanding of evangelical ethics in
conjunction with the work of Lutheran bioethicist Gilbert Meilaender.
We will then thoroughly examine the work of contemporary Roman

Catholic thinker, Lisa Sowle Cahill. Finally, we will then go out on a limb and note how the buds and leaves of both the disjunctive and conjunctive modes of ethical reflection overlap and intertwine, and at this point I will suggest that proleptic ethics bears the best fruit.

It is my proposal that the field of Christian ethics should be founded on our vision of the promised Kingdom of God. Ethics should be founded on eschatology. The world that constitutes our present reality is slated for transformation, a transformation promised to us by God and proleptically anticipated in the Easter resurrection of Jesus Christ. The advent of God's kingdom will bring new life and healing, a new creation. Christian ethical thinking begins with the disjunction between present and future realities. It begins by looking forward, to the new, the transformed, the healed, the saved. The eschatological vision draws us toward what is better, and it is this inspired striving for what is better that energizes creativity in Christian living.

Included in the eschatological vision is the promise of resurrection and the image of a spiritual body. First came the physical but now comes the spiritual, writes Paul in 1 Cor. 15:45–49. Spirit transcends biology. We pass from being people of dust to people of heaven. We pass from being the children of Adam and Eve to becoming brothers and sisters of Christ. Although Paul's contrast between body and spirit can be misused when pressed into the service of escapism, I believe it makes one vital point relevant to the concerns raised in this book: Our ultimate destiny with God is determined not by our past biology but rather by our future transformation in the divine spirit. Our definition or identity as human beings is determined not by the DNA we have inherited but rather by our vision of the network of relations that will constitute the Kingdom of God.

I believe that the essential structure of Christian ethical thinking is prolepsis. A *prolepsis* is a concrete actualization within present reality of what we envision will be the case in the future-transformed reality. "Thy kingdom come," we ask in the Lord's Prayer, "thy will be done on earth as it is in heaven." Ethical deliberation begins by projecting a vision of new creation saved by divine grace and then works back to our present situation and the responsibility we need to shoulder now. The posture to Christian ethics should be future oriented, transformatory, active, creative, expectant, and hopeful. It is out of a vision of hope for a better reality that we deliberate over genetics and the use of reproductive technology when asking: Who are we in light of our biological inheritance and our promised destiny with God?

Humanism: Joseph Fletcher
and the Field of Bioethics

The advantage to the theological approach is that it can take account of our relationship to God; whereas in the humanist approach, the advantage is that it presumably places religious and nonreligious ethicists in conversation with one another. Let us look very briefly at an example of each, first Joseph Fletcher along with the widely recognized principlist school of biomedical ethics. Then, for contrast, we will turn to the work of Trutz Rendtorff.

Famed for his controversial book of 1966, *Situation Ethics,* Joseph Fletcher offers us today a strictly humanist set of ethical first principles that is not intended to be antithetical to a religious or theologically grounded ethic. He says that his humanist perspective "is not religious and claims no knowledge of God's will beyond the conviction that any God worth believing in wills the best possible well-being for humans."[2] That is, if there is a God worthy of ethical attention, this God must conform to an anthropocentric criterion, namely, "well-being for humans." Fletcher believes that this criterion of human well-being is in fact what the Bible means when it sponsors love and concern for persons, but by no means does the authority of the Bible serve to ground the principle here. This is an ethic created by humans for the benefit of humans.

When applied to specific moral situations, Fletcher factors in wisdom for determining what is ethically good. Fletcher is not satisfied with an ethic that merely helps us negotiate our way through gray areas wherein we feel we must choose the lesser of two evils. Rather, by deciding on behalf of the "wisest" path to human well-being, we decide on behalf of what is itself good. Fletcher holds that "if any act or policy is the wisest as measured by human need and well-being, then it is *positively* good, *positively* the right thing to do. There will be no reason to have to defend it by some twisty kind of casuistry. This holds whether it is abortion, sterilization, artificial insemination, embryo implants, cloning, [etc.]."[3]

Fletcher is a futurist. Biological science and reproductive technology are increasing the quality of human well-being for the future. "The biological revolution is a quantum or dialectical leap in human change," he writes, "it is an instance of . . . the transformation of quantity into quality."[4] We are re-forming ourselves. He dubs the human race as *homo auto fabricus.* The self-transformation of humanity will be facilitated by making fewer babies and better ones, whether they are made naturally or by new artificial modes. The natural method—that is, making babies through sexual intercourse—is not intrinsically superior to the artificial method—making babies by using alternative reproductive techniques. The ultimate court of appeal for Fletcher is not our biological history; rather, it is the criterion of human well-being envisioned for the future.

The criterion of well-being for human beings may sound minimalist, but it easily garners maximum adherence in the field of ethics and is most closely associated with the issues we raise in this book, namely, biomedical ethics. Over the last three decades, this field has attained a very high level of sophistication and provides an admirable model for integrating humanist values with medical science. Beginning usually with concrete moral dilemmas that arise during medical treatment or laboratory research, bioethicists work back to general normative principles that provide justification for the moral judgments they render. A handful of principles—nonmaleficence, beneficence, autonomy, and justice—seem to have stood test after test and continue to typify ethical deliberation in the medical setting.[5]

The first of these general normative principles is *nonmaleficence* and its twin, *beneficence*. Nonmaleficence is rooted in the ancient and often-repeated maxim from the Hippocratic Oath, "Above all, do no harm" (*Primum non nocere*). In the medical field this oath means that we should not, by carelessness, malice, inadvertence, or avoidable ignorance, do anything that will cause injury or increase the suffering of a patient. In practice, however, the physician or nurse may in fact do harm—such as prick the skin to take a blood sample—but as they do so, they are constantly balancing eventual positive goods over temporary, inflicted harms. Nonmaleficence is a negative principle that says, if we cannot do good then we should at least avoid doing harm.

Beneficence is the flip side of nonmaleficence. The principle of beneficence says that we should take positive actions that will promote the well-being of people. We have a duty to further the best interests of others. In medical practice and research, this principle means that we should pursue better health for those entrusted to our care. Some theorists argue that nonmaleficence and beneficence belong together in a single principle, seeing the first as a passive complement to the second more active moral task.[6]

The Enlightenment principle of *autonomy* is fundamental to modern thinking. The Institute of Medicine defines autonomy as "self-determination, self-rule, or self-governance."[7] In medical practice this principle means that rational individuals should be permitted to be self-determining—that is, they should be permitted to make their own decisions regarding their healthcare based on the best available medical information. The autonomous person gets choice. In order to avoid constrictions on self-determination, such as we find in paternalism, obtaining *informed consent* from patients before beginning treatment is the primary way in which autonomy is protected. When it comes to genetic testing, selective abortion, and other such concerns, autonomy and its correlate, informed consent, are applied to the parents, not the child.

The principle of *justice* has to do with the allocation of limited resources, the distribution of benefits and burdens. Justice here comes in two forms: noncomparative justice and comparative justice. In noncomparative justice, treatment services are rendered according to a standard that is independent of the claims of others, for example, the simple administering of emergency first aid. Anyone who needs first aid should get it. In comparative justice, however, what one person or group receives is determined by balancing the competing claims of others. When overwhelmed with multiple medical needs, the triage nurse in a hospital emergency room may have to make decisions regarding who gets priority in treatment and who must wait. A medical system with limited resources may have to balance basic health services needed by large numbers of people with exotic or expensive treatments, such as kidney dialysis, that affect only a small number of patients. This is the task of distributive justice.

With regard to prenatal diagnosis and issues surrounding selective abortion, bioethicist John C. Fletcher [not to be confused with Joseph Fletcher] performed a cross-cultural study in 19 nations. The following set of agreed-upon ethical principles emerged as a result of his study: (1) parental autonomy; (2) noninfliction of harm on individuals or families; (3) full disclosure of findings of prenatal diagnosis; and (4) offering voluntary programs of prenatal diagnosis and genetic counseling.[8] These ethical policies seem to apply the four basic normative principles.[9]

What is noteworthy here is that these normative principles also seem to function quite well in a society often described as pluralist, divided into separate and competing value systems. Hospitals and other medical settings are frequently pluralist in their professional makeup, mixing together healthcare professionals and patients from a wide spectrum of religious traditions and moral commitments. Yet these general normative principles work reasonably well, and they have received cultural reinforcement in the courts. These principles help constitute a public moral code of a sort.[10] The values they presuppose are humanist—that is, by focusing on various dimensions of human well-being, they become anthropocentric values.

Theological Ethics:
Trutz Rendtorff

If we understand ourselves as human beings in relation to God, however, a strictly humanist foundation for ethics or a general normative bioethics will not be adequate. We will need to press for more than anthropocentric wisdom; ethics will have to include theology. Munich ethicist Trutz Rendtorff argues that to understand the human situation as truly human, we must recognize

> that human life is not something that exists in and of itself, but rather depends in an elementary fashion on the social nature of life. . . . The communicative structure of the reality of life is in its essence that of a life in communion with God. In ethics the recognition of this basic situation is at issue. The task of an ethical theology is to provide an explication and a basis for this state of affairs and to support it through argumentation. Ethics is thus an intensified form of theology.[11]

To think of ethics as an intensified form of theology does not require it to sever ties with humanist or secular approaches to ethical issues, however. Conversation must remain open, says Rendtorff.

> Theology must resist the temptation to address the theoretical and practical atheism of the world in such a manner as to suggest that only where the theological form of ethics is consciously present do we encounter theologically relevant issues involving the ethical reality of life. On the contrary theology must, as a consequence of its own premises, enter into an open debate with other theoretical approaches to the study of the reality of human life.[12]

Rendtorff begins with three basic elements—three basic observations about life—that form the tripod on which the ethical stool stands: the *givenness of life*—that is, we receive life from the hand of its creator, God; *the giving of life,* contributing to the life and well-being of others—that is, loving; and the *reflection on life*—that is, the reflection on the split between the way life currently is and the expectation of a future good that has not yet fully become reality.[13]

The givenness of life translates into the status of givenness that is ascribed to marriage. Marriage is an example of human community, Rendtorff says, and the communal relation between husband and wife comes prior to the pursuit of individual self-fulfillment or even prior to setting goals for marriage. In the history of the church, marriage has frequently been thought of as having a goal or purpose, most often the legitimate channeling of lust and procreation. More recently, the purpose of marriage is described in terms of human flourishing through a loving relationship. But Rendtorff rejects all such purposes, even noble purposes, on the grounds that subordinating the marriage as a means to a further end undermines the definition of marriage as community. He believes that the communal bond comes first, and all other goals or purposes come second. Rendtorff wants to avoid a crisis wherein a couple, judging that the goal has not been achieved, would judge the marriage as a failure and dissolved.[14]

The marital community includes children. Rendtorff takes a "family planning" approach to family ethics, approving contraception to determine when children should arrive but disapproving of abortion to prevent them entirely. Rendtorff assumes that parents can decide *when* they will have children, but they cannot decide *what kind* of children they will have. "Within certain limits it is possible to plan when and whether parents will have children," he writes, "but by contrast, what kind of children they will have cannot be planned."[15] I find this to be a curious ambiguity: Either he is saying this is technically impossible—which would be a mistake in assessing what reproductive technology can in fact do—or he is placing an imperative within an indicative to say: Thou shalt not plan what kind of child to have. Regardless, the Rendtorff position is that the means of family planning—that is, deciding what reproductive technology to use—is ethically secondary to the overall point of view of the parents doing the planning.

The Rendtorff proposal can be described as an *evangelical ethic* because it begins with the evangel of God's love for us that becomes transmitted in our love for one another. Once we realize how steadfast is the love of the giver of our life, then we become liberated from devotion to ourselves and free to love others for their own sake. Evangelical ethics begins with Paul's understanding of a justifying "faith working through love" (Gal. 5:6).

> Faith is trust in Christ as trust in this freedom of justification. It sets humans free from the compulsion for self-realization. The christological basis of this freedom is that it has as its content the

reality of community with God. That is the specifically theological meaning of love.[16]

In contrast to Fletcher's anthropocentric ethic, Rendtorff's ethic requires the acknowledgment that faith gives human communion with God. Despite this difference regarding first principles, however, Fletcher's wisdom and Rendtorff's love both strive to serve the well-being and even the flourishing of the human race.

Evangelical Ethics:
Karl Barth and Gilbert Meilaender

Distinctive to evangelical ethics is the triple structure: faith, freedom, and love. Through faith, the believer is bound to Christ and by God's grace realizes that his or her salvation is a free gift. This means, among other things, that the moral life need not be pursued with the reward of salvation as its goal. Salvation is assured; it can no longer be earned. Faith in God's grace bestows freedom, freedom from striving to establish a saving relationship with God. The ongoing temptation for us humans is to disbelieve in God's grace, to deny God's grace by building ethical ladders that we, in our delusion, think we need to climb to earn divine favor. The building of such ethical ladders constitutes an unnecessary return to bondage. Paul trumpets this propensity to deny grace and its accompanying freedom, "For freedom Christ has set us free. Stand firm, therefore, and do not submit again to a yoke of slavery" (Gal. 5:1).

Faith in its freedom is like a fertilized tree that bears juicy fruit. The key fruit is love. And love, here, is understood as disinterested love—that is, love that is guided not by the interest of the lover but rather by the interest of the beloved. Freed from the need to pursue moral living to satisfy one's own need, the person of faith can devote himself or herself strictly to the need of the neighbor. We willingly serve "another without hope of reward," writes Martin Luther, emphasizing that the person of faith considers nothing except the need and the advantage of the neighbor.[17] Nächstenliebe becomes the German term for neighbor love. Exactly how we should meet the neighbor's need becomes a practical concern, one to be met freely and creatively and not by any slavish adherence to impersonal moral principles. "The only thing that counts is faith working through love" (Gal. 5:6).[18]

Karl Barth outlines the evangelical foundation for ethics with three propositions. First, God is free. God is free because God is sovereign, and because of this sovereignty, God has chosen to commit the Godself to human well-being. Second, our human freedom is a gift from this free God. We gain freedom along with joy when we appropriate God's election on our behalf. We are God's creature and God's partner. Third, evangelical ethics is a reflection on God's call for human action that is implied by the gift of freedom. This freedom is essentially not *freedom from* but rather *freedom for,* in this case freedom for loving. Evangelical ethics, even when engaged in interpreting Scripture, defies enslavement to a set of rules. Rather, it seeks concrete action in concrete situations, action taken out of freedom and love.[19]

Ethicist Gilbert Meilaender characterizes "the Christian life as one of faith that gives rise to faithfulness."[20] What is central is "focus on the neighbor."[21] He writes, "faith must be active in love, and love, in turn, must seek justice for the neighbor. Hence, in its social mission the church engages in works of mercy that serve human need and works of witness that condemn injustice."[22]

Evangelical ethics begins with the recognition of the other as other. It takes an extra effort, which is based on extra trust and extra sensitivity, to love the neighbor who lies beyond kinship, to love benevolently someone who is clearly other to us. This is not to deny the validity of the preferential love we give to those who are close to us. These two loves—particular attachment and sheer affirmation of another—are both indicative of the life of faith. Yet the difficult one is clearly the latter, the benevolent love we extend to those outside the pale of kinship or even friendship.

Meilaender identifies four alternative strategies that ethicists have used for affirming the two loves—mutual love and benevolence—within the Christian life. The problem all ethicists face here is the connection, or nonconnection, between particular attachments and the global mandate to love all our neighbors even when those neighbors are our enemies. In the context of this book, this applies to the connection between those with whom we identify, according to the inheritance myth, and others who are biological outsiders.

The first strategy, according to Meilaender, is to connect mutual love and benevolence closely, but to do so without deriving either from the other. In this case, benevolence is employed as an external limit principle that opens up an arena for preferential love. As long as we do neither harm nor injustice to any neighbor, this method permits giving ourselves in the special bonds of clan or tribe.

The second strategy stems from a general principle of benevolence. We start with a universal love that embraces every human being equally. Within this broad scope we telescope down more particular loves. Because we are finite and cannot actually love each and every person in the world equally, so the argument goes, we can translate universal benevolence into special relationships with those particular persons who exist in close proximity to us. We love them as we would all others, namely, we love them disinterestedly. We do not demand mutuality.

The third strategy is to reverse the direction, to telescope up from preferential love toward benevolent love. One might decide to marry a particular person on the basis of passion, on the basis of a particular attraction, rather than seeing the beloved as a single instance of a more universal principle of benevolent love. But having committed oneself to loving a husband or a wife, the habit of loving could gradually expand to become more inclusive.

The fourth strategy is the Franciscan understanding of love. It begins with the observation that the spirit of self-giving is common to mutuality and benevolence. By affirming the importance of special attachments for finite, embodied human beings, and without questioning the necessity of universal neighbor love, this strategy recognizes that some Christians emphasize one, while other Christians emphasize the other. Self-spending occurs in both, of course, but some individuals declare that they are called to a special vocation that emphasizes benevolence. The advantage here is that the church, which includes both the vocations of mutuality and benevolence, witnesses to both types of love, while not trying to hold them together in a single life.

Meilaender notes that the first two strategies seem more characteristic of Protestantism, whereas the latter two strategies are more likely to appear in Roman Catholic circles. It has been the genius of Catholicism to combine the third and the fourth strategies. Catholics recognize that for most of us the necessary movement is one that builds up from particular attachments to benevolence; yet there may be some who are called to live even now as if particular and partial loves were no longer essential in human life. As we saw earlier, Don Browning's *caritas* builds on the strengths of kin love to construct an ethic of altruism and neighbor love.

In developing his own constructive position, Meilaender argues that we ought not think that there must be an opposition either between self-love and neighbor love or between between kin love and stranger love. The commandment of Jesus that we love others as we love ourselves includes love of self and love of one's own; it simply makes self-love the model for comprehending what love of the other might look like. Self-referential love is not forbidden to Christians but rather making ourselves an object of our love—that is, making others the means toward our self as the end. In practice there is no sharp line, of course; for one cannot tell where joy in someone else's well-being begins and desire for our own stops. They overlap and merge and need not be sorted out when life is lived by faith in God's grace.

What I find significant in Meilaender's work for our task here is the assumption that Christian ethics must take with utmost seriousness the mandate to love the other, to love the stranger and even the enemy. It seems to me that built right into this concept of benevolent love is a trajectory that takes us beyond the fence of preferential love, beyond the borders fixed by shared genes. It seems to me that the preemptive move on the part of parents who are bringing a child into the world is to initiate a loving relationship with someone who is both other and yet kin. The otherness is determined by the child's dignity and its kinship is determined by the love of the parents. And this should be the case whether the child shares DNA with both parents, one parent, or neither. Dignity claims otherness and requires benevolence; mutual love, not biology, creates true kinship.

Too bad Meilander himself fails to draw these implications out of his own commitments. Like me, Meilander cautions against "quality control" in baby making so as to preserve the dignity of children. But unlike me he grounds it in "marriage as a basic form of life within which procreation ought to take place. . . .We will view all forms of collaborative reproduction as dehumanizing, as a violation of a basic form of human life."[23] I find this to be a non sequitur. Marriage as a form of life does not necessarily preclude collaborative reporduction. Meilander seems to slip into the inheritance myth, forfeiting the gains of evangelical ethics.

The method of evangelical ethics seems on the face of it to be exclusively Christian, yet its proponents contend that it extends more broadly. If faith in Jesus Christ and trust in God's grace is the prior condition for "faith active in love," one would think that this ethic would belong strictly to those professing this particular faith. Meilaender does not draw this limiting conclusion, however. He argues, "Christians must begin from faith, though this starting point need not imply a wisdom available to them alone. . . . Faith may broaden our vision and enable us to see what might otherwise have remained hidden to sight; it may enrich and enlarge our understanding of the moral life, and this enlarged understanding is, in principle at least, able to be shared with anyone and everyone."[24]

A Roman Catholic Natural
Law Ethics: Lisa Sowle Cahill

The most penetrating and edifying analysis of the Christian tradition regarding the relation between baby making and companionship in marriage, in my judgment, is the work of ethicist Lisa Sowle Cahill. I have frequently cited her insights regarding various issues in earlier chapters. Here we will look at the foundations on which she constructs her ethical superstructure.

Cahill stated the basic challenge in 1989: "If the prophetic message of today's Church is to be that sexual expression should arise from personal commitment which, barring extraordinary circumstances, is open to and responsible for children, it will have to find a language to ground the meanings of sex and parenthood convincingly in the personal devotion of the partners."[25] This grounding language, she believes, can be drawn from the alphabets of natural law, cross-cultural observation, and a personalist interpretation of human experience that leads to an ideal of conjugal love as a form of committed friendship.

The Cahill method is distinctively Roman Catholic and, thereby, makes universal claims that can be shared by Catholics and non-Catholics alike. Whereas a distinctively evangelical approach appears to limit ethical discourse to the community of faith that seeks to live consciously in response to God's love, a Roman Catholic approach that relies on a version of natural law posits ethical principles that can be shared by believers and unbelievers alike. Despite the attempts by secular humanists in the media to dismiss Roman Catholic moral pronouncements—especially pronouncements regarding abortion—as mere sectarian religious interest, the actual method employed by Catholic theologians seeks honest and authentic public discourse over moral matters. Ethics based on natural law is intended to appeal to all intelligent and good-willed persons. Cahill writes,

> Catholic natural law ethics is specifically not a "religious" ethics in any way that intentionally marks off Catholic Christian behavior from that of other intelligent and good-willed persons. Scriptural warrants, therefore, are not used to point out a distinctive way of Christian moral living, but are used to support the validity of moral obligations regarded as binding on everyone.[26]

In sum, ethical foundations are laid on grounds accessible to all people of good will, and the distinctively Christian contribution is to validate

and enhance already existing human insights regarding what constitutes healthy human flourishing.

Postmodern Pluralism and
Universal Natural Law

The fundamental task Cahill takes up in her recent scholarly work is
to ground the ethics of marriage in a concept of natural law that, on the
one hand, benefits from the cross-cultural sensitivity and passion for
justice demanded by deconstructionist postmodernism on the behalf of
women while, on the other hand, not surrendering to a pluralist relativity that forbids lifting up a universal vision of what constitutes human flourishing. The value of postmodernist philosophy is that it provides us with the hermeneutic of suspicion, and this suspicion permits
an unintimidated re-thinking of the tradition; it permits a critical reassessment of the preconscious patriarchal and oppressive cultural
forms perpetuated by the tradition. It also encourages a retrieval of the
fundamental, egalitarian commitments inherent in the Christian gospel.
Cahill's feminist ethic, committed to social equality of men and women,
works with a critical dialectic between the patriarchal and egalitarian
(sub)traditions within Christianity. Appealing to the universal human
experience of embodiment and its articulation in her own version of
natural law, she adjudicates between these two subtraditions within the
Christian tradition. The result is an ethic of marriage and nuclear family relations within which sexuality contributes to human flourishing
through procreation and companionship.

To follow this road, Cahill needs to jump the postmodern hurdle
placed in the path by philosopher Michel Foucault. The assumption of
this version of postmodernism is that all human thinking is inextricably historical, relative, contextual, socially produced, and susceptible to
the pressure of powerful ideologies.[27] Applied to the issues at hand,
Foucault pictures our modern obsession with sexuality as socially constructed and socially distorted by the preceding Christian tradition. The
Christian practice of confession, wherein the penitent confesses sex's secrets to a powerful authority such as a priest, inadvertently leaves the
impression that sexuality is fundamental to human ontology. Modern
culture is no help here because it promotes the illusion that we can escape ecclesiastical repression and attain sexual liberation through talking about sex in public. Such talk of human fulfillment through sexual
liberation only reinforces the social construction. Sexuality is not a sim-

ple biological given; rather, it is a social construction. And social constructions differ from context to context, with our particular sexual construct as an expression of bourgeois power.[28]

So Foucault engages in cultural iconoclasm that denies any foundation for rendering normative value judgments. The difficulty for feminists who are striving for social justice is that this refusal to acknowledge a normative foundation undermines the very concept of justice across ethnic, racial, or gender lines. The difficulty for humanist bioethicists, it would follow, would be that postmodernists would describe what bioethicists in fact are currently doing as impossible, namely, working out of a set of principles that garners general support across diverse religious and cultural lines.[29]

Feminists identify numerous injustices involving women that need transformation: the plight of poor rural women in the two-thirds world, oppressive customs and marriage structures in various societies, sexual exploitation, genital mutilation, prostitution and sex tourism, hierarchical structures in churches, and cultural forms that confine women's roles. To combat these injustices in differing social contexts requires a vision of the human good toward which transformatory action could be taken. But no consistent feminist critique of injustice can maintain such a good if it assumes matters of sex and gender are reducible to cultural constructions and thereby subject their very roots to the relativity of values.

Cahill locates two related problems within the pluralist postmodern program that make it internally incoherent. First, despite what they call themselves, these postmodernists are actually still modernists. Foucault and his disciples retain the ethical and transformative interest of the Enlightenment, using Enlightenment values to critique the deadening effects of bureaucratic, technological, late capitalist culture. In doing so, they continue to rely on modern ideals such as individual autonomy (even while deconstructing the individual self), while appealing to human solidarity in resisting oppressive or repressive cultural regimes. Reason may be given a more historicized and pluralist twist, but the Enlightenment trust in critical reason is not abandoned.

The second problem Cahill identifies in the postmodern program feeds directly into her own proposed revision of feminism. Feminists, many of whom take advantage of the postmodern hermeneutic of suspicion for the purposes of critically rethinking the Christian tradition, also embrace the modern Enlightenment values of rights, equality, autonomy, freedom, and tolerance. The coherence problem arises when we acknowledge that these are universal values—that is, they imply a vision of what is good for the human race applicable to all people of all times. These values are inescapably universalistic and totalistic. Even though they arose within a specific historical context, namely, modern western bourgeois society, their intent is to liberate all people regardless of culture, gender, or race. Are these values compatible with the radical pluralism of this brand of postmodernism? Clearly not. Yet the postmodern critique of universalism comes together in the same package with this affirmation of universalism.[30]

The result is that academics and advocates stumble philosophically because, while they reject any notion of universal human nature or even of sexual nature, they still work with the assumption that they operate with moral force when demanding that equality and freedom are human values that ought to characterize sexual relationships.

Cahill's correction consists of building a universal perspective by retrieving and remodeling the concept of natural law. Her concept of natural law is constructed on a combination of Thomistic foundations and cross-cultural observations. Thomas Aquinas defined natural law as the inclination of every creature toward the proper ends and actions intended for it by God. In human beings this inclination is not merely physical or instinctual but also intellectual and rational.[31] The first undemonstrable precept of the moral law based in natural law is clear: to do good and avoid evil. The way to do good in part is determined by our conformity to our natures, in this case our sexual natures. "Sexual intercourse is a natural expression of the committed love of a woman and a man; generally speaking, the action has an intrinsic or natural potential for the birth of children who become part of the love relationship of the parents."[32] Cahill finds this natural tie between sex, love, and parenthood everywhere in human experience, in culture after culture; so she concludes that it is fundamentally bodily or physical in origin. The result is a modest use of natural law applied across cultural-context lines, which speak universally to the human condition.[33]

Cahill fears that some might object to her reliance on Aquinas because of his anachronistic and patriarchal assumptions regarding women. In order to meet this possible objection, she suggests that we start where Aquinas did and then proceed to destinations beyond what he himself had foreseen. To retrieve Aquinas as a resource for a feminist and historically sensitive approach to sex and gender requires a readiness to forgive or look beyond his reductionist assumptions about sex and women.[34] The task is to begin with his inductive epistemology and vision of the human person as embodied and social, and then to expand this epistemology and vision toward a more complete and egalitarian ethic.

The Procreative and Unitive
Dimensions of Marriage

Inductive observations in the service of natural law theory lead Cahill to draw the following conclusions regarding human nature that pertain to sex and family. In trying to find our "essential" humanity, we need to note that, cross-culturally, all human beings come in some way or other from the bodies of other human beings, and, barring exceptional circumstances, exist in relations of dependency and interdependency to certain networks—kin networks—to which they belong. Moreover, at least for the foreseeable future, the combination of one female and one male parent will be indispensable to produce members of each subsequent generation. Sex, birth, and family are intrinsic to human nature. These are simply facts of the human condition that are basic to our experience of who we are as human beings. Any social ethic, especially a feminist social ethic, is not well served by neglecting this fact.[35]

In addition to biology, Cahill adds personal relationship, and in addition to the procreative purpose of marriage, she adds the unitive dimension. "Human beings are not *only* interested in genetic self-perpetuation or in maximizing their sexual and reproductive opportunities. They care about the establishment of long-term interpersonal relationships, especially to spouse, children and family members."[36] With this premise as a cross-cultural observation that reinforces what can be discerned through natural law, Cahill can proceed to argue that the first task of Christian sexual ethics is to enhance the genuine mutuality of woman and man; the second task is to present the potential parental aspect of human sexual intimacy in an attractive and encouraging, rather than a prohibitive and oppressive, way.[37]

Cahill's overall proposal, in sum, is to establish a foundation for normative ethics in the universal human experience of embodiment as it manifests itself in sexuality and family relations, a transhistorical and transcontextual human experience which constitutes a form of natural law ethics.

> My proposal is essentially that while human sexual differentiation and sexual reproduction have no doubt been vastly exaggerated in their importance for identity and social organization, they do stand

as experiences which begin in humanity's primal bodily existence, and which all cultures institutionalize (differently) as gender, marriage, and family. Human flourishing, as sexually embodied, depends on the realization of the *equality of the sexes*, male and female; and in their sexual union, on the further values of *reproduction, pleasure,* and *intimacy*. The institutions of gender, marriage, and family should *ethically and normatively* be responsive to and should enhance these values.[38]

From Foundation to Application

The task of the ethicist goes beyond foundations, beyond even projecting the ideal. It includes what I call the formulation of middle axioms—that is, principles that help us move from the vision of the ideal toward action in the concrete situation in which we find ourselves. Cahill agrees with this formulation and puts it this way: "The crucial task of the moral philosopher or the reflective moral person is to discover where to set priorities and when to make judicious sacrifices."[39] Even if we were to agree that, according to natural law, the best form of procreation is a fertile sexual act between loving spouses who are committed to sharing in the nurturing of the resulting child, we would still need ethical guidance when confronted with people who do not conform to this ideal. The present controversy over reproductive technology takes place in an epoch characterized by the relative absence of this ideal.

So, let us ask: With her commitment to look to nature, especially biological or genetic nature, what moral judgments will Cahill render regarding reproductive issues? What about artificial insemination, for example? Consistent with her foundational principles, she approves of artificial insemination with husband's sperm (AIH) but not artificial insemination with donor sperm (AID). The biological connection between parents and children is decisive. She can approve of the use of artificial reproductive technology—presumably because it enhances the unitive or personal relationship of wife and husband—but she disapproves of third-party semen donations on the procreative grounds that it breaks the genetic tie between parents and children.

> It is wrong in the process of formulating moral norms to take human biology and dissociate it from total personal existence. To treat a donor as an anonymous nonpersonal provider of a commodity which can be introduced without further consideration into two of the most crucial and most intimate relationships of

other persons, marriage and parenthood, is to do just that. On the other hand, I do not find the integrity of the biological process by which conception usually occurs to be so morally compelling as to prohibit artificial techniques which subordinate that process to the desire of a married couple to give birth to a child genetically related to both of them.[40]

Cahill concludes that homologous reproductive techniques that maintain the genetic bond between parents and children are morally permissible because they help fulfill the ideal relation between love, sexuality, and parenthood. But she opposes heterologous methods such as donors and surrogates that introduce a third party. The biological role of the third party invades and breaks up the biological family unity. Thus, she lays down a middle axiom: The limit of justified compromise in linking marriage, sex, and procreation should be set at the point where one's physical procreative capacity is realized outside the spousal relation and within a physical relation of reproductive cooperation with a third party.[41]

Is There Room
for Nongenetic Inheritance?

Cahill asks the question that I also ask in this book regarding the necessary connection between biology and love for children. She notes how the increase in prevalence of nontraditional families, including homosexual unions, single-parent families, and blended families created by remarriage after divorce, prompt consideration of whether biological parenthood creates or should create a lasting social commitment to one's children, and, conversely, whether a biological basis is really necessary for family or parental love and commitment. She observes that families, everywhere in the world, are based in biology. Despite cultural differences or even differences between families within a culture, the fundamental experience of family is universal because it is a bodily experience. Making a kind of is-ought move, she then argues that the biological relationship *should,* ideally, be the foundation of the social family; but, recognizing the imperfections that cause us to fall short of the ideal, she affirms adoption and similar nonbiological family ties.

Families can have the following features: (1) may vary in size from small and simple to large and complex; (2) their boundaries between inclusion and exclusion may be flexible; (3) familial and marital ties may or may not be a primary factor in the social organization of authority and goods; and (4) the roles of "kin" may be exchangeable or extendable so that persons with no biological tie may function in the family as "fictive kin"—that is, analogously to blood kin or relations by marriage. Yet, argues Cahill, *family* has a basic and constitutive relation to biological relationship for which other relations, however valid, are only analogues. The biological family fixes the paradigm. Families that include nonbiologically connected persons still mimic the paradigm. All families, cross-culturally, are based on the biological realities of sex, reproduction, shared male-female parenthood, the experience of being a child with two older parents, with brothers and sisters, and with a wide range of relatives.

Even if there is room in Cahill's ethics for nongenetic inheritance, this nonbiological bond would still draw energy from its analogy with the biological bond. She is drawing a picture of the family in general— a picture of the ideal family—without rendering a negative judgment about specific families that include nonbiologically connected members. Building a family around adoption, for example, is a laudable thing for Cahill, but it draws its energy from the biological family it mimics. The biological tie remains essential.

From the Inheritance Myth to Adoption

Just how deeply entrenched is Cahill's reliance on the parent-to-child biological connection in establishing a Christian approach to family ethics? She writes, "A Christian perspective on reproductive technologies can appreciate the human and moral importance of biological kinship, without either absolutizing it or making its level of importance to social parenthood totally dependent on individual choice."[42] That she wants a *via media* between absolutizing the biology and absolutizing personal choice sounds admirable. Yet a Cahill disciple might want to know just how much weight to give the biological connection and just how much choice to take away. She does not offer us a formula. When it comes to the procreative versus unitive sex values, she gives clear priority to the unitive value.[43] Yet when it comes to taking a stand on reproductive issues in ethics, she tends to grant decisive weight to biological parenting.

The inviolability of genetic inheritance in Cahill's ethical proposal leads her to advocate a severe reassessment of reproductive technologies, especially AID, gamete donation, and surrogate motherhood. She recommends a public policy that refuses "to let donors totally off the hook and out of the picture" by (1) making their identities available to the children when they grow up; (2) declining to make gamete donation a research-funding priority; (3) denying insurance coverage to these technologies; (4) setting an age limit for recipients as well as donors; and (5) discouraging or denying ovum donation to single women.[44]

What about adoption? Cahill is a supporter, for she herself is the mother of five children, three of whom are adopted. Her egalitarian sense of the common good comes into play when she puts together the needs of homeless children with the desires of families who want children. She says that, given the availability and need of parentless children worldwide, adoption is a viable way to channel one's parental aspirations. Adoption can be the antidote to those couples suffering from infertility disappointment.

> Adoption can transform a reproductive "failure" on the one side, and a disrupted birthing situation on the other, into a constructive reconformation of family relationships. The matching of adults' needs and children's needs is an equation in which a double negative can become a positive accomplishment.[45]

I think Cahill is absolutely correct, of course. Yet one might ask just how her earlier-mentioned commitment to biological inheritance fits in here. To be consistent, one might think that infertile couples who adopt are still failing to fulfill their sexuality. Cahill's answer would be that adopted children still help constitute a family because they, by analogy, follow the model of biological children. Children who are the genetic extension of the marital pair remain the norm for Cahill, and adopted children meet this norm by analogy.

In contrast to Cahill, I see no need to appeal to biological procreation as that which norms adoptive relationships. Whether children are born into a family or adopted into a family, the other family members have to commit themselves to love the children and shoulder the appropriate responsibility for rearing them. On a practical level, parents should affirm that they love their adoptive children no less than their biological children, and the distribution of family assets in the will should demonstrate this equality. In an emerging postmodern society where choice is inescapable, parents must choose to love or not to love both their genetic and their adoptive children.

Sexual Flourishing
versus Becoming a Parent

What about the connection between sexuality and parenting? How can Cahill consistently persist in pressing two nearly incompatible points: (1) the flourishing and fulfillment of women must be found in dimensions of life beyond motherhood and (2) sexuality should be defined as necessarily entailing the procreation of children? The logic is this: If sex, then motherhood. Any flourishing beyond motherhood that includes sexuality seems precluded. Although Cahill makes room for homosexuality and even gay or lesbian couples establishing households, she does not apparently permit sexual fulfillment for heterosexual women apart from motherhood, except perhaps by accident. The intent of sexual relations must include at least the openness to baby making, and raising children is also included in her definition of full sexuality. Evidently nonmotherhood flourishing must be nonsexual flourishing. To me this seems unnecessary. It is my judgment that we should keep the former and jettison the latter—that is, we should affirm that the fullness of a woman's life may be found in her being a mother, but certainly need not be. We should affirm that female flourishing may very well include a rich sexual life regardless of whether or not she gives birth to her own biological offspring.

Cahill's response to this, I think, would be to distinguish between a general paradigm and specific instances. According to the paradigm, sex and parenthood are inextricably linked, linked for both fathers and mothers. Yet, in specific cases, not every man or woman can or need become a parent. If by accident of biology or by some other factor a woman enjoys a fulfilling sex life but does not become a parent, Cahill would agree that this is a good to be celebrated. My own position differs slightly. In our era of advancing reproductive technology and overpopulation, I see less of a need for this biological paradigm.

I can wholeheartedly agree with Cahill when she exclaims, "If the state of childhood implies vulnerability and dependency on the protections of adults, then those adults responsible for the existence of a child have a duty to ensure as far as possible that the basic components of his or her identity and welfare as a human person not be sacrificed to the adults' ends."[46] Yes, I say. But then Cahill goes on to add what I believe is a non sequitur. "Thus being raised in a context of mutual support and loved by one's biological parents is a valuable component of the welfare of the child." It's the weight she gives to "one's biological parents" that seems at times to be excessive. Yet she concludes, as I do, that "sexual intercourse is not a morally necessary means of conception" and that "it is morally commendable in many circumstances to parent genetically unrelated children."[47]

The biology is given priority of place for Cahill, but it is not an absolute value that trumps all others. When arguing for the best interests of children as the first criterion for judging third-party arrangements, Cahill writes,

> Sometimes it is morally commendable to set aside these physical substrata of identity and relatedness, when to give them explicit social recognition causes disproportionate damage to the child or its natural family, or interferes with the child's psycho-social welfare. This is the case in adoption, or in the denial of custody or visiting rights to destructive parents. However, generally speaking, it serves the welfare of both parent and child to be able to build an interpersonal relation on their biological one.[48]

Biology, Theology, and Universal Ethics

If this biological kin connection is as essential as Cahill says it is, and if this essential connection is discernible through natural law theory, then I ask: Have we arrived at a point where natural law ethics and evangelical ethics must part company? Evangelical ethicist Gilbert Meilaender would see the admittedly restrictive tendencies of kin selfishness as an inescapable liability to the natural law approach to ethics. If by nature we are disposed to serve the interests of our genetically bound kin group before serving those of our nonkin neighbor or even our enemy, then the distinctively Christian accent in ethics cannot be accounted for. A natural law ethic "cannot capture successfully one of the great themes of the Christian life: self-giving and even self-sacrifice on behalf of the neighbor, done with a glad and willing heart."[49]

Cahill, in contrast, accepts as a given the natural priority of self-interest aimed toward genetic kin, but she then proceeds to expand this outward, toward a wider circle that includes nonkin neighbor and enemy love:

> Our biological inheritance furnishes us both with tendencies to selfishness (self-interest) and the capacities for empathy and altruism. What sociobiology offers to theological ethics is a stronger appreciation of the fact that both sin and virtue are conditioned by

our embodiment, and not only by our freedom of will. But to refer back to genetic development as a base of either morally virtuous or vicious capacities does nothing to undermine their moral
character. Their rootedness in our embodiment neither requires
nor guarantees that any one capacity will in reality govern the integration of our multiple bodily, personal, and social potentials.
The human capacity is to order, shape, prioritize and encourage
certain dispositions over others.[50]

What we have here is a version of Meilaender's third strategy, telescop-
ing out from a biologically determined preferential love in the direction
of altruism and benevolence.

The distinctively Christian family ethics that Cahill sponsors takes
biological kinship as a base, but not as a limit. Baby making fulfills a
couple's unitive bond to one another, and their commitment to inter-
generational embodiment establishes a human bond with the wider
community. The family becomes a "domestic church" wherein the
gospel of Jesus Christ is shared and the values leading to human flourishing are taught. Like a stone tossed into a lake that makes ever-widen-
ing ripples, love within the family ripples out to become a love that im-
bues the wider society. The family as a bounded kinship group offers a
constant opportunity to sublimate each member's self-interest into dedication to one's mate, children, or other relatives. If the family is made
up of disciples of Christ, then it reflects the transforming power of kingdom life. It educates in solidarity and compassion for those excluded
from the social, material, psychological, and spiritual conditions of human flourishing. In this fashion the Christian family becomes the
church in the world.

What is called for at this moment in history is the church's affirmation of full equality between men and women and for full reciprocity
in the marriage relationship. Although Cahill herself endorses the Roman Catholic proscription against abortion, she complains loudly that
the manner in which the church renounces abortion, so as to define
woman's role strictly in terms of motherhood, only perpetuates patri-
archialism. Although Cahill herself endorses the Roman Catholic
emphasis on procreation, she endorses, as ever more important, the
unitive value of marriage as well, endorsing this value in personalist
terms. A woman is more than a mother, and the enjoyment of sexuality is more than merely an act to beget children. Marriage and family
should contribute to her flourishing as a person, as it should for the
husband-father.

> To argue for motherhood as a distinctive experience of women is not to argue that women are defined only or primarily by motherhood: that authentic mothering has to begin with genes and pregnancy (not adoption); that women who are not literally mothers cannot be fulfilled; or that men's fulfillment does not integrally involve sharing parenthood with women. Paternity, if different in texture, should still be as strong a component of male sociability as motherhood is for women. For neither should parenthood mean ownership or control, but rather for both care-filled connection to and responsibility for mate and child.[51]

The more-than-just-a-mother personhood presumed here is in jeopardy, however, not just by the church's antiabortion rhetoric but also by third-world poverty and customs that limit a poor woman's social prestige to her accomplishments as a mother. A theology that restricts sexuality and marriage to biological procreation reinforces the oppressive weight of poverty. Poor health, physical exhaustion, and the unending struggle to provide materially for her children, when combined with submission to her man, leaves the woman of the underclass little access to personal joy beyond that offered by motherhood. The Christian social message that Cahill wants to deliver is this: Full reciprocity between women and men in loving marital bonds will create families that will be genuine schools of transforming values for the whole of society. In this school of transforming values, she adds, the Christian family should teach inclusive love for the outsider, for the marginalized, for those beyond our kin connection.

Sex and family are not merely private relationships; they are social institutions. The strength of Roman Catholic thought, through the centuries, is that it has affirmed the value of family for society and the body politic.

> The family must be seen, neither as a "haven" from the world, nor as a nexus of social control, but as a school for critical contribution to the common good. To place parenthood in social context would also mean, from a Christian standpoint, asking how Christian values transform the family, and shape the family's contribution to society.[52]

Cahill's agenda is to declare infertility therapy and reproductive technology to be a matter of social as well as of sexual ethics. Her position is feminist and nonindividualist. It is also "objectivist" in the moderate sense of affirming the possibility and importance of establishing a public conversation about the good—individual human goods and the common good—involved when families make reproductive decisions.

Toward a
Proleptic Ethic of Dignity

Where does the love of children fit in all of this? The normative principles invoked by humanist bioethicists impart some protective limits. The principles of nonmaleficence and beneficence can be appealed to protect the child coming into the world from inordinate suffering and even stir us to look out for his or her best welfare. However, for the most part, these two principles—along with autonomy and justice—have been applied to existing parents, family, and society rather than to children who do not yet exist. Evangelical ethics and natural law ethics, in their different though complementary ways, seek to ground loving human relations by providing a foundation for social institutions. Here children find their place in ethics designed for institutions such as marriage, family, or society.

Two categories will help bring children into sharper focus, human dignity and the future. Theologically, these two categories belong together. The concept of human dignity, however, is not just one in a long list of Enlightenment innovations. It was built on biblical and theological foundations. Three Christian doctrines in particular undergird dignity: creation, incarnation, and sanctification.

First, the whole cosmos with all its magnificent grandeur is understood to be the creation of God's Word; yet, there is a special divine "delight" taken in humanity (Prov. 8:27–31). The vastness and complexity of the natural world does not prevent the heavenly sovereign from paying particular heed to the human creature.

> When I look at your heavens, the work of your fingers,
>   the moon and the stars that you have established;
> what are human beings that you are mindful of them,
>   mortals that you care for them?
>   (Psalm 8:3–4)

Existentially, this makes us feel that God attends to each of us, that God cares for each of us. Luther, when commenting on the first article of the Apostles' Creed, "I believe in God, the Father Almighty, maker of heaven and earth," asks, "what does this mean?" He answers: "I believe that God has created me and all that exists."[53] Note the order of consciousness here. First God creates me and then, oh yes, God creates all that exists.[54] Built into the Christian understanding of creation is a special focus on the human race, even on the human consciousness that each of us individually enjoys.

Second, the incarnation reiterates in an even more dramatic way not only God's love for the world but God's love for us humans in the world. "For God so loved the world," goes the gospel in miniature, "that he gave his only Son" (John 3:16). Because of the trinitarian structure of the divine reality affirmed by Christian theology, this giving of the Son is understood as internal to God's life. Love drew God toward the world and into the world, and the incarnation in Jesus Christ constitutes God's having become human. Through the historical act of incarnation, God has defined the divine self as including the human. Add to this the kenotic self-emptying (Phil. 2:7), the suffering and death, and the atoning work on behalf of our salvation, and the result is a picture of God engaging in a form of benevolence on behalf of us. We have become the end toward which divine action is the means. This divine act imputes worth to us, among other things. It establishes the ground for us to affirm our own dignity.

Third, sanctification and its goal, the full attainment of the image of God in us, invokes the dynamic of the future here. The Athanasian formula—that God became human so that we might become divine—locates us on the trajectory toward a divinely empowered fulfillment. The phrase "image of God" or *imago dei* can refer to a number of things, but here I will attend to its identification with Jesus Christ. Jesus Christ is the *eikon tou theou*, the image of God (2 Cor. 4:4). He is the New Adam. Whereas in the first Adam we received life, in Christ we will receive eternal life (Rom. 5:12–21). Eschatologically, we will share the one image of God with Christ.

> Thus it is written, "The first man Adam became a living being"; the last Adam became a life-giving spirit. But it is not the spiritual that is first but the physical, and then the spiritual. The first man was from the earth, a man of dust; the second man is from heaven. As was the man of dust, so are those who are of the dust; and as is the man of heaven, so are those who are of heaven. Just as we have borne the image of the man of dust, we will also bear the image of the man of heaven. (1 Cor. 15:45–49)

We look to the future, not the past, to find the true *imago dei* in us. Our true identity is determined not by our biological genesis but by our spiritual epigenesis. That we will be conformed to Christ, that we will be enspirited and enjoy life eternal, is an eschatological promise. The fulfillment of this promise lies in our future. That God would make such a promise to us imputes to us the ultimate dignity. When we embrace this promise in faith, we affirm our dignity by embracing our eternal worth.

Jesus Christ is the prolepsis of this eschatological future. As he rose from the dead on Easter, so too will we rise into the everlasting Kingdom of God (1 Cor. 15:20). Christ embodies ahead of time the reality we will become. We will become like Christ; we will become one with Christ. We can experience proleptically some of that likeness and oneness in advance through faith; we can walk now in "newness of life" (Rom. 6:4).

This is the christological grounding of human dignity. But, one might ask, what does this have to do with ethics? The answer is that ethics takes on a proleptic structure. Ethics begins with a vision of God's eschatological future and the divine action whereby we are given eternal worth. Ethics continues by encouraging us to confer worth upon persons now on the basis of God's promise for confirmation of this worth in the future. That human dignity begins with conferring worth is decisive for understanding the practical situation in which we find ourselves, namely, relating to persons such as children yet to be born who do not already claim such worth for themselves. They cannot. They are as dependent on us to grant them this worth as the human race is dependent on its creator and redeemer God to do the same.

This makes Christian ethics forward looking in two senses. The first sense has to do with a conferring of dignity today that depends on God's confirmation tomorrow. The effort and strain we invest to love and nurture an as yet nearly unresponsive bundle of unborn protoplasm is built on our confidence that the future will redeem our action by confirming that it was worthwhile. Even if the child is genetically defective, suffering from disease, and likely to die after a short life, we confer worth because of God's promise that he or she will be of eternal worth in the divine scheme.

The second sense of future characteristic of proleptic ethics is thinking positively about creating something new. Not only do we confer dignity on persons who already exist, we use our imaginations to anticipate persons yet to be born who will enjoy participating in God's destiny. We human beings created in the image of God are, to use the words of theologian Philip Hefner, *created co-creators*.[55] We embrace a certain optimism regarding our human responsibilities toward the future that is expressed in engaging in creative enterprises. One such enterprise is the bringing of new children into the world and educating them to enjoy God and God's world.

Of course, we must distinguish quite decisively between a particular person who exists and the general concept of persons who may exist in the future. We have been working with the assumption all along here that a decisive threshold is crossed at the point of egg fertilization by the sperm. Once the DNA is set, a particular blueprint is written that is unique and virtually unalterable for an individual and his or her identical twin. We are no longer talking about general human potential; we are now talking about a specific person or persons. Even if we grant a developmentalist view of human personhood, we are still talking about one distinctive person or persons and no others. At every stage in a person's development proleptic ethics inspires us to treat him or her as a person of worth, as having some degree of dignity. The sheer existence of an individual with unique DNA invites us to make this conferral of worth.

This does not apply equally to sperm or ova prior to fertilization. Sperm and ova are valuable, to be sure, but dignity associated with personhood simply does not apply. Nor does it apply to any vision we might have of a child yet to be conceived in the future, even a vision of the perfect child. It only applies to actual living children, living in utero or on the school playground. It does not apply to a vision because a vision is just that, a vision and not a person. We must project good healthy visions, to be sure. We simply reserve the category of dignity for existing persons. In reserving dignity for existing persons, I in no way want to inadvertently endorse a conservatism that fails to look creatively toward future newness.

As created co-creators, we engage in creating, and this includes sponsoring the birth of new children. Each of these new children will then become the object of our conferring worth and, hopefully, will eventually embrace dignity for themselves. This should be the case whether the child is conceived through sexual intercourse or carefully designed through genetic selection and engineering. Let me be clear on one point: Regardless of the reproductive technology employed or avoided, our ethical responsibility is to love existing children. The way in which we express this love is by conferring intrinsic worth so that they might embrace a sense of their own dignity.

The second orientation toward the future mentioned above, the orientation toward newness, has some implications for reproductive technology. The most significant implication is the disavowal of the inheritance myth. There is no theological basis for committing any passion toward producing heirs who will carry our DNA into future generations. It is not built into the divine order of things to demand that we become parents for the purpose of perpetuating our genes. Our connection to God's eschatological future is not biological. Our biology belongs finally to the dust. Rather, the connection is spiritual. What *spiritual* means here is that the connection of our present moment to God's eschatological future is one God will establish; it will be a dramatic divine action that will both cancel and affirm our contribution to the human race. This implies that the biological family does not trump the social family. Biological inheritance on earth is but a prelude to our spiritual inheritance in heaven. To live proleptically is to allow our earthly life to be influenced by this heavenly vision.

The theological disavowal of the inheritance myth has implications for the practice of such things as AID, in vitro fertilization, genetic selection, and surrogate motherhood. Proleptic ethics is not conservative. Proleptic thinking does not grant endorsement to a tradition that is formulated in a prescientific era when having children through sexual intercourse became tacitly and then dogmatically identified with God's will. By embracing created co-creativity as a distinctively human responsibility, proleptic ethics can appreciate the desire we have to bring children into the world who may be exempt from the genetic diseases that plagued so many of us in previous generations. To envision a better world tomorrow that includes better human health and greater self-fulfillment is an appropriate response to a God who promises to do new things in the future. It is also appropriate to attempt to bring that vision of a better future to bear on the agenda of scientific research and the implementation of newly developing technologies. Rather than appeal to reactionary variants of biological essentialism to obstruct the creative use of reproductive technologies, proleptic ethics encourages their use as means toward a further end. That end is the love of children regardless of their genetic makeup or reproductive origin.

Notes

Chapter 1. Choosing for Children in an Era of Disintegrating Families

1. Don Browning and Carol Browning, "The Church and the Family Crisis: A New Love Ethic," *The Christian Century* 108 (August 7–14, 1991):747.
2. Ron Rosenbaum, "Staring into the Heart of Darkness," *New York Times Magazine* sect. 6 (June 4, 1995):36. Susan Smith was convicted of murder and sentenced to life imprisonment.
3. Don Browning and Ian Evison, "The Family Debate: A Middle Way," *The Christian Century* 110 (July 14–21, 1993):713. Since 1973 the Children's Defense Fund (CDF), headed by Marian Wright Edelman, has sought to draw attention to economic and political neglect of children in poverty. "Leave No Child Behind" names the nonpartisan campaign of CDF. Shannon P. Daley, writing on behalf of the CDF, says that every child needs a *healthy start* (basic health), a *head start* (quality child care and preschool), a *fair start* (a family with enough food and shelter to survive), and a *safe start* (protected from abuse) ("On the Welfare of Children," *Word and World* 15 [Winter 1995]:24–31).
4. "Americans don't hate their children—they just forget about them when they enter a voting booth" (*Focus on Children: The Beat of the Future,* Report of the 1992 Media Conference at the Columbia University Graduate School of Journalism sponsored by the Prudential Foundation, 14). Herbert Anderson and Susan B. W. Johnson contend that we need to foster a transformation from the *indifference that is* to the *interdependence that ought to characterize* our attitudes toward children and families in society (*Regarding Children: A New Respect for Childhood and Families* [Louisville, Ky.: Westminster John Knox Press 1994]).
5. See Arland Thornton, "Changing Attitudes Toward Family Issues in the United States," *Journal of Marriage and Family* 51 (1989):873–93.
6. David Popenoe, *Disturbing the Nest: Family Change and Decline in Modern Societies* (Hawthorne, New York: Aldine De Gruyter, 1988), xii.
7. Ibid., 31.
8. Ibid., 72.
9. Ibid., 47. See also pp. 58–89.
10. Ibid., 289.

11. Ibid., 52.
12. Ibid., 315.
13. Ibid., 301.
14. Ibid., 300.
15. Ibid., 326.
16. Ibid., 302.
17. Ibid., 309.
18. Ibid., 330.
19. Ibid., 331.
20. Ibid., 331.
21. Robert N. Bellah et al., eds., *The Good Society* (New York: Alfred A. Knopf, 1991), 46.
22. Ibid., 47.
23. Ibid., 48.
24. Ibid., 260.
25. Stanley Hauerwas, *A Community of Character* (Notre Dame, Ind.: University of Notre Dame Press, 1981), 161.
26. Ibid., 172.
27. Ibid., 191.
28. The category of unwanted children can also be formalized statistically as we approach the population-carrying capacity of the planet. "World population, now 5.7 billion, will rise to 8.5 billion by the year 2025. Family planning is no longer something we can ignore or fail to teach as stewards of the global family. We humans are becoming a menace to all other life and the non-human world. We are placing burdens on the environment that go beyond its carrying capacity. With the new discoveries being made in genetics, we must develop an ethic of gene stewardship" (Jerry L. Schmalenberger, "The Stewardship of the Family," *Currents in Theology and Mission* 22 [April 1995]:105).
29. Judith Bruce et al., eds., *Families in Focus: New Perspectives on Mothers, Fathers, and Children* (New York: The Population Council, 1995), 3.
30. Ibid., 41.
31. Ibid., 59.
32. Ibid., 75.
33. Ibid., 71.
34. Jean Bethke Elshtain and David Popenoe, *Marriage in America: A Report to the Nation* (New York: Institute for American Values, 1995), 3.
35. Ibid., 8.
36. Ibid., 11.
37. Don Browning, "The Family and the Male Problematic," *Dialog* 34 (Spring 1995):125.
38. "Though bound by allegiance to a compact and coherent set of doctrines, they [sociobiologists] go by different names: behavioral ecologists, Darwinian anthropologists, evolutionary psychologists, evolutionary psychiatrists" (Robert Wright, *The Moral Animal* [New York: Pantheon Books, 1994], 6).

39. Ibid., 127.

40. One of the interesting by-products of increased sophistication in DNA testing is the high frequency with which laboratories now uncover family secrets such as false paternity. When a fetus or child is being tested for genetic inheritance, quite frequently it is determined that the man purported to be the child's father is not. Cuckoldry may be more widespread than ordinarily thought. "Blood tests show that in some urban areas more than one fourth of the children may be sired by someone other than the father of record" (Wright, *Moral Animal*, 70). This creates ethical dilemmas in genetic counseling regarding to whom this information should be disclosed and under what conditions.

41. Evolutionary ethicist Michael Ruse makes this clear, "When it comes to ultimate foundations, the evolutionist and the Christian part company. For the evolutionist, morality—that which yields standards of right and wrong—rests in the contingencies of human nature. In an important sense, therefore, there are no ultimate foundations, just a biological illusion of objectivity. For the Christian, morality simply has to be more than this . . ." ("Evolutionary Theory and Christian Ethics," *Zygon* 29 [March 1994]:5–24, 23). Robert Wright would agree, "Brotherly love in the literal sense comes at the expense of brotherly love in the biblical sense; the more precisely we bestow unconditional kindness on relatives, the less of it is left over for others" (*Moral Animal*, 160).

42. Thomas Aquinas, *The Summa Contra Gentiles*, III:ii, trans. English Dominican Fathers (London: Burns, Oates & Washbourne, 1928), 117.

43. Ibid., 118.

44. Martin Luther, "The Estate of Marriage," in *Luther's Works*, vol. 45, ed. Helmut T. Lehman (Minneapolis: Augsburg Fortress Press, 1962):39.

45. Browning, "The Family and the Male Problematic," 128.

46. Don Browning, "Altruism and Christian Love," *Zygon* 27 (December 1992):421–36, 423.

47. Ibid., 435.

48. Well, perhaps a sociobiologist might have an explanation. Cain would not have killed Abel had they been identical twins and shared all their genes. But as mere brothers, they shared only half their genes. So, murder becomes an option. "Even pure sibling love—brotherly love—isn't love," says Robert Wright. He recalls J.B.S. Haldane saying that he would never die for a brother—but rather for two brothers or eight cousins (*Moral Animal*, 165). According to this theory, suicide (at least prior to reproduction) should never happen.

49. Evolutionary psychologist Robert Wright argues, "At some point . . . *male parental investment* [MPI] entered our evolutionary lineage. We are, as they say in the zoology literature, high in MPI. . . . Genes inclining a male to love his offspring—to worry about them, defend them, provide for them, educate them—could flourish at the expense of genes that counseled continued remoteness" (*Moral Animal*, 57–58). Yet, today father remoteness is the problem. How do we explain this genetically? We don't. Or, do we?

In a *Time* cover article addressed in part to the Unabomber's ego by clobbering modern technological society, Wright argues that there is a mismatch between our genetic makeup and the modern world. Evolution had intended for us to live in small intimate communities, not in the individual isolation pressed upon us by the industrial way of life. This explains the prevalence of stress, anxiety, and depression ("The Evolution of Despair," *Time,* 146 [August 28, 1995]:50–57). It may also explain deadbeat dads: deadbeat dadism would be due not to genes but to technological society. But, I might ask, do genes explain technological society? By adding enough auxiliary hypotheses to the hardcore theory, sociobiology seems to be able to explain just about everything, *ex post facto* that is.

50. "In Whose Best Interest?" was the way Nancy Gibbs titled her treatment of the legal debacle that saw Baby Jessica taken from her adoptive parents, Jan and Roberta DeBoer, and returned to her biological parents, Dan and Cara Schmidt (*Time* 142 [July 19, 1993]:44–51).

51. Michelle Stanworth, *Reproductive Technologies: Gender, Motherhood, and Medicine* (Minneapolis: University of Minnesota Press, 1987), 20.

52. Ibid., 21.

53. John Calvin, *Institutes of the Christian Religion,* Library of Christian Classics, vol. 20, ed. John T. McNeill and trans. Ford Lewis Battles (Louisville, Ky.: Westminster/John Knox Press, 1960), 418–19. The love commandment in this strong sense is incompatible with kin altruism in sociobiology. "The exhortation is to love everyone: family, friend, nodding acquaintance, and enemy, and apparently no distinctions are to be drawn. Indeed, one is to forgive enemies, virtually without limit. . . . This is unacceptable to the evolutionist" (Ruse, "Evolutionary Theory and Christian Ethics," 17).

54. This is the theme of Paul R. Sponheim's helpful work, *Faith and the Other* (Minneapolis: Fortress Press, 1993).

55. Assertion made during the annual "Religion, Culture and Family Project" meeting hosted by the University of Chicago, September 17, 1995. Elsewhere she writes, "the goal of feminism at its best has always been a better human community, not just a defense of women" (*After Eden: Facing the Challenge of Gender Reconciliation,* ed. Mary Stewart Van Leeuwen et. al. [Grand Rapids: Wm. B. Eerdmans Publishing Co., 1993] 106).

Chapter 2. Multiple Choice in Baby Making

1. Christopher Morse, *Not Every Spirit: A Dogmatic of Christian Disbelief* (Valley Forge, Penn.: Trinity Press International, 1994), 274.

2. Not all infertility stories finish with a happy ending. When they don't we should not allow stigma—even the stigma we might hold against ourselves—to make matters worse. James Dobson's *Focus on the Family* (November 1994) sensitively draws attention to the deep grief some infertile

couples feel when they try the various reproductive technologies but still fail to bring a child into the world. It just may be God's will to remain childless, says Dobson, and our task as persons of faith is to accept God's will. Yes, infertility is a major life crisis, but the status of parenthood does not define who we are before God; nor should it before our friends and colleagues.

3. A most unusual success story occurred with an IVF in March 1993 that resulted in twin boys, Teun and Koen, for a small town family in the Netherlands. Though born together, Teun is white and Koen black. The reproductive clinic apologized for the mistake saying, "We suspect that a technician broke the rules and used a pipette that was not clean," thereby adding the sperm of a man from Aruba to the sperm of the Dutch father. Terrified at the thought that the AID father might want to claim Koen for himself, the social family has hired a lawyer. They said they love the child and would not dream of giving him up. See Marlise Simons, "Uproar Over Twins, and a Dutch Couple's Anguish," *New York Times,* International Edition sec. A (June 28, 1995):3.

4. "Fetal Egg-Cell Research Scare," *Science* 265 (July 29, 1994):608.

5. David M. Feldman, "The Ethical Implications of New Reproductive Techniques," in *Jewish Values in Bioethics,* ed. Levi Meier (New York: Human Sciences Press, 1986), 181.

6. Joseph Fletcher, *Ethics of Genetic Control* (Buffalo, N.Y.: Prometheus, 1988), 41.

7. Resolve, Inc., P.O. Box 474, Belmont, MA 02178.

8. Carol Gilligan, *In a Different Voice: Psychological Theory and Women's Development* (Cambridge: Harvard University Press, 1982).

9. John A. Robertson, *Children of Choice: Freedom and the New Reproductive Technologies* (Princeton: Princeton University Press, 1994), 5.

10. Ibid., 35.

11. Ibid.

12. Ibid., 150.

13. Ibid., 151.

14. Ibid., 150.

15. Ibid., 151.

16. Lisa Sowle Cahill, *Sex, Gender, and Christian Ethics* (Cambridge: Cambridge University Press, 1996), chapter 7; cited here in prepublication manuscript form.

17. Ibid.

18. Lisa Cahill does not fit squarely in the essentialist camp, as we will see when we look more closely at her important work in a later chapter. Rather than emphasize the exclusive mother-fetus bond as essential and inviolable, it is the bond between the child and the two parents that demands her attention.

19. Robertson, *Children of Choice,* 229. Radical or anti-essentialist feminism— to be distinguished from liberal socialist feminism or cultural feminism

wherein women have an essential nature distinguishable from men— translates what we previously thought was *natural* into *political* terms. From a radical feminist perspective, for a woman to pursue fulfillment through motherhood is a political, not a natural, desire. Embracing this view, Janice G. Raymond attacks John Robertson and the concept of procreative liberty. She says that choice does not in fact amount to self-determination for women, because the range of choices offered by reproductive technology is determined by a patriarchal system of exploiting women's bodies. "What defenders of new reproductive techniques regard as natural, feminists challenge as political. . . . Feminists oppose the idea that reproduction is a biological imperative. . . . The new reproductive technologies represent an appropriation by male scientific experts of the female body, depoliticizing reproduction and motherhood by recasting these roles as fundamental instincts that must be satisfied. . . . Much of technological reproduction is brutality with a therapeutic face" (*Women as Wombs* [San Francisco: Harper San Francisco, 1993], xviii–xix).

20. Pope John Paul II, "The Gospel of Life," *Evangelium vitae,* III: 60 (New York: Random House, Times Books, 1995), 107.

21. Robertson, *Children of Choice,* 166.

22. Ibid., 233.

23. If babies are persons, we may love them but we do not own them. However, we might forget this when thinking in terms of production—what Vanderbilt University ethicist Bonnie J. Miller-McLemore dubs "generativity"—because we inadvertently think we own what we produce. "Generativity implies that one owns what one produces. Yet we never own our children. Children come to us as gifts; in their case, not even biology can determine ownership" ("Produce or Perish: Generativity and New Reproductive Technologies," *Journal of the American Academy of Religion* 59 [1992]:39–69, 56).

24. Congregation for the Doctrine of the Faith, *Instruction on Respect for Human life in Its Origin and on the Dignity of Procreation: Replies to Certain Questions of the Day,* in Thomas A. Shannon, *Bioethics,* 3rd ed. (Mahwah, N.J.: Paulist Press, 1987), 591–92.

25. According to some views, creationism also refers to the creation of the soul at birth. It has been upheld since the days of Jerome in opposition to two alternative views, pre-existence and traducianism (sometimes called generationism). Origen and others held that each soul pre-exists and becomes incarnate at birth. Traducianists, such as Tertullian and Gregory of Nyssa, held that the human soul is transmitted by parents to children, usually through the physical act of generation. The Vatican today apparently adheres to the creationist position.

26. *Instruction,* in Shannon, *Bioethics,* 3rd ed., 595.

27. Ibid., 591–92.

28. Ibid., 609. The focus on the individual sex act is characteristic of the Vat-

ican but not of Lisa Sowle Cahill's ethics, as we will see when we return to this issue.

29. Ibid.

30. Vladimir Solovyev, *The Meaning of Love,* trans. Jane Marshall (London: Geoffrey Bles, The Centenary Press, 1945), 30.

31. Ibid., 31.

Chapter 3. Surrogate Motherhood: An Ethical Puzzle

1. Margaret Atwood, *The Handmaid's Tale* (New York: Fawcett Crest, 1985).

2. Congregation for the Doctrine of the Faith, *Instruction on Respect for Human Life in Its Origin and on the Dignity of Procreation. Replies to Certain Questions of the Day,* II:A:2 in *Bioethics,* 3rd ed., ed. Thomas A. Shannon (Mahwah, N.J.: Paulist Press, 1987), 604. See also Thomas A. Shannon and Lisa Sowle Cahill, *Religion and Artificial Reproduction* (New York: Crossroad, 1988), 160.

3. *Instruction* in Shannon, *Bioethics,* 3rd ed., 605.

4. A feminist reading says that the "real moral of the story of Abraham, Sarah, and Haagar" is patriarchy. "Nobody ever questioned that Haagar was the mother, but what earthly difference did it make who was the mother? Abraham was the father. The children, whether they came through Sarah, through Haagar, or from the sky, were Abraham's children and that is what counted; they were his seed. Mothers are pretty much dismissable" (Barbara Katz Rothman, "Reproductive Technologies and Surrogacy: A Feminist Perspective," *Creighton Law Review* 25 [1992]:1601).

5. Jon D. Levenson, *The Death and Resurrection of the Beloved Son* (New Haven, Conn.: Yale University Press, 1993), 92. Walter Brueggemann's interpretation differs. He sees Abraham and Sarah as so overwhelmed by the scandal of God's promise that they cannot reasonably maintain their faith in it. "Israel stands before God's word of promise but characteristically finds that word beyond reason and belief. Abraham, and especially Sarah, are not offered here as models of faith but as models of disbelief. For them, the powerful promise of God outdistances their ability to receive it" (*Genesis,* Interpretation (Louisville, Ky.: Westminster/John Knox Press, 1982), 158.

6. Levenson, *Death and Resurrection,* 92. Note that Sarai and Abram were not renamed Sarah and Abraham until Genesis 17.

7. Ibid., 41–42.

8. Shannon and Cahill, *Religion and Artificial Reproduction,* 136.

9. Instructive here is the work of John A. Robertson, *Children of Choice: Freedom and the New Reproductive Technologies* (Princeton, N.J.: Princeton University Press, 1994) and, also by Robertson, "Surrogate Mothers: Not So Novel After All," *The Hastings Center Report* 13 (October 1983):28–34; and Herbert T. Krimmel, "The Case Against Surrogate Parenting," *The Hastings*

Center Report 13 (October 1983):35–39. Both articles were reprinted in *Taking Sides: Clashing Views on Controversial Bioethical Issues,* 4th ed., ed. Carol Levine (Guilford, Conn.: Dushkin, 1991), 40–57. See also Maura A. Ryan, "The Argument for Unlimited Procreative Liberty: A Feminist Critique," *The Hastings Center Report* 20 (July/August 1990):6–12.

10. Bruce R. Reichenbach and V. Elving Anderson, *On Behalf of God: A Christian Ethic for Biology* (Grand Rapids: Wm. B. Eerdmans Publishing Co., 1995), 157.

11. Leon R. Kass, M.D., "Making Babies Revisited" in Shannon, *Bioethics,* 3rd ed., 466.

12. Ibid.

13. Paul Lauritzen, *Pursuing Parenthood: Ethical Issues in Assisted Reproduction* (Bloomington, Ind.: Indiana University Press, 1993), 111–12.

14. Robertson, *Children of Choice,* 140.

15. Sharon Elizabeth Rush, "Breaking with Tradition: Surrogacy and Gay Fathers," in *Kindred Matters: Rethinking the Philosophy of the Family,* ed. Diana Tietjens Meyers et al. (Ithaca, N.Y.: Cornell University Press, 1993), 127.

16. Reichenbach and Anderson, *On Behalf of God,* 154.

17. Robertson, *Children of Choice,* 227. The sworn enemy of Robertson's procreative liberty, Janice G. Raymond, argues that the issue of surrogacy payment cannot be divorced from the wider issue of economic oppression of women. "Choice is not the same as self-determination. Choice can be conformity if women have little ability to determine the conditions of consent. . . . A woman who signs a surrogate contract, agreeing to bear a child for a contracting couple, consents to the arrangement, but she has little self-determination if she cannot find sustaining and dignified work and resorts to surrogacy as a final economic resort. Feminists must go beyond choice and consent as a standard for women's freedom" (*Women as Wombs* [San Francisco: Harper San Francisco, 1993], 103).

18. Barbara Katz Rothman, *Recreating Motherhood: Ideology and Technology in a Patriarchal Society* (New York: W.W. Norton, 1989), 236.

19. Rush, "Breaking with Tradition," in *Kindred Matters,* 132–33.

20. Ibid., 138.

21. Elizabeth S. Anderson, "Is Women's Labor a Commodity?" in *Contemporary Issues in Bioethics,* ed. Tom L. Beauchamp and LeRoy Walters (Belmont, Calif.: Wadsworth, 1994), 237–38.

22. Ibid., 240.

23. Rothman, *Recreating Motherhood,* 233. But Rothman is thinking here only of genetic-gestational surrogacy where the surrogate mother provides her own ovum. Admittedly, this calls for serious examination. Rothman's judgment about baby selling does not apply necessarily to IVF-gestational surrogacy, however, where the surrogate has no genetic relationship to the child she carries. In general, Rothman is very helpful in warning us against the dangers of commodifying children. "While on the one hand we are trying to think of children as people, deserving respect and needing care, on

the other hand our society is also coming to think of children as products . . . as objects, as commodities . . . " (Ibid., 19).

24. Rush, "Breaking with Tradition," in *Kindred Matters,* 124.

25. *New York Times* (January 28, 1983):18; cited by Robertson in "Surrogate Mothers," 32.

26. Krimmel, "The Case Against Surrogate Parenting," 35.

27. Ibid., 36–37.

28. *In re Baby M,* 217 NJ 313, 525 A2d 1128 (1987).

29. George J. Annas sharply criticizes Judge Sorkow for inconsistencies and for bias in favor of the upper middle-class Stern family and against the lower middle-class Whitehead family. "Baby M: Babies (and Justice) for Sale," *The Hastings Center Report* 17 (June 1987):13–15. Feminists would add that a residual patriarchy pervades the whole incident, because the genetic and gestational mother was not given treatment equal to that of the genetic father. Rothman writes about Mr. Stern, "had that man gone into a bar and picked up a devout seventeen-year-old Catholic girl who would not have an abortion, seduced her, sent her two maternity smocks, a layette, and a basket of flowers, he could then claim paternity and take the baby from her in a custody battle. He would have been exactly where he ended up—with custody of a child even though the mother is still legally the mother" ("Reproductive Technologies and Surrogacy, 1602).

30. *In re Baby M,* 109 NJ 396, 537 A2d 227 (1988).

31. *In re Baby M,* 525 A2d 1159.

32. Lisa Sowle Cahill, who wants to protect the role that biological inheritance plays in parenting, is critical of Judge Sorkow. "The best interests standard has the potential to reconcile consideration both of intentional commitment and of socially recognized biological relation, by focusing on the need of a child for both and on the necessity to balance these needs within the parameters of the options practically available in specific cases. However, in Judge Sorkow's interpretation of best interests, the interrelational aspects of parenthood not only take precedence over the biological, as they properly should, but function as virtually the sole criterion of best interests, as they should not" ("The Ethics of Surrogate Motherhood: Biology, Freedom, and Moral Obligation," *Law, Medicine, and Health Care,* 16:1–2 [Spring 1988]:67–68).

33. *In re Baby M,* 525 A2d 1164.

34. *Johnson v. Calvert,* 63 Orange County Superior Court, CA 31, 7 (1990).

35. Ibid., 5.

36. Ibid., 8.

37. That this is a propitious time for undertaking this fundamental re-thinking of the parent-child relationship is the position taken by Walter J. Wadlington, "Contracts to Bear a Child: The Mixed Legislative Signals," *Idaho Law Review* 29 (1992–1993):382–410.

38. According to Wadlington, "Our expanded understanding of genetics and

biology may force us to further review the already eroding law that relies so heavily on blood kinship" (Ibid., 407).

39. Policy Statement, National Coalition Against Surrogacy, 1130 17th St., NW, Suite 630, Washington, DC 20036.

40. Andrew Kimbrell, "The Case Against the Commercialization of Child-bearing," *Willamette Law Review* 24 (Fall 1988) 1035–49, 1036.

41. Ibid., 1049–50.

42. Juliette Zipper and Selma Svenhuijsen, "Surrogacy: Feminist Notions of Motherhood Reconsidered," in *Reproductive Technologies: Gender, Motherhood, and Medicine,* ed. Michelle Stanworth (Minneapolis: University of Minnesota Press, 1987), 126.

43. Michelle Stanworth, "Editor's Introduction," in *Reproductive Technologies,* 4.

44. Ibid., 15–16.

45. Lisa Sowle Cahill, *Sex, Gender, and Christian Ethics,* (Cambridge: Cambridge University Press, 1996), chap. 8.

46. Ibid., 52.

47. Jean Bethke Elshtain, "Reflections on Abortion, Values, and the Family," *Abortion: Understanding Differences,* ed. Sidney Callahan and Daniel Callahan (New York: Plenum Press, 1984), 59.

48. Ibid., 62.

49. Ibid., 66.

50. Maura A. Ryan, "The Argument for Unlimited Procreative Liberty: A Feminist Critique," *The Hastings Center Report,* 20 (July/August 1990):6–12, 11.

51. James Lindemann Nelson, "Parental Obligations and the Ethics of Surrogacy: A Causal Perspective," *Public Affairs Quarterly* 5 (January 1991): 49–61, 54.

52. Hilde Lindemann Nelson and James Lindemann Nelson, "Cutting Motherhood in Two: Some Suspicions Concerning Surrogacy," *Hypatia* 4 (Fall 1989):85–94, 87.

53. Ibid., 90.

54. Rothman, *Recreating Motherhood,* 239.

55. Ibid., 237–38.

56. Ibid., 241. Paul Lauritzen follows Rothman here. "We need not invoke any mystical notions about pregnancy nor infant-mother bonding to acknowledge that pregnancy is both unique and not properly described by the language of gestational services. A pregnant woman does not simply provide a womb for rent. She puts her entire body to the task of nurturing the developing fetus for nine months. . . . Gestational motherhood is not really a service, certainly not a commodity; rather, it is a relationship" (*Pursuing Parenthood,* 105).

57. Robertson, *Children of Choice,* 131–32. Not everyone is likely to be convinced by Robertson's paternalist argument favoring surrogacy. Paul Lauritzen, for example, says that "the argument that surrogacy should be per-

mitted because any state restriction would be unjustifiably paternalistic ultimately rests on a false or misleading view of pregnancy" (*Pursuing Parenthood*, 103). Pregnancy is not like other commercial services we human beings can render for sale, he contends; rather, it is a unique experience of bonding between mother and child. So Lauritzen would outlaw surrogacy. His argument against surrogacy does not call into question a woman's right to bodily autonomy or her rational capacity to make decisions. "Rather, the argument is that certain rights should be inalienable because to put a price on these rights and offer them for sale is essentially dehumanizing" (Ibid., 104).

58. Cahill does not belong squarely in the essentialist feminist camp. She is a biological essentialist with regard to parenting in general, but she is reluctant to grant maternal essentialism to the woman in particular. She writes, "Although I concur with the basic feminist critique of the patriarchal family and of notions of women's maternal nature that served to perpetuate it, I do not believe it is necessary to give up appeals to nature altogether, including parental nature. . . . I think it is a mistake to argue against reproductive technologies (especially the use of women as donors and surrogates) by returning to social definitions of maternal nature. . . . In any event, maternal nature would have as its corollary paternal nature. . . . I see the common bonds and obligations of parental nature as morally and experientially more important than the differences in styles of parenthood that men and women may well have" (Lisa Sowle Cahill, "Women, Marriage, Parenthood: What Are Their Natures?" *Logos: Philosophic Studies from Santa Clara University* 9 [1988]:32).

59. Cahill, "The Ethics of Surrogate Motherhood," 69.

60. Ibid., 71.

61. Ibid., 71.

62. Lisa Sowle Cahill, "Manufactured Motherhood," *Santa Clara Magazine* 31 (Winter 1989), 13.

Chapter 4. Designer Genes and Selective Abortion

1. Theodore G. Tappert and Helmut T. Lehman, eds.: *Luther's Works*, vol. 54, trans. Theodore G. Tappert (Minneapolis: Augsburg Publishing House, 1967), 158.

2. "Although the old eugenic generalizations have been cast off, the logic behind them persists, refueled by evidence from diagnostic tests and justified in terms of efficiency, effectiveness, and cost" (Dorothy Nelkin and Laurence Tancredi, *Dangerous Diagnostics* [New York: Harper, Basic Books, 1989], 13).

3. "Genetic tests could foster a new eugenics in which pressure is exerted on women whose offspring would be at risk to avoid their conception or birth" (Neil A. Holtzman, *Proceed with Caution: Predicting Genetic Risks in*

the Recombinant DNA Era [Baltimore: Johns Hopkins University Press, 1989], 8).

4. "Designing Genetic Information Policy: The Need for an Independent Policy Review of the Ethical, Legal, and Social Implications of the Human Genome Project," Sixteenth Report by the Committee on Government Operations (Washington: U.S. Government Printing Office, April 2, 1992), 15, 19.

5. Ibid., 21.

6. National Center for Human Genome Research, *Genetic Information and Health Insurance,* NIH Publication No. 93–3686 (Washington, D.C., May 10, 1993), 2.

7. The threat of extra costs of raising a child with a genetic disorder "might increase the pressure on parents and adoption agencies to provide more complete genetic profiles of babies who are up for adoption, which in turn might increase the incidence of rejecting infants because of their genetic propensities" (Holtzman, *Proceed with Caution,* 192).

8. Sheryl Stolberg, "Insurance Falls Prey to Genetic Bias," *Los Angeles Times* sec. A (March 27, 1994):20.

9. Choice of language here is important, though in itself not morally decisive. Bioethicist John C. Fletcher reminds us that "abortion kills the fetus, an act that cannot be disguised by applying such qualifying terms as 'selective,' 'elective,' or 'therapeutic,' or referring to the act as 'termination of pregnancy'" ("Moral Problems and Ethical Guidance in Prenatal Diagnosis," in *Genetic Disorders and the Fetus* 2nd ed., ed. Aubrey Milunsky [New York: Plenum Press, 1986], 824). George McKenna observes that even those who favor abortion want it to be "safe, legal, and rare." Why rare? He takes note of expressions substituted for the word *abortion* such as *termination of pregnancy* as well as references to abortion clinics as *reproductive health clinics.* He asks whether this language is trying to cover up something troubling. "The obvious answer is that abortion is troubling because it is a killing process. Abortion clinics may indeed be places of healing and care, as the Planned Parenthood counselor maintains, but their primary purpose is to kill human fetuses" ("On Abortion: A Lincolnian Position," *The Atlantic Monthly* 276 [September 1995]:54). The language battle described here is fought at the professional and ideological level. The genetic counselor confronts women or couples dealing with existential decisions at a personal level. At this level human intuition seems to presume that the unborn fetus is a person deserving regard, if not devotion. This can remain true even when the decision to abort is made.

10. According to Milunsky, "over 95 percent of such couples do not need to consider elective abortion. The few who are initially ambivalent almost invariably move to terminate the pregnancy following detection of a serious fetal defect" (*Genetic Disorders,* 9). Genetic disorder is not the only grounds for selective abortion. Increasingly pregnancy reduction has become a normative practice. When twin, triplet, or more embryos are discovered im-

planted in the mother's womb, and it is thought that not all can be brought to viability, the number of fetuses will be reduced in order to increase the chance that one, or perhaps two, will survive in healthy fashion. Rather than use the term *abortion,* this is called *selective feticide* in behalf of *selective birth* (Ibid., 830).

11. Compassion need not be applied only to the unborn child in question but rather to all involved. John C. Fletcher warns that "choosing not to abort in pregnancies of high genetic or social risk can result in serious harm for the woman, the couple, the family, and the affected individual . . . with consequences that cannot be put aside by referring to the outcome as a 'gift of God' or as an event that draws family members together" ("Moral Problems," in Milunsky, *Genetic Disorders,* 824).

12. Currently half of all pregnancies in California are terminated by abortion, with the vast majority due simply to the choice of the mother and not because of medical reasons. If this practice continues, then the total number of abortions may not rise dramatically, just the number in the genetic selection category.

13. Marsha Saxton, "Prenatal Screening and Discriminatory Attitudes About Disability." *Genewatch* 4 (1987):8–10; cited by Holtzman, *Proceed with Caution,* 216.

14. Caring for discarded or marginalized persons is the clear Christian mandate. It is the work of redemption in a world that is already a mess. At a more abstract level, the ethicist can ask: Should we create a mess? To this Paul Ramsey answers: no. "Men and women have no unqualified right to have children. The treatments for the prevention of cystic fibrosis, Huntington's chorea, achondroplasia, some forms of muscular dystrophy, PKU, amaurotic [familial] idiocy, and other chromosomal abnormalities . . . are continence, not getting married to a particular person, not having any children, using three contraceptives at once, or sterilization" (*Fabricated Man: The Ethics of Genetic Control* [New Haven, Conn.: Yale University Press, 1970], 120).

15. A woman's choice may be further influenced by procedural requirements. At issue in *Planned Parenthood of Southeastern Pennsylvania v. Casey* (112 US 2791 [1992]) is the right of the state to regulate abortion. Pennsylvania was requiring that doctors give prescribed information to women seeking abortions; that a woman wait 24 hours between counseling and undergoing the abortion procedure; that minors obtain parental consent; and that married women notify their spouses. The U.S. Supreme Court upheld the first three regulations but rejected the fourth: spousal notification.

16. Stephen L. Carter, *The Culture of Disbelief* (New York: HarperCollins, Basic Books, 1993) 252–53.

17. This answer was not good enough for the key person in *Roe v. Wade,* namely, Jane Roe. Changing her name to Norma McCorvey, "Jane Roe" changed her mind. On Tuesday, August 8, 1995, she was baptized by Reverend Flip Benham of the antiabortion group, Operation Rescue. Ms.

McCorvey now opposes abortion after the first trimester of pregnancy. See Sam Hverhovek, "New Twist for a Landmark Case: *Roe v. Wade* Becomes *Roe v. Roe,*" *New York Times* sec. A (August 12, 1995):1, 7; and Mark A. Kellner, "Jane Roe Plaintiff Joins Pro-Life Movement," *Christianity Today* 39 (September 11, 1995):70.

18. British Council of Churches, *Human Reproduction,* 1962. See British Medical Association, *Medical Ethics Today* (London: British Medical Journal, 1993):102. In the United States, radical pro-choice feminists fear the advance of reproductive technology because it draws attention to the child-to-be, the fetus, independently of the mother. Because maintaining the woman's right to choose an abortion is the bottom line, the scientific distinction between the fetus and the mother's body is perceived as a political threat. Janice G. Raymond's attack against procreative liberty is a case in point. "Whether in the womb or outside, attention is riveted on the fetus as an individual entity. . . . Reproductive technologies and contracts augment the rights of fetuses and would-be fathers. . . . Those who *support* and *promote* technological and contractual reproduction are *undermining* women's reproductive rights, especially women's right to abortion" (*Women as Wombs* [San Francisco: Harper San Francisco, 1993]), xi, author's italics).

19. John T. Noonan, Jr., statement before the New York State Legislature during debate on a bill to reform the state's abortion law in Spring 1968; cited by Daniel Callahan, *Abortion: Law, Choice and Morality* (New York: Macmillan Publishing Company, 1970), 379.

20. John T. Noonan, Jr., "Abortion and the Catholic Church: A Summary History," *Natural Law Forum* 12 (1967):128–29; cited by Callahan, *Abortion,* 379.

21. Paul Ramsey, "The Morality of Abortion," in *Life or Death: Ethics and Opinions,* ed. Edward Shils et al. (Seattle: University of Washington Press, 1968), 61–62, cited in Callahan, *Abortion,* 379. Ramsey writes, "Microgenetics seems to have demonstrated what religion never could; and biological science to have resolved an ancient theological dispute. . . . Thus, it might be said that the individual is whoever he is going to become from the moment of impregnation. Thereafter, his subsequent development may be described as a process of becoming the one he already is. Genetics teaches that we are from the beginning what we essentially are in every cell . . . " ("The Sanctity of Life: In the First of It," *The Dublin Review* [Spring 1967]:1–2).

22. Callahan, *Abortion,* 383.

23. Congregation for the Doctrine of the Faith, *Instruction on Respect for Human Life in Its Origin and on the Dignity of Procreation: Replies to Certain Questions of the Day* in *Bioethics,* 3rd ed., ed. Thomas A. Shannon (Mahwah, N.J.: Paulist Press, 1987), 597.

24. James Dobson, "Who We Are and What We Stand For," *Focus on the Family* (August 1993):12.

25. *Time* 146 (September 11, 1995):35.
26. John A. Robertson, *Children of Choice: Freedom and the New Reproductive Technologies* (Princeton: Princeton University Press, 1994), 50–53.
27. Malcolm Potts, "The Problem of Abortion," in *Biology and Ethics* ed. F. J. Ebeling (New York: Academic Press, 1969), 77–78; see Callahan, *Abortion,* 385.
28. Robertson, *Children of Choice,* 158.
29. Fletcher, "Moral Problems," in Milunsky, *Genetic Disorders,* 826.
30. Callahan, *Abortion* 388–89.
31. Garrett Hardin, "Abortion—Or Compulsory Pregnancy?" *Journal of Marriage and Family* 30 (May 1968):250, cited by Callahan, *Abortion,* 391.
32. More recently Beverly Wildung Harrison at Union Seminary in New York has argued against describing a fetus prior to the midpoint of pregnancy as "a person" and that "the constitutive foundations of personality are bound up not with biological maturation of the human species life form but with the quality of our social relations." She argues that rights are to be socially conceived, and that the victimage of women in history is as much a factor in abortion as the biological status of the fetus as a human life ("Our Right to Choose," in *Taking Sides: Clashing Views on Controversial Bioethical Issues,* 4th ed., ed. Carol Levine [Guilford, Conn: Dushkin, 1991]), 6. Sidney Callahan, in contrast, argues for a pro-life feminism that goes beyond the pro-choice feminist reliance on the individual woman's choice to a more relational vision, according to which both the fetus and the pregnant mother share in social community. She claims "good feminist principles" require opposition to abortion ("Abortion and the Sexual Agenda: A Case for Prolife Feminism," in Levine, *Taking Sides,* 9).
33. Callahan, *Abortion,* 396.
34. Ibid., 397.
35. For Callahan to see abortion as a first line of defense against pregnancy fails to acknowledge that many women who seek an abortion had been using a contraceptive method that for some reason or another did not work. Abortion is still a second line of defense.
36. Daniel Callahan, "An Ethical Challenge to Prochoice Advocates," *Commonweal* 117 (November 23, 1990):681–87; reprinted in Shannon, *Bioethics,* 4th ed. (Mahwah, N.J.: Paulist Press, 1993), 21–35. M. Christian Green, seeking a way through the impasse between pro-choice and pro-life advocates, recommends that just war theory be applied to the ethical debate. Although frequently unacknowledged, Green observes that ethicists on both sides, as well as Supreme Court decisions, appeal to some if not all just war criteria when deliberating abortion issues. Because this is the case, a conscious appeal to just war theory may lead to increased common ground and cooperation ("The Function of Just War Theory in the Abortion Debate," M.T.S. Thesis, Candler School of Theology, Emory University, 1995).
37. Pope John Paul II, *Evangelium Vitae* (The Gospel of Life) (New York:

Random House, Times Books, 1995), 104. The pope is skeptical about the morality of capital punishment even when a crime has been committed, and following Pius XII, he is reluctant to view the fetus as the unjust aggressor against the mother—even when the fetus endangers the mother's life—thus deserving of the death penalty.

38. Sidney Callahan, "Value Choices in Abortion," in *Abortion: Understanding Differences,* ed. Sidney Callahan and Daniel Callahan (New York: Plenum Press, 1984), 296.

39. Pope John Paul II, *The Gospel of Life,* 113.

40. Ibid., 114.

41. Ibid., 107.

42. Ibid., 108.

43. Ibid., 97.

44. Ibid., 112.

45. Ibid.

46. *Instruction* in Shannon, *Bioethics,* 3rd ed., 596.

47. Lisa Sowle Cahill, "*In Vitro* Fertilization: Ethical Issues in Judeo-Christian Perspective," *Loyola Law Review* 32 (1988):348, 350.

48. Ibid., 349. Because recent discussion has focused on the prospect of twinning between fertilization and implantation since this passage was written, Cahill today would substitute "from implantation" for "from fertilization."

49. Ibid., 353. See Thomas A. Shannon and Lisa Sowle Cahill, *Religion and Artificial Reproduction* (New York: Crossroad, 1988).

50. Sissela Bok, analyzing *Roe v. Wade,* writes, "I find I cannot use words like 'deprived,' 'deny,' 'take away,' and 'harm,' when it comes to the group of cells. . . . If, therefore, very early abortion does not violate these principles for the protection for life, but infanticide does, we are confronted with a new kind of continuum in the place of that between less human and more human. . . . It would be preferable to encourage early abortions rather than late ones. . . . For this purpose, the two concepts of *quickening* and *viability*—so unsatisfactory in determining when humanity begins—can provide such limits" ("Ethical Problems of Abortion," in Shannon, *Bioethics,* 3rd ed., 32–33.

51. Lisa Sowle Cahill, "The Embryo and the Fetus: New Moral Contexts," *Theological Studies* 54 (March 1993):128.

52. Bruce R. Reichenbach and V. Elving Anderson, *On Behalf of God: A Christian Ethic for Biology* (Grand Rapids: Wm B. Eerdmans Publishing Co., 1995), 166.

53. Ibid., 116.

54. Norman M. Ford, *When Did I Begin?* (Cambridge: Cambridge University Press, 1988), 170. "It seems that the biological evidence leads to the philosophical conclusion that a human individual, our youngest neighbour and member of the human community, begins at the primitive streak stage and not prior to it, but most certainly by the stage of gastrulation when the human embryo's primitive cardiovascular system is already functioning and blood is circulating" (Ibid., xviii).

55. Ibid., 172.

56. Thomas A. Shannon and Allan B. Wolter, O.F.M., "Reflections on the Moral Status of the Pre-Embryo," in Shannon, *Bioethics*, 4th ed., 43. Following Roman Catholic tradition Shannon and Wolter distinguish active conception, physical union of egg and sperm, from passive conception at the moment when the rational soul is infused into the physical body (Ibid., 48).

57. Ibid., 53.

58. Evangelical Lutheran Church in America, "A Social Statement on Abortion" adopted at the meeting of the second biennial Churchwide Assembly of the Evangelical Lutheran Church in America, Orlando, Fla., August 28–September 4, 1991). Hereinafter referred to as Lutheran.

59. United Methodist Church, "Genetic Task Force Report to the 1992 General Conference." Hereinafter referred to as Methodist.

60. World Council of Churches, "Biotechnology: Its Challenges to the Churches and the World," (Geneva, Switzerland: August 1989), 31–32. World Council of Churches, P.O. Box 2100, 1211 Geneva 2, Switzerland. Hereinafter referred to as WCC.

61. The Division of Mission in Canada, "A Brief to the Royal Commission on New Reproductive Technologies on behalf of The United Church of Canada" (January 17, 1991) 13–14.

62. United Church of Christ, "The Church and Genetic Engineering" (Pronouncement of the Seventeenth General Synod, Fort Worth, Tex., 1989), 4. Hereinafter referred to as UCC.

63. Ronald Cole-Turner, "Genetics and the Church," *Prism* 6 (Spring 1991): 57.

Chapter 5. Sex and Baby Making in Christian Thought

1. Augustine, "On the Good of Marriage" (*De Bono Conjugali*), 31; "On Marriage and Concupiscence" (*De Nuptiis et Concupiscientia*), 19; and "On Original Sin" (*De Peccato Originali*), 44. Thomas A. Shannon and Lisa Sowle Cahill comment, "More definitively than in any other author, the Christian tradition in Augustine sets parenthood as the agenda of the sexual life, and establishes the marriage of one man and one woman as the framework within which this agenda is to be fulfilled" (*Religion and Artificial Reproduction* [New York: Crossroad, 1988], 36).

2. Augustine, "On the Good of Marriage," 8.

3. Augustine, "On the Good of Marriage," 6, 8.

4. Augustine, *City of God*, XIV:22.

5. Commenting on Augustine, classicist Peter Brown writes, "Adam and Eve had originally enjoyed a harmonious unity of body and soul. Their bodies had followed the dictates of their wills with the same loving and

familiar concord as they themselves had followed the will of God" (*The Body and Society: Men, Women, and Sexual Renunciation in Early Christianity* [New York: Columbia University Press, 1988], 405).

6. Augustine, *City of God,* XIV:24. The metaphor of sowing the seed in sex, analogous to a farmer's sowing the seed in the soil, presumed the widespread belief in the ancient world that the sperm contained what was necessary to make a human being. The seventeenth century saw a variant: the idea of a homunculus—a miniature person that simply grew bigger through time—present on the tip of the sperm. That the woman provides an egg, the ovum, and half of what we biologically inherit had to wait until the medical discoveries in the eighteenth and nineteenth centuries.

7. Augustine, "On the Good of Marriage," 7.

8. Note that for Augustine marriage is sacramental because it is permanent, indissoluble. Later generations expanded on this idea. Aquinas like Augustine dubbed marriage as sacramental—using the Vulgate translation of *mysterion* in Eph. 5:32 as *sacramentum,* rather than today's translation as "mystery"—and then added that as a sacrament, marriage confers an extra measure of supernatural grace in the form of power to maintain the marital bond (*Summa Theologica,* II:iii:Q.42:2). Although some voices have tried to tie sacramentality to sexual intercourse per se, Aquinas follows Augustine in holding that it is specifically the indissolubility of marriage that constitutes its sacramental character. See John T. Noonan, *Contraception: A History of Its Treatment by the Catholic Theologians and Canonists* enlarged ed. (Cambridge: Harvard University Press, 1986) 286–88.

9. Augustine, "On Marriage and Concupiscence," 16.

10. Ibid., 11.

11. Philo, *The Special Laws,* 3.20.113. It was not until Constantine's reign on November 16, 318 that the murder of a son or daughter was referred to as parricide; and it was not until February 7, 374 that infanticide was declared by law as homicide.

12. Tertullian, "Apology," 9.

13. Ibid. Elsewhere Tertullian describes in detail the mechanical devices used to abort the unborn. See "A Treatise on the Soul" (*De Anima*), 25.

14. One argument against sex-for-pleasure is the one we present here, namely, to prevent infanticide. However, the argument of Augustine that usually garners attention has to do with his personal and theological struggle with concupiscence as described in his *Confessions.* Certainly this is the focus of Peter Brown's interpretation, see *The Body and Society,* 418–19. The spiritual wrestling between concupiscence and continence, as Augustine describes it, seems to fit men, but it ignores women. Margaret R. Miles, dean of the Graduate Theological Union and Augustine scholar, writes, "A gendered reading of the *Confessions* reveals that it contains no depictions of women who, like Augustine, suffer and struggle to define and achieve their own goals." *Desire and Delight: A New Reading of Augustine's Confessions* (New York: Crossroad, 1992), 92. Elaine Pagels, a patristics popu-

larizer, registers a related complaint against the bishop of Hippo: He took his own experience and made it a paradigm for all human experience. This led to the doctrine that spontaneous sexual passion is not due to our nature but rather due to our fall from nature. This implies bondage to sin. Whereas early church history saw Christians basking in the gospel as a message of freedom—*autoexousia,* the freedom to rule oneself—with Augustine we are returned to bondage and to the need for external government. To Pagels it is Augustine's theology, not sexual desire, that constitutes the fall. See *Adam, Eve, and the Serpent* (New York: Random House, 1988) 99, 106, 111, 130.

15. Augustine, "On Marriage and Concupiscence," 17.
16. Noonan, *Contraception,* 136.
17. For Aquinas the natural law is rational, universal, and divine, making all sin unnatural. Any sexual pleasure outside intercourse—*coitus interruptus,* masturbation, homosexual activity, bestiality—is sinful because it conflicts with right reason and because it conflicts with the natural pattern of sexuality, which is to procreate. "A lustful man intends a sex pleasure, not human fruitfulness, and he can experience this without a generative act; this is what he seeks in unnatural vice" (*Summa Theologica* II:ii:Q.154: A.11). Lisa Sowle Cahill describes natural law ethics in the Thomistic tradition: "In a fundamental way it is an empirical approach. Human experience reveals what is most fulfilling for humans. Reason and intelligence are needed to interpret experience, however, in order to distinguish what is *essentially* natural (morally appropriate) human conduct, as differentiated from behavior that humans may often exhibit, but which is not in conformity with their true nature or highest ideals" (*Religion and Artificial Reproduction,* 37, Cahill's italics).
18. Aquinas says that an unnatural act (*contra naturam*) "is any complete sex-act from which of its nature generation cannot follow" (*Summa Theologica,* II:ii:Q.154:A.1). Fascinating here is Aquinas' treatment of the sin of lust as if applicable only to the man. Even though he is satisfied that moral distinctions drawn between fornication, adultery, incest, and rape are due strictly to the status of the woman involved—that is, whether she is single, married, related, or unwilling—the question of lust or sin for the woman involved is not raised. A woman who leaves her husband for another man is deemed an adulteress (II:ii:Q.154:A.8). For the most part, it seems that the category of mutuality does not play a role in Aquinas' deliberations. Fordham feminist Elizabeth A. Johnson, commenting on his limiting of the value of women to procreation, says, "The effective history of Aquinas' theology in the Catholic church illustrates how powerfully androcentric thought functions to legitimate patriarchy. As an intellectual model it constructs the world in language, mindset, imagery, and the distribution of value in such a way as to marginalize women and justify structures that exclude them for full and equal participation" (*She Who Is* [New York: Crossroad, 1993], 25).

19. Thomas Aquinas, *Supplement,* Q.41, A.3 and 4.
20. Thomas Aquinas, *Summa Contra Gentiles,* IV:83, 88. Lisa Sowle Cahill comments, "Thomas downplays sexual pleasure and even the intimacy and love of the partners as motives for sexual expression, tolerating the former as a venial sin, and speaking of the latter primarily in relation to the total project of married life. This is probably as it should be, but the importance of sexual intimacy as an expression and enhancement of the friendship of which Thomas speaks surely deserves more attention than he gives it" (*Between the Sexes: Foundations for a Christian Ethics of Sexuality* [Minneapolis: Fortress Press, 1985], 113).
21. Seduction is defined as the nonviolent deflowering of a virgin and is a particularly despicable crime because it may prevent the victimized maiden from entering a legitimate marital relationship later. Rape may or may not coincide with seduction, but it always applies when violence is involved. "Wherever an element of violence enters," writes Aquinas, "there you have the quality of rape" (*Summa Theologica,* II:ii:Q.154:A.7). "Raping a virgin is worse than seducing her, and raping a wife is worse than committing adultery" (Ibid., II:ii:Q.154:A.12). In such cases we have crimes with victims, and these acts are described as "unnatural" in the sense that all immoral acts are unnatural.
22. "Sins against nature are sins against God" (Aquinas, *Summa Theologica,* II:ii:Q.154:A.12).
23. Ibid. Thomas Aquinas, "Concerning Evil" (*De Malo*), 15:2. See Noonan, *Contraception,* 238–41; 279–82. Noonan notes, "While for analysis here a distinction may be made between the rationale appealing to nature, the rationale based on the protection of life, and the rationale defending the purposes of marriage, a sharp line between them cannot be attributed to the scholastic writers. What was treated as a sin of homicide or what was viewed as an attack on nature was also considered destructive to the marital relation" (Ibid., 247). Hence, the focus on children I am developing here is the cultivation of seeds sown by the theological tradition, not the harvest of ripe thought.
24. Noonan, *Contraception,* 281.
25. Martin Luther, "Large Catechism," in *The Book of Concord,* ed. Theodore G. Tappert (Minneapolis: Fortress Press, 1959), 393.
26. Thus, theologian Gerhard Forde may be slightly overstating the case when he comments, "The tradition has always insisted that the estate of marriage is divinely ordained and thus especially God-pleasing. It is simply not the case that marriage was looked upon as a kind of necessary evil, a hedge against lust. Luther, for instance, used the 1 Cor. 7:9 passage that 'it is better to marry than to burn' primarily as a criticism of Roman attempts to claim celibacy as a state higher than marriage. It was better to marry than to burn under the burden of falsely required laws" ("Law and Sexual Behavior," *Lutheran Quarterly* 9 [Spring 1995]:10).

27. John Calvin, *Institutes of the Christian Religion,* vols. 20 and 21, The Library of Christian Classics, ed. John T. McNeill and trans. Ford Lewis Battles (Philadelphia: Westminster Press, 1960), 406.

28. Martin Luther, *Genesis Chapters 1–5,* in *Luther's Works,* vol. 1, ed. Jaraslov Pelikan and trans. George V. Schick (St. Louis: Concordia, 1958), 135. Changing contexts can result in changing meanings. In the sixteenth century, Luther sought to liberate healthy sexuality by locating it in marriage. In the late twentieth century, the church that bears Luther's name in North America seeks to constrict sexual activity within marriage. This means that gay and lesbian sexual activity outside of marriage is judged to be illegitimate. This line of argumentation is key to justifying the position of the Evangelical Lutheran Church in America against the ordination of gay and lesbian clergy. See the fascinating description of uses of Luther's theology for such purposes in Christian Albert Batalden Scharen, "A Blessed and God-Pleasing Estate: An Investigation of the Grounds and Consequences of Lutheran Theological Formulations of Marriage," M.A. Thesis, Graduate Theological Union, Berkeley, California, April 1995.

29. Luther, "The Estate of Marriage" in *Luther's Works,* vol. 45, ed. Walter I. Brandt and Helmut T. Lehman (Philadelphia: Fortress Press, 1962), 36.

30. Ibid., 18–19. Interpreting Luther here Gerta Scharffenorth writes, "The common bond between men and women follows from the Creator's word. God's word creates the mutual love which embraces all of humankind and enables mutual responsibility between the sexes. This assignment to one another in the course of history corresponds to their equality before God, who created man and woman in his own image" (*Becoming Friends in Christ: The Relationship Between Man and Woman as Seen by Luther* [Geneva: Lutheran World Federation, 1983], 41). Cahill adds, "Despite Luther's positive view of women as originally equal to men, some decided sexist implications of his theory cannot be overlooked. Luther basically accepts the subordination of women as the way things are now, even though not the ideal. Further, though he does praise motherhood, his exaltation of it as a cross by which to glorify God could be read as an endorsement of an attitude of passive resignation on the part of women who suffer real injustices in the domestic sphere. To be fair to Luther, he does make similar recommendations for the husband and father" (*Between the Sexes,* 130). Pamela D. Couture at Emory University shows Luther's influence on John Wesley who, on the one hand, saw marriage and family as an obstruction to a life devoted to God's ministry while, on the other hand, draws our attention to the needs of children and their marginalized mothers. "Together, Luther and Wesley create a voice within classical theology for shared responsibility on behalf of poor women and children" (*Blessed are the Poor? Women's Poverty, Family Policy, and Practical Theology* [Nashville: Abingdon Press, 1991], 134).

31. Steven Ozment, *Protestants* (New York: Doubleday, 1992), 151–52.

Reformation scholar Heiko A. Oberman would also agree. See *Luther: Man Between God and the Devil* (New York: Doubleday, 1989), 272–89.

32. Martin Luther, "A Sermon on the Estate of Marriage," in *Luther's Works,* vol. 44, ed. Franklin Sherman and Helmut T. Lehman (Minneapolis: Fortress Press, 1966), 10. Reprinted in *Martin Luther's Basic Theological Writings,* ed. Timothy F. Lull (Minneapolis: Fortress Press, 1989), 633.

33. Ibid.

34. "Since marriage has existed from the beginning of the world and is still found among unbelievers," writes Luther, "there is no reason why it should be called a sacrament of the New Law and of the church alone. The marriages of the ancients were no less sacred than are ours, nor are those of unbelievers less true marriages than those of believers, and yet they are not regarded as sacraments" (Martin Luther, *Luther's Works,* vol. 36, ed. Abdel R. Wentz and Helmut T. Lehman [Minneapolis: Fortress Press, 1959], 92). Philip Melanchthon distinguishes sacraments of the New Testament from other noble religious practices such as matrimony and prayer in his "Apology of the Augsburg Confessions," in Tappert, *Book of Concord,* 213.

35. Martin Luther, "On Marriage Matters," in *Luther's Works,* vol. 46, ed. Robert G. Schulz and Helmut T. Lehman (Minneapolis: Fortress Press, 1967), 265–67. The Lutheran reformers transformed the Roman Catholic approach to marriage. How? Emory University law professor John Witte says that the Reformers rejected the sacramental concept of marriage and the subordination of marriage to celibacy and removed many marriage laws based on these assumptions; they introduced a social concept of marriage; they shifted jurisdiction over marriage from the ecclesiastical to the civil sphere; and they revised the role of parents, priests, and peers in the process of marriage formation and dissolution. See John Witte, Jr., "The Transformation of Marriage Law in the Lutheran Reformation," in *The Weightier Matters of the Law: Essays on Law and Religion,* ed. John Witte, Jr., and Frank S. Alexander (Atlanta: Scholars Press, 1988), 57–97. I would qualify the Witte description by observing that the sacramental feel of marriage remained, while authority in marriage matters shifted from the church to the state. This shift did not constitute a secularization of marriage, however, because the state was enjoined to carry out God's law. Ozment adds another point here: "It is a gross exaggeration to say that Luther removed the pope from the bedroom only to put the state there. Foundations were laid in Protestant lands for a more realistic and charitable treatment of marriage" (*Protestants,* 158).

36. Calvin, *Institutes,* 1483.

37. Luther, "A Sermon On the Estate of Marriage," 44:8; or Lull, *Basic Theological Writings,* 631.

38. Luther, "A Sermon on the Estate of Marriage," 44:9; or Lull, *Basic Theological Writings,* 632.

39. Luther, *Luther's Works,* 45:33–34.

40. Luther, *Luther's Works,* 1:126. Cahill makes us aware that "Luther does seem of two minds about sex. Sexual passion, with what he perceives as its near irresistibility, appears always sullied by lust. Still, he marvels at the miracles of pregnancy and birth, extols the maternal labors that nourish offspring, enjoins participation by the father, and speaks freely and affectionately of wife and children. . . . We find a man [Luther] unafraid to challenge the presuppositions of received traditions, to return to sources, and to re-create both religious foundations and the meanings of human existence that they undergird and enhance" (*Between the Sexes,* 133).

41. Ozment, *Protestants,* 168.

42. Citation and translation in Oberman, *Luther,* 312, from *D. Martin Luthers Werke: Kritische Gesamtausgabe, Tischreden* (Table Talk), vols. 1–6 (Weimar, 1912–21), No. 5, 549oc; 186.

43. Luther, *Luther's Works,* 45:46. Scharffenorth observes that Luther presumed mutuality and equality between father and mother when raising children, not a brute authoritarianism of the father. She writes, "Criticism of Luther today is thus often set off by the importance he attached to obedience and orders of precedence, particularly in view of recent depth psychological findings. But close perusal of sources shows that the special position claimed to the father is a subsequent addition to Luther's view of parent-child relations" (*Becoming Friends in Christ,* 40).

44. Luther, "A Sermon On the Estate of Marriage," *Luther's Works,* 44:13; or Lull, *Basic Theological Writings,* 635–36. See also Luther, "A Sermon on Keeping Children in School," *Luther's Works,* 46:223, 230. The Roman Catholic Catechism of 1566, which embodied counter-Reformation theology, argued similarly: The purpose of "the appetite of procreation [is] not so much indeed that heirs of property and riches be left, but that worshippers of the true faith and religion be educated" (*Roman Catechism,* 2.18.13, as cited in Noonan, *Contraception,* 313).

45. Pius XI, *Casti Connubii,* in *Papal Teachings: Matrimony,* ed. Benedictine Monks of Solesmes (Boston: St. Paul Editions, 1963), 273–74, cited with comments by Cahill, *Religion and Artificial Reproduction,* 43.

46. Pius XI, *Casti Connubii,* 23–24.

47. Lisa Sowle Cahill, *Sex, Gender, and Christian Ethics* (Cambridge: Cambridge University Press, 1996), chap. 7, p. 6.

48. *Gaudium et Spes* (Pastoral Constitution on the Church in the Modern World) in *The Documents of Vatican II,* ed. Walter M. Abbot, S.J., (New York: America Press, 1966), sections 47–52, pp. 249–58.

49. Ibid.

50. Ibid.

51. Paul VI, *Humanae Vitae* (Mahwah, N.J.: Paulist Press, 1968), 11.

52. Richard A. McCormick, S.J., *The Critical Calling: Reflections on Moral Dilemmas Since Vatican II* (Washington: Georgetown University Press, 1989), 213–14.

53. Cited by Shannon and Cahill, *Religion and Artificial Reproduction,* 45.

54. Lisa Sowle Cahill, "Catholic Sexual Ethics and the Dignity of the Person: A Double Message," *Theological Studies* 50 (1988):122.

55. Paul Lauritzen, *Pursuing Parenthood: Ethical Issues in Assisted Reproduction* (Bloomington, Ind.: Indiana University Press, 1993), 6. Lauritzen wants to separate the argument of body-soul unity from the argument of natural law, but in the context of the Vatican document the former is certainly a plank in the latter's platform.

56. Congregation for the Doctrine of the Faith, *Instruction on Respect for Human Life in Its Origin and on the Dignity of Procreation: Replies to Certain Questions of the Day,* in *Bioethics,* 3rd ed., ed. Thomas A. Shannon (Mahwah, N.J.: Paulist Press, 1987), 593.

57. *Instruction,* in Shannon, *Bioethics,* 3rd ed., 595. Because creationism is only one among other respectable theological positions within the history of Roman Catholic theology, it is not presented here in a decisive fashion. The subtlety is that it is more or less assumed. Pope John Paul II hints at traducianism but reiterates creationism in *Evangelium Vitae,* II:43. "In procreation, therefore, through the communication of life from parents to child, God's own image and likeness is transmitted, thanks to the creation of the immortal soul." When does ensoulment occur? *Donum Vitae* seems to assume at fertilization. Yet, on an earlier occasion, the Congregation for the Doctrine of the Faith left open "the question of the moment when the spiritual soul is infused. There is not a unanimous tradition on this point" (Declaration on Abortion, 13).

58. Augustine, *City of God,* XI: 232.

59. Tertullian, "A Treatise on the Soul," (*De anima*), XXVIII. On this Tertullian was reflecting the common ancient Roman belief that sex makes the blood boil. Brown describes the belief: "To make love was to bring one's blood to the boil, as the fiery vital spirit swept through the veins, turning the blood into the whitened foam of semen. It was a process in which the body as a whole . . . was brought into play. . . . The genital regions were mere points of passage. They were the outlets of a human espresso machine" (*The Body and Society,* 17).

60. Augustine, "On Free Will," XXI:59; "Letters," CLXVI:6–12.

61. *Instruction,* in Shannon, *Bioethics,* 3rd ed., 606, italics added.

62. Ibid., 608.

63. Ibid., 603.

64. Ibid., 593.

65. Lauritzen, *Pursuing Parenthood,* 8.

66. *Instruction,* in Shannon, *Bioethics,* 3rd ed., 607.

67. Lauritzen, *Pursuing Parenthood,* 8.

68. McCormick, *The Critical Calling,* 337.

69. Pope John Paul II, *Evangelium Vitae* (The Gospel of Life) (New York: Random House, Times Books, 1995), 22, pope's italics.

70. Ibid., 164–65, pope's italics.

71. Ibid., 166.

72. Ibid., 176.

73. Pope John Paul II, *Crossing the Threshold of Hope* (New York: Alfred A. Knopf, 1994), 206–7. See *Evangelium Vitae,* 177–78.

74. Shannon and Cahill, *Religion and Artificial Reproduction,* 52–53. See also pp. 45–53.

75. Joseph Fletcher, *The Ethics of Genetic Control* (Buffalo: Prometheus, 1988), 15. Anthony Giddens gives a name to sexuality now liberated by reproductive technology from procreation, "plastic sexuality." It can be molded to the personality, especially by women engaged in the process of self-definition. "Sexuality is at last fully autonomous. . . . [It] can become wholly a quality of individuals and their transactions with one another" (*The Transformation of Intimacy: Sexuality, Love and Eroticism in Modern Societies* [Stanford, Calif.: Stanford University Press, 1992], 27).

76. Sidney Callahan, "Value Choices in Abortion," in *Abortion: Understanding Differences,* ed. Sidney Callahan and Daniel Callahan (New York: Plenum Press, 1984), 288.

77. Ibid., 289.

78. Ibid., 304.

79. Ibid., 305.

80. Shannon and Cahill, *Religion and Artificial Reproduction,* 24.

81. Ibid., 138.

82. Ibid., 53.

83. Forde, "Law and Sexual Behavior," 17.

84. Pursuing a distinctively *healthy* understanding of sexuality and an appropriate ethic will by no means be easy. What we have inherited from the tradition is twisted and convoluted and sometimes mean spirited. French philospher Michael Foucault makes this clear when advancing his "repressive hypothesis" regarding the transformation by modernity of the Christian practice of confession. "We must not forget that by making sex into that which, above all else, had to be confessed, the Christian pastoral always presented it as the disquieting enigma: not a thing which stubbornly shows itself, but one which always hides. . . . What is peculiar to modern societies, in fact, is not that they consigned sex to a shadow existence, but that they dedicated themselves to speaking of it *ad infinitum,* while exploiting it as *the* secret" (*The History of Sexuality,* vol. 1 [New York: Random House, 1978], 35).

85. Vladimir Solovyev, *The Meaning of Love,* trans. Jane Marshall (London: Geoffrey Bles, The Centenary Press, 1945), 7.

86. Ibid.

87. Ibid., 25.

88. Ibid., 44.

89. Ibid., 58–89.
90. Ibid., 75–76.

Chapter 6. Visions of the Future
and Ethical Foundations

1. Wolfhart Pannenberg, *Anthropology in Theological Perspective* (Louisville, Ky.: Westminster/John Knox Press, 1985), 242.
2. Joseph Fletcher, *The Ethics of Genetic Control* (Buffalo: Prometheus, 1988), xviii.
3. Ibid., 31; italics in original.
4. Ibid., 3. If he were alive today, Reformed ethicist Paul Ramsey would likely object to Fletcher's technological tranformationism for two reasons. First, it invests too much optimism in the power of science and technology to improve the human situation. Such futurism constitutes an idolatry of human creativity. Second, it cuts us off from the biological dictates of nature—that is, creation—in the parenting process. "To be debiologized and recombined in various ways, parenthood must first be broken or removed. When the transmission of life has been debiologized, human parenthood as a created covenant of life is placed under massive assault and men and women will no longer be who they are" (*Fabricated Man* [New Haven, Conn.: Yale University Press, 1970], 135). To say this, Ramsey must presume that God speaks to us through creation—creation here understood as biology—at a level more trustworthy than through human reason or through the spirit. He criticizes futurism for promoting another form of dualism wherein human reason tries to gain control over physical reality. He thinks he can solve the problem of dualism by subordinating human reason to pretechnological physical processes. I do not believe this will work. For good or ill, I believe we are condemned to be futurists. Our task is to employ reasoning in the pursuit of the good over the ill.
5. Some ethicists in the field of biomedical ethics are beginning to withdraw somewhat from the principlist approach and develop an "ethics of care." Tom L. Beauchamp and James F. Childress are shifting the justifying ground for the four principles away from the overlapping consensus of utilitarianism and deontology toward what they call a "principle-based, common morality theory." Autonomy, beneficence, nonmaleficence, and justice are said to be embedded in common moral beliefs. See *Principles of Biomedical Ethics* (New York: Oxford University Press, 1994). Reviewer Ezekiel J. Emanuel suggests that shifting the ground underlying the principles may itself herald the end of principlism, giving the work of Beauchamp and Childress a schizophrenic character until the break becomes complete ("The Beginning of the End of Principlism," *Hastings Center Report,* 25 [July–August 1995] 37–38).

6. Tom L. Beauchamp and LeRoy Walters combine the principles of non-maleficence and beneficence in their textbook, *Contemporary Issues in Bioethics,* 4th ed. (Belmont, Calif.: Wadsworth, 1994), 24–25; Ronald Munson distinguishes these principles in *Intervention and Reflection: Basic Issues in Medical Ethics,* 4th ed. (Belmont, Calif.: Wadsworth, 1992), 32–35. For a particularly clear and helpful summary of normative bioethical principles, see Thomas A. Shannon, *Bioethics* 3rd ed. (Mahwah, N.J.: Paulist Press, 1987), 3–16.

7. Lori B. Andrews et al., eds., *Assessing Genetic Risk* (Washington, D.C.: National Academy Press, 1994), 248. The four principles important to the Institute of Medicine are autonomy, confidentiality, privacy, and equity.

8. Fletcher, "Moral Problems," in *Genetic Disorders and the Fetus,* 2nd ed., ed. Aubrey Milunsky (New York: Plenum Press, 1986), 842.

9. Ibid., 845.

10. The lack of public controversy over these general normative principles is amazing. "That we are morally obligated on some occasions to assist others—at least in professional roles such as nursing, medicine, and research—is hardly a matter of moral controversy" (Beauchamp and Walters, *Contemporary Issues in Bioethics,* 25).

11. Trutz Rendtorff, *Ethics,* 2 vols. (Minneapolis: Fortress Press, 1986), 1:7.

12. Ibid., 1:25.

13. These three basic elements, which are derived from observation, appear to function for Rendtorff akin to the way empirical observation and natural law function in the work of Lisa Sowle Cahill, whose foundational theory we will examine later. In fact, Rendtorff acknowledges that his approach is similar to contemporary Catholic natural law ethics, which seeks "to win for itself a basis for responsibilities that take precedence over the concept of autonomy" (*Ethics,* 1:37), and he further asserts that the recent revisions of Roman Catholic natural law theory, which include application to all law, makes the sixteenth-century sectarian dispute between Lutherans and Catholics largely irrelevant today (*Ethics,* 1:119).

14. "It is not possible to single out and establish any one purpose, or even any clear priority of purposes, that could serve as a basis for marriage as a living community. . . . Marriage is to be a lifelong relationship. It is not possible to designate a point in time when marriage would have fulfilled its purpose and thus come to an end before the living community itself was at an end" (Rendtorff, *Ethics,* 2:11–12).

15. Ibid., 2:83.

16. Ibid., 1:64.

17. Martin Luther, "The Freedom of a Christian," in *Luther's Works,* vol. 51 ed. Helmut T. Lehman and John W. Doberstein (Minneapolis: Fortress Press, 1959), 365, or in *Martin Luther's Basic Theological Writings,* ed. Timothy F. Lull (Minneapolis: Fortress Press, 1989), 617.

18. See George W. Forell, *Faith Active in Love* (Minneapolis: Augsburg Publishing House, 1954).

19. Karl Barth, "The Gift of Freedom: Foundation of Evangelical Ethics," in *The Humanity of God,* trans. Thomas Weiser and John N. Thomas (Richmond: The Westminster Press, 1968), 69–96.
20. Gilbert C. Meilaender, *Faith and Faithfulness* (Notre Dame, Ind.: University of Notre Dame Press, 1991), ix.
21. Ibid., 106.
22. Ibid., 147.
23. Gilbert Meilander, "Products of the Will," *Washington and Lee Law Review,* 52:1 (1995)173–95, 188.
24. Meilander, *Faith and Faithfulness,* 126–27. Luther Seminary systematic theologian Paul Sponheim's position is similar: "The Christian is driven by the passion of faith in God. 'Because [God] first loved us' (1 John 4:19) the Christian is impelled to the hungry, the imprisoned, the naked—all these 'least', in whose suffering Christians face their brother Jesus (Matthew 25)" (*Faith and the Other* [Minneapolis: Fortress Press, 1993], 131). Although this love begins with the passion of faith, its moral claims can be shared with nonbelievers because it is a "public character of faith" (Ibid.).
25. Lisa Sowle Cahill, "Catholic Sexual Ethics and the Dignity of the Person: A Double Message," *Theological Studies* 50 (1989):147–48.
26. Lisa Sowle Cahill, *Love Your Enemies: Discipleship, Pacifism, and Just War Theory* (Minneapolis: Fortress Press, 1994), 3.
27. The term *postmodern* has multiple meanings, which is something that is ignored by the totalizing attitude of the pluralist postmodernists, an attitude that contradicts their own principles. There are two main branches of postmodern thought: holism and pluralism. What these two branches have in common is an agreed-upon definition of *modernity* that is rooted in the dualistic separation of subject from object in Cartesian philosophy. They both also have a tendency to de-center the self in philosophical reflection. The holist postmoderns presume the fragmentation of the modern world to be less real and less desirable than unity, so they reaffirm unity in the form of integrative wholeness at all levels of reality. This leads to a global ethic, emphasizing human unity across race, gender, and nation as well as unity between humanity and nature. The pluralist postmoderns, however, presume that the fundamental and indelible reality is the fragmentation of the human race into separate, ethnic cultures, gender competition, and other struggles for social power. Each attempt to present a vision of global unity is judged to be just one more attempt by one group to exert ideological power over another. Pluralist postmodernists therefore oppose all attempts to lift up a universal ethic. They contradict themselves by asserting that their anti-universalism applies universally. Pluralist postmodernists also pretend that holist postmodernists do not exist.
28. Michael Foucault, *The History of Sexuality,* 3 vols. (New York: Random House, 1980–1986).
29. In his work on ethical foundations, William O'Neill, S.J., ethicist at the Graduate Theological Union, takes up the problem of pluralism, accord-

ing to which the Christian faith would constitute one manifestation of "self-interest" with no legitimate claim to universal applicability. By invoking the hermeneutical theory of Hans-Georg Gadamer, O'Neill believes a proper understanding of the relation of prejudice to reason can explain how a particular position taken by Christian faith can have universal meaning. A kingdom of ends discerned through the fusion of horizons establishes the link. "Our mutual interest in a whole of ends in systematic conjunction is fulfilled in a fusion of our intentional horizons, in our attaining and sustaining a rational consensus about what can be made actual by our conduct, i.e., the *universale concretum* of a kingdom of ends" (*The Ethics of Our Climate: Hermeneutics and Ethical Theory* [Washington, D.C.: Georgetown University Press, 1994], 119).

30. Cahill finds support from philospher Charles Taylor who writes, "Foucault's analyses seem to bring evils to light; and yet he wants to distance himself from the suggestion which would seem inescapably to follow, that the negation or overcoming of these evils promotes a good" (Charles Taylor, "Foucault on Freedom and Truth," in *Foucault: A Critical Reader* ed. David Couzens Hoy [London: Basil Blackwell, 1986], 69).

31. Thomas Aquinas, *Summa Theologica,* I:ii:Q.91:A.2.

32. Thomas A. Shannon and Lisa Sowle Cahill, *Religion and Artificial Reproduction* (New York: Crossroad, 1988), 137. "Natural law thinking in ethics makes claims about those moral purposes or goals which are ideal or fulfilling for human persons" (Lisa Sowle Cahill, "Moral Traditions, Ethical Language, and Reproductive Technologies," *The Journal of Medicine and Philosophy* 14 [1989]:509). "The real basis of Catholic sex and gender ethics is a certain interpretation of human nature and of what is naturally fulfilling and appropriate for human relationships" (Lisa Sowle Cahill, "Is Catholic Ethics Biblical? The Example of Sex and Gender," in *Warren Lecture Series in Catholic Studies* 20 [March 15, 1992]:1).

33. "In the postmodern period, conceding the historical contextualization of all thinking and knowledge, a credible natural law method cannot claim to provide absolute certainty over all particular cultures and historical perspectives. Yet it can hope for the gradual reduction of cultural bias by means of a critical interaction of experience and reflective thinking. Defined broadly, a natural law ethical approach is one that depends on reasonable and critical reflection on experience and that aims at as broad as possible a consensus about the good life or flourishing (in Aristotelian terms) for human beings" (Lisa Sowle Cahill, "Women, Marriage, Parenthood: What are their Natures?" *Logos: Philosophic Issues in Christian Perspective* 9 [1988]:11).

34. With regard to gender equality, Cahill's approach is to draw on Aquinas' strengths but jettison his weaknesses. "The stress on the mutual friendship that should characterize marriage also helps counteract the subordinationist view of women which Aquinas preserves from both Aristotle and from Augustine, and which goes more or less unchallenged in his writings" (*Religion and Artificial Reproduction,* 39).

35. Lisa Sowle Cahill, *Sex, Gender, and Christian Ethics,* cited here in its pre-published manuscript form, chapter 3, "Particular Experiences, Shared Goods."

36. Cahill, *Sex, Gender, and Christian Ethics,* chap. 4, p. 29.

37. Cahill, "Is Catholic Ethics Biblical?" 14.

38. Cahill, interlude and proposal in *Sex, Gender, and Christian Ethics,* 3.

39. Cahill, "Women, Marriage, Parenthood," 16.

40. Lisa Sowle Cahill, "*In Vitro* Fertilization: Ethical Issues in Judeo-Christian Perspective," *Loyola Law Review* 32:2 (1988):348.

41. Cahill, "Women, Marriage, and Parenthood," 23.

42. Cahill, *Sex, Gender, and Christian Ethics,* chap. 8, p. 55.

43. "The primary significance of sex in marriage is to express the spousal union, however critically related to procreation sex may be" (Cahill, "Moral Traditions," 515).

44. Cahill, *Sex, Gender, and Christian Ethics,* chap. 8, p. 54.

45. Ibid., 49.

46. Ibid., 57–58.

47. Ibid.

48. Lisa Sowle Cahill, "The Ethics of Surrogate Motherhood: Biology, Freedom, and Moral Obligation," *Law, Medicine, and Health Care* 16 (Spring 1988):70.

49. Meilaender, *Faith and Faithfulness,* 123.

50. Cahill, *Sex, Gender, and Christian Ethics,* chap. 4, p. 35.

51. Ibid., 22.

52. Cahill, *Sex, Gender, and Christian Ethics,* chap. 7, p. 36.

53. Martin Luther, "Small Catechism," in *The Book of Concord,* ed. Theodore Tappert (Minneapolis: Fortress Press, 1959), 344–45. Pannenberg makes the connection in related fashion. "The invocation of God's rights as the divine Majesty makes the inviolability of human dignity immune against human caprice" (*Anthropology,* 242).

54. This human focus within the wider world of nature does not by any means entail an anthropocentric disregard for the environment through a brute, exploitative attitude toward the ecosphere. When presenting proleptic ethics elsewhere, I emphasize that a future-oriented concept of human dignity is a component in an ecologically oriented ethic. See my work in systematic theology, *GOD—the World's Future* (Minneapolis: Fortress Press, 1992), chap. 12, especially pp. 371–74.

55. Philip Hefner, *The Human Factor* (Minneapolis: Fortress Press, 1993), 35–42.

Acknowledgments

Grateful acknowledgment is made to the following publishers:

Augsburg Fortress, for permission to reprint excerpts from *Luther's Works*, vol. 44, edited by James Atkinson, copyright © 1966 Fortress Press; *Luther's Works*, vol. 45, edited by Walther I. Brandt, copyright © 1962 Muhlenberg Press; *Martin Luther's Basic Theological Writings*, edited by Timothy F. Lull, copyright © 1989 Augsburg Fortress.

Cambridge University Press, for permission to reprint excerpts from Lisa Stowe Cahill, *Sex, Gender, and Christian Ethics*, copyright 1996 © Cambridge University Press.

Concordia College, for permission to reprint excerpts from Jaroslav Pelikan, ed., *Luther*, vol. 1, translated by George V. Schick, copyright © 1958 Concordia College.

Doubleday, for permission to reprint excerpts from Steven Ozment, *Protestants: The Birth of a Revolution*, copyright © 1992 Doubleday.

Index of Authors

Index of Subjects